Praise for previous editions of

Nebraska
Off the Beaten Path®

"The book provides a good beginning for those who want to explore the diversity Nebraska has to offer."

—*Nebraska History* magazine (Lincoln)

Help Us Keep This Guide Up to Date

Every effort has been made by the author and editors to make this guide as accurate and useful as possible. However, many things can change after a guide is published—establishments close, phone numbers change, and facilities come under new management.

We would love to hear from you concerning your experiences with this guide and how you feel it could be improved and be kept up to date. While we may not be able to respond to all comments and suggestions, we'll take them to heart, and we'll also make certain to share them with the author. Please send your comments and suggestions to the following address:

The Globe Pequot Press
Reader Response/Editorial Department
P.O. Box 480
Guilford, CT 06437-0480

Or you may e-mail us at:
editorial@globe-pequot.com

Thanks for your input, and happy travels!

OFF THE BEATEN PATH® SERIES

Nebraska

FOURTH EDITION

Hannah McNally

The
Globe
Pequot
Press

GUILFORD, CONNECTICUT

Text design by Laura Augustine
Maps created by Equator Graphics © The Globe Pequot Press
Illustrations by Julie Lynch
Excerpt from *The Nebraska Bean Cookbook* reprinted with permission from the Nebraska Dry Bean Growers Association.

ISSN 1539-6932
ISBN 0-7627-2663-6

Manufactured in the United States of America
Fourth Edition/First Printing

To my mother, Mary Agnes,
my sister, Monica Mary,
and my niece, Jodi Lynn.

May they be together,
giggling, gossiping, and grousing,
on the next stage of their journey.

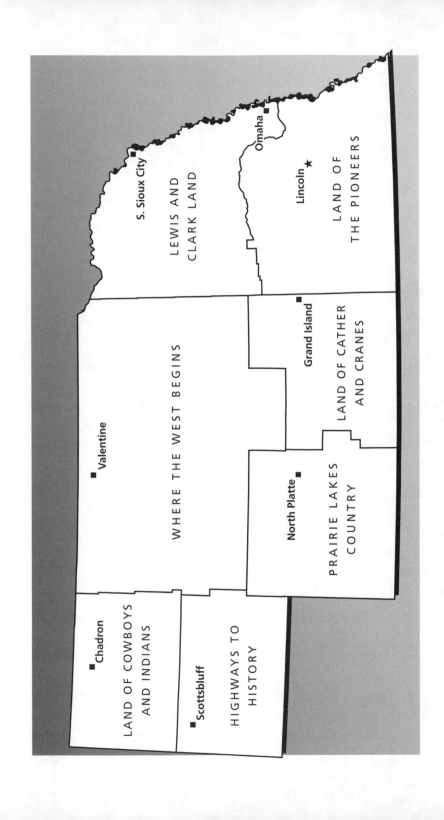

LAND OF COWBOYS
AND INDIANS

■ Chadron

HIGHWAYS TO
HISTORY

■ Scottsbluff

WHERE THE WEST BEGINS

■ Valentine

PRAIRIE LAKES
COUNTRY

■ North Platte

LAND OF CATHER
AND CRANES

■ Grand Island

LEWIS AND
CLARK LAND

■ S. Sioux City

LAND OF
THE PIONEERS

★ Lincoln

■ Omaha

Contents

Introduction ix

Land of the Pioneers.   1

Lewis and Clark Land. 41

Where the West Begins. 77

Land of Cowboys and Indians. 105

Highways to History 123

Prairie Lakes Country. 139

Land of Cather and Cranes 157

Index. 181

About the Author. 192

Introduction

After Maj. Stephen H. Long of the Army Engineers completed his expedition to the Rocky Mountains in 1819, a member of his group described the lands west of the Missouri River as the "abode of perpetual desolation." About 175 years later a late-night comedian described her New York–to–Los Angeles car trip and concluded that, after driving through Nebraska, she had proof that "the dead walk the earth."

Nebraskans are both used to and bemused by such comments about our state. And we are accustomed to living in a state offering a friendly and safe environment, abundant cultural and recreational activities, ethnic and geographic diversity, and reasonable prices. So we can easily afford to lightly shrug and smile at less-than-generous or downright inaccurate comments about Nebraska; we know better.

If you substitute *Nebraska* for *Midwest* in futurist Faith Popcorn's following comments, you'll know why this state is a good place in which to live . . . and travel: "The uncluttered, unbridled lives of Midwesterners will be the envy of the rest of the nation well into the next century. Living on the coasts used to be the aspiration, but not any longer. Today, everything that everybody wants—big family, good food, regular people, nothing hyped up—is all in the Midwest."

Nebraskans are not prone to braggadocio (the one exception is the Nebraska Cornhuskers, who won back-to-back college football championships in 1970 and 1971, in 1994 and 1995, and one more in 1997), and we are not given to gushing about the loveliness of our state and our quality of life. We accept Nebraska like we accept air; it is something so subtle, so natural that it merits little conscious consideration.

Although we are far too modest about Nebraska, we are more than willing to share. It is hoped that this book will let others in on the secrets and charm of Nebraska. Take the time to explore state parks, bicycle along portions of the Cowboy Trail (when completed it will be the nation's longest rail-to-trails path), float down the Niobrara River (one of the best canoeing rivers in the country), pull up a chair in a mom-and-pop cafe or be seated at a four-star restaurant, take a covered-wagon ride along the Oregon Trail, tee off at some the best golf courses around, be awed at an IMAX theater, sink into a comfortable bed at a B&B, experience the intense magic of the world's largest concentration of Sandhill cranes each spring, see where Kool-Aid was invented (in Hastings), lose your inhibitions by entering the cluck-off competition at the Wayne Chicken Show, take part in a cattle drive in the Sandhills, take in an opera, or stroll though the world's largest indoor rain forest at Omaha's Henry Doorly Zoo.

As you travel in Nebraska, please take the time to discover for yourself these off-the-beaten-path places. This book cannot pretend to be a comprehensive collection of all the things to see and do in Nebraska, but it is a good place to start. You'll find a variety of little-known places and a smattering of more famous attractions that should not be missed.

Your trip may be affected by the weather. Nebraskans enjoy a wide variety of climatic conditions. The highest temperature ever recorded in the state was a steamy 118° F at Geneva in 1934 and in both Hartington and Minden in 1936. Nebraska folklorist and tall-tale collector Roger Welsch says that old-timers claim that sometimes it was so hot the hens laid hard-boiled eggs, a situation remedied by feeding them cracked ice. The coldest temperature in Nebraska is recorded as a numbing minus 47°F at Camp Clarke in 1899 and Oshkosh in 1989. Welsch reports that it was once so cold, lawyers were seen with their hands in their own pockets, and people went to church just to hear about hell.

So if you're traveling in Nebraska in the summer, bring clothes for hot weather. If it's winter, bring clothes for cold weather. In the spring or fall, which are pretty, although admittedly a bit too brief, bring something for both climates. (Residents have extensive wardrobes, with clothes suitable for every weather vagary.) Keep in mind there have been January days when it's been shorts–and–shirt sleeves weather, but there also have been occasions when late spring and early fall bring freak blizzards. And although Interstate 80 rarely closes for winter storms, it can happen. Long-distance truckers don't call I–80 the "Snow Chi Minh Trail" for nothin', you know.

It's a good idea to travel with a Nebraska state map as you use this book. Most of the places listed are not on I–80, so you'll need a map to help you navigate. If you'd like a free packet of tourism materials, including a map and a catalog of events, please call the Nebraska Division of Travel and Tourism toll-free at (877) NEBRASKA. Or you can write to them at P.O. Box 98907, Lincoln, NE 68509–8907. Their Internet address is www.visitnebraska.org; the e-mail address is tourism@visitnebraska.org. All the larger cities have a convention and visitors bureau from which you can obtain additional information. Their Internet sites are linked to the Division of Travel and Tourism, as are hundreds of other communities and attractions. Several visitors centers on I–80 are staffed from Memorial Day weekend through Labor Day weekend, and the staff there will be able to answer questions, point you in the right direction, and help you find lodging across the state.

As you drive in rural areas, don't be mystified by the "finger wave." You are likely to be greeted by fellow travelers with their index fingers raised briefly in a friendly salute. Try it yourself; you'll likely find yourself inexplicably happier.

Enjoy yourself in Nebraska. And as you learn more about us, you might come to agree with a much more accurate assessment of Nebraska than those offered by early explorers or television comics. Rev. Val Peters, the director of Girls and Boys Town, has written, "Anyone can sit back at the seashore and be inspired because it shouts at you—so do the mountains. But the prairie only whispers. You must listen closely and not miss the message."

Helpful Information

Nebraska Association of Bed and Breakfasts
(877) 223–NABB
Web site: www.nabb1.com

Nebraska Department of Roads
1500 Highway 2
Lincoln, NE 68502
(402) 471–4567
Web site: www.dor.state.ne.us/
Road and weather conditions, 511

Nebraska Game and Parks Commission
2200 North Thirty-third Street
Lincoln, NE 68503–0370
(800) 826–7275 or (402) 471–0641
Web site: www.ngpc.state.ne.us/

Nebraska Historical Society
Fifteenth and R Streets
Lincoln, NE 68501
(402) 471–4746
Web site: www.nebraskahistory.org

INTRODUCTION

Daily Newspapers in Nebraska

Alliance Times Herald	*McCook Gazette*
Beatrice Sun	*Nebraska City News-Press*
Columbus Telegram	*Norfolk Daily News*
Fremont Tribune	*North Platte Telegraph*
Grand Island Independent	*Omaha Daily Record*
Hastings Tribune	*Omaha World-Herald*
Holdrege Citizen	*Scottsbluff Star-Herald*
Kearney Hub	*Sidney Sun-Telegraph*
Lincoln Journal Star	*York News-Times*

Public Transportation

Only the two largest cities, Omaha and Lincoln, have fairly extensive bus routes and taxi service. A handful of communities, including Omaha, Lincoln, Nebraska City, and Kearney, have trolley lines that serve the downtown areas.

Famous Nebraskans, Born or Bred

Grace Abbott, social reformer

Bess Streeter Aldrich, novelist

Grover Cleveland Alexander, baseball player

Kurt Andersen, co-founder of *Spy* magazine

Fred Astaire, actor and dancer

George Beadle, Nobel prize winner for physiology/medicine

Ward Bond, actor

Marlon Brando, actor

William Jennings Bryan, three-time presidential candidate and prosecutor in the Scopes Monkey Trial

Lloyd Bucher, Boys Town graduate and captain of the USS *Pueblo*

Warren Buffett, financier and second richest man in the United States

Mark Calcavecchia, professional golfer

Johnny Carson, former talk-show host

Willa Cather, Pulitzer prize–winning novelist

Dick Cavett, entertainer

Dick Cheney, vice president of the United States

Montgomery Clift, actor

James Coburn, actor

Buffalo Bill Cody, Pony Express rider, scout, buffalo hunter

Wahoo Sam Crawford, baseball player

Crazy Horse, Oglala Sioux war chief

Chip Davis, founder of Manheim Steamroller

Sandy Dennis, actress

Mignon Good Eberhart, mystery novelist

Loren Eiseley, naturalist and writer

Ruth Etting, vaudeville performer and movie star

Joe Feeny, Irish tenor on the *Lawrence Welk Show*

Father Edward Flanagan, founder of Boys Town

Henry Fonda, actor

Gerald Ford, former President of the United States

Bob Gibson, baseball player

Rodney Grant, actor

Rollie, Will, and *Joyce Hall,* founding brothers of Hallmark Cards

Howard Hansen, composer and conductor

Robert Henri, painter

L. Ron Hubbard, founder of the Church of Scientology

Richard Janssen, actor

Swoosie Kurtz, actress

Evelyn Lincoln, private secretary to former President John F. Kennedy

Harold Lloyd, actor

Pierce Lyden, actor

Malcolm X, civil-rights leader

Randy Meisner, member of the Eagles rock group

Wright Morris, novelist and photographer

J. Sterling Morton, founder of Arbor Day

John G. Neihardt, novelist and poet

Nick Nolte, actor

Senator George Norris, credited with planning the Tennessee Valley Authority

Rose O'Neill, creator of the Kewpie Doll

Edwin Perkins, inventor of Kool-Aid

Susan LaFlesche Picotte, first female Native-American medical doctor

Charles Purcell, designer of the Oakland–San Francisco Bay Bridge

Thurl Ravenscroft, voice of Tony the Tiger

Red Cloud, Oglala Sioux chief

Mari Sandoz, novelist

Gale Sayers, football player

William Sessions, former director of the FBI

Ted Sorenson, speechwriter/ political strategist for former President John F. Kennedy

Standing Bear, Ponca Indian chief

Matthew Sweet, rock musician

Robert Taylor, actor

George Raymond Wagner, better known as "Gorgeous George," professional wrestler

Sam Yorty, former mayor of Los Angeles

Daryl Zanuck, co-founder of 20th Century-Fox

Nebraska Fast Facts

- The Reuben sandwich was invented in Omaha's Blackstone Hotel.
- Cliff's Notes originated in Lincoln.
- Cabela's, located in Sidney, says that it has the largest and fastest growing mail-order outdoor sporting-goods business in the world.
- Nebraska measures 387 miles across. It is 459 miles diagonally from the northwest to the southeast.
- Frisbees were first tossed about in Lincoln.
- The Vise-Grip was invented in DeWitt.
- Nebraska comes from the Oto Indian word Nebrathka, meaning "flat water."
- In 1986, Nebraska was the first state to have two women, Kay Orr and Helen Boosalis, run against each other for governor.
- Nebraska ranks first in the nation for the production of alfalfa meal and great northern beans.
- Three Indian tribes, the Santee Sioux, the Omaha, and the Winnebago, have reservations in Nebraska.
- The B-29s that dropped atomic bombs on Japan, the Enola Gay and Bocks Car, were assembled at a plant in Bellevue.
- Omaha has been the home of the College World Series since 1950.

- The first paved transcontinental highway, Lincoln Highway (US 30), goes through Nebraska.

- There are approximately 2,500 lakes in the state.

- Kool-Aid was invented in Nebraska.

- The state's only Frank Lloyd Wright building is a private home in McCook.

- One of the nation's first female pilots, mail carrier Evelyn Genevieve Sharp, was from Nebraska.

- Nebraska has 23,686 miles of streams, rivers, and canals, ranking it tenth in the nation.

- Chief Crazy Horse was killed at Fort Robinson, which is now a state park.

- Most of the state sits squarely atop the huge Ogallala (also called the High Plains) Aquifer. This vast "underground sea" stretches from South Dakota to Texas.

- The 911 system of emergency communications was first developed here.

- The world's largest elephant fossil was found in Nebraska.

- Fort Atkinson, now a state historical park, was established on a site recommended by Lewis and Clark. It was the first military fort built west of the Missouri River and had the state's first school.

- The only member of the British royalty buried in the state, Lady Evelyn Brodstone Vestey, is at perpetual rest in her hometown of Superior.

- The state is crossed by the Pony Express, the Oregon Trail, the Mormon Trail, the Ox-bow Trail, a Ponca Trail of Tears, the Sidney-Deadwood Trail, and the Texas-Ogallala Trail.

- The Lewis and Clark Trail follows Nebraska's eastern border, the Missouri River.

- The Nebraska legislature is the only nonpartisan, one-house (or unicameral) system of state government in the country.

- A sculpture by Klaus Oldenburg is located on the University of Nebraska-Lincoln campus.

- Two world-famous architects designed buildings in Lincoln: Phillip Johnson designed the Sheldon Art Gallery, and I. M. Pei designed the NBC Center.

- Black calvary men, or "Buffalo Soldiers," were stationed at Fort Robinson during the Plains Indian Wars. They were first called Buffalo Soldiers by Native Americans because their hair reminded the Indians of buffalo hair.

- The first lawsuit in Nebraska was a dispute over stolen cheese.

- The world's first test-tube tigers were raised at the Henry Doorly Zoo in Omaha.

- Chicken pot pies were first developed by Swanson Foods in Omaha.

- The largest gathering ever of Native Americans (more than 10,000) was in 1851 at Horse Creek near Morrill.

- The world's largest collection of windmills is at the 2nd Wind Ranch near Comstock.

Recommended Nebraska Reading for Children

My Daniel by Pam Conrad

Prairie Songs by Pam Conrad

The Sandhill Crane by Colleen Gage

Dark Arrow by Lucille Mulcahy

Night of the Twisters by Ivy Ruckman

The Horsecatcher by Mari Sandoz

The Covered Wagon and Other Adventures by Lynn Scott

The Historical Album of Nebraska by Charles A. Wills

The prices and rates listed in this guidebook were confirmed at press time. We recommend, however, that you call establishments before traveling to obtain current information.

Land of the Pioneers

outheast Nebraska, a lovely land of rolling hills and forested river banks, has witnessed several historic events that shaped the future of the West. From original homestead cabins to blazing gunfights, from architectural wonders to ethnic festivals, from the Pony Express to the Oregon Trail, the Land of the Pioneers is a rich and exciting land for you to discover. Historic attractions, state parks, hiking and biking trails, B&Bs in tiny towns, and deluxe hotels in cities complement your prairie experience in southeast Nebraska.

Cass County

e'll begin our southeastern tour at **Platte River State Park,** located near Louisville just south of Interstate 80 and Highway 50. There's great hiking in the woods and a place to rest up at the lodge. Guests can stay in cabins or in a tepee village. (Tepee guests will need to bring their own sleeping bags, towels, soap, ice chests, and any other modern luxury.) Because of the rugged terrain, there are no camping facilities at Platte River State Park, but there are camping facilities at **Louisville Lakes State Recreation Area,** just a few minutes away. The restaurant at Platte River State Park offers buffalo entrees daily from Memorial Day through Labor Day. Activities in the park include swimming, hiking, paddle boating, tennis, archery, volleyball, and horseback trail rides. A Game and Parks permit is required. Before you get too far from Platte River State Park, please go see the one that didn't get away. At the **Ak-Sar-Ben Aquarium and Outdoor Education Center** at Schramm Park there's a catfish that makes me never want to put my feet in any water that is not crystal clear. Big fish with many sharp teeth live in the Missouri River where this giant fish was caught. At ninety-five pounds and 54 inches long, she's the largest catfish in captivity in the country. She has a 34-inch waist; if she had any fashion sense (really, those *whiskers!*), we could wear the same clothes. She's probably about thirty years old, and she doesn't have a name because the people who work there suspect if she were

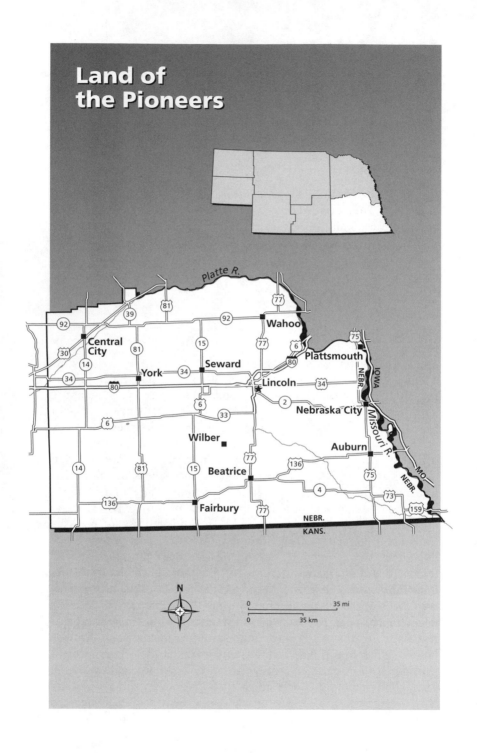

Land of
the Pioneers

Platte R.

92

39

81

92

77

Wahoo

Central
City

81

15

77

6

75

30

14

81

Seward

Plattsmouth

York

34

80

34

Lincoln

NEBR.

IOWA

34

80

6

2

Nebraska City

Missouri R.

6

33

Wilber

Auburn

14

81

15

77

136

75

MO

Beatrice

136

4

73

NEBR.

Fairbury

77

159

NEBR.
KANS.

N

0   35 mi

0   35 km

LAND OF THE PIONEERS

given a name it might somehow hex her longevity. In other tanks are the very weird-looking paddlefish and sturgeon. There are lots and lots of normal-looking fish in lots of other tanks. Two snapping turtles with sharp claws occupy one tank with goldfish intended as turtle snacks. Children often report to the staff when the turtles are "fighting." But they're not fighting, they're trying quite vigorously to make little snappers. The Education Center is fun, too, with lots of critter and bird parts to learn about. There's also a movie theater where you can see all sorts of wildlife-oriented films. It's located 9 miles south of Interstate 80, exit 436. The aquarium and center are open at various times and dates throughout the year; summer hours are Monday through Friday, 10:00 A.M. to 4:30 P.M.; and Saturday, Sunday, and holidays, 10:00 A.M. to 5:00 P.M. Admission is only $1.00 for adults and 50 cents for children ages six through fifteen. The number is (402) 332–3901. The Web site is www.ngpc.state.ne.us/parks/aquarium.html.

If you're staying at Platte River State Park from May through October, a short drive south will bring you to *Weeping Water* and the *Lofte Community Theater,* a setting for the "Born in a Barn" players, who have produced more than 300 plays in a converted 1924 hog barn since 1977. Four major productions run from May to October each year. The Lofte Community Theater is 3 miles north and 1/2 mile west of Weeping Water on Highway 1. If you want to be one of the more than 10,000 people who enjoy the productions each year, call (402) 267–5400 for tickets or more information. The Web site is www.lofte.com.

Weeping Water, local legend holds, gets it name from the voluminous tears shed by Native American women upon the death of their warriors after a fierce battle. They wept so long and so hard their tears began to form little streams and ultimately a larger stream. Sit quietly by the falls of the Weeping Water Creek, and hear the sound of ancient grief.

If you're hungry, head over to *Mom's Cafe* at 422 Main in *Plattsmouth* (junctions of Highways 66 and 34 in eastern Cass County) for the best chicken-fried steak in the world. Check it out; it costs $6.79 with all the fixin's. If you're there for breakfast, check that out, too. Mom's Cafe opens at 5:30 A.M. Monday through Saturday and at 6:00 A.M. on Sunday. They close at 8:00 P.M. Tuesday through Saturday and at 2:00 P.M. Sunday and Monday. The phone number is (402) 296–3000.

If you're a Lewis & Clark Expedition fan, Plattsmouth has something for you. In late July 1804, the expedition reached the mouth of the Platte River, or the "Great River Platt" as indicated in the journals. Historian Stephen Ambrose noted this event as a milestone since the mouth of the Platte "was the Missouri riverman's equivalent of crossing the equator" since it meant entering a new ecosystem and territory of the Sioux. The journals mentioned the Platte's great velocity as well as the amount of sand it dumped into the Missouri River and noted "a great number of wolves" at that evening's campsite. You won't typically see wolves today, but you can stand at the Platte's mouth at *Schilling Wildlife Management Area* by going from Plattsmouth's Main Street east over railroad tracks and by taking the first left onto Refuge Road. It's not hard at all to imagine the expedition and its excitement at this milestone. The phone number is (402) 755–2284.

Head back west on Highway 66 to *South Bend,* population ninety-seven. The *Round the Bend Bar* (it's the only business on the south side of the highway) serves big lunches for a little money and some of best prime rib dinners around. Its biggest claim to fame is the Testicle Festival, a feast of Rocky Mountain Oysters held annually on, ironically enough, Father's Day. The phone number is (402) 944–9974.

If you're a golfer, you'll want to go north from South Bend toward Interstate 80 and watch for signs to *Quarry Oaks* at 310th Street/Quarry Oaks Drive. This dramatic, scenic course has craggy terrain and rolls through a burr oak forest. Many holes overlook the Platte River, and there are striking elevation changes. Fees for eighteen holes range from $55 to $65, including a cart. Call (402) 944–6000 to make a reservation for a tee time about a week ahead of time.

If you're not a golfer, you should head directly to *Louisville* (Highways 66 and 50) to the *The Coop* lunchroom at 127 Main Street and the *Coop de ville Gallery* next door. The restaurant's decor is wildly and whimsically eclectic, and you are encouraged to rummage in the back room to select hats, jewelry, scarves, and gloves to get dressed up for lunch. You will need reservations, so if you're reading this prior to your trip, call right now. The number is (402) 234–2669. Lunches are wonderful, and the desserts divine. After lunch everyone in the place, this means you, dances around in a conga line and does the Chicken Dance. It's hilarious.

The owners are women artists who firmly believe women don't take the time to play, and The Coop restaurant is designed to alleviate that. Stop by next door to see some pretty, one-of-a-kind pieces at the Coop de ville Gallery. When you're exhausted from shopping, the gallery's *Cafe Poulet* serves specialty coffee drinks and cookies. The phone number is (402) 234–2717. The Web site for all these places is www.artchicksgallery.com.

Your next stop is *Elmwood,* the home of Bess Streeter Aldrich, one of many famous Nebraska authors. (To get to Elmwood from Louisville, take Highway 50 south to Highway 34. Go west on Highway 34 for 6 miles, and then turn north on Highway 1 for 2 miles.) Her works include *A Lantern in Her Hand* and several other novels. She published 160 short stories (her first financial success as a writer was a $175 check for winning a 1911 short-story contest sponsored by *Ladies Home Journal*). Most of her works are about what she knew best: the lives of pioneers in her adopted state of Nebraska and her home state of Iowa. At present visitors can see her *Home and Museum* at 204 East F Street, which is open for tours on Wednesday, Thursday, Saturday, and Sunday from 2:00 to 5:00 P.M. or by special appointment. The telephone number is (402) 994–3855. The *Bess Streeter Aldrich Museum* is housed in the Elmwood Library at 204 East F Street. It contains original manuscripts, awards she won, a gift shop with her books, and a duplicate model of the bust of her which is in the Nebraska Hall of Fame in Lincoln's State Capitol Building. Hours are the same as the Home and Museum. The Web site is www.lincolnne.com/nonprofit/bsaf.

If you'd like to speed up the pace a bit, head west on Highway 34 and stop at *Eagle Raceways,* just 12 miles west of Eagle on Highway 34 or 11 miles south of exit 420 on Interstate 80. From April through September races are held on the world's fastest ⅓-mile dirt track. Races begin on Friday and Saturday at 7:30 P.M.; the gates open at 5:30 P.M. For details call (402) 484–7704 or visit www.eagleraceway.com.

My golfing friends prevailed upon me to mention *Woodland Hills Golf Course,* just west of Eagle on Highway 34. Me, I'm inclined to agree with Mark Twain that golf is "a good walk spoiled," but I've seen the rapturous looks on my buddies' faces after a game at this course. Plus, it comes recommended by *Golf Digest,* which gave it a four-and-a-half-star rating as a result of its readers' survey of public-access golf courses. Four stars, translated from the survey, means, "Outstanding. Plan your next vacation around it." It's the only course in Nebraska with this rating. If you golf, you'll have that same rapturous look on your face. Prices are $25 to $35. The telephone number is (402) 475–4653. The Web site is www.woodlandhillsgolf.com.

Saunders County

The **Willow Point Gallery and Museum** in **Ashland** at 1431 Silver Street is a unique store with a waterfall, a stream, a wishing pond, fish, and native plants, which make visitors feel as though they've stepped outside from, well, the outside. See the seasons unfold at this indoor setting with nearly thirty mounted animals, including moose, black bear, mountain lion, white fox, and a huge polar bear, found among their natural habitats. Also featured is work by nationally known artist Gene Ronka. Ashland is on Highway 63; take one of three I–80 exits to reach town. The hours are Monday through Saturday, 10:00 A.M. to 6:00 P.M.; and Sunday, noon to 4:00 P.M. Call (402) 944–3613 or (800) 861–4260.

About 30 miles northwest of Ashland is **Wahoo,** the hometown of five internationally known men, each of whom achieved prominence in vastly different fields. The five famous sons include Darryl Zanuck, cofounder of 20th Century-Fox and winner of seven Academy Awards; "Wahoo" Sam Crawford, who was named to the Baseball Hall of Fame in 1957; Clarence W. Anderson, who wrote dozens of books about horses, starting with *Billy and Blaze;* Dr. George Beadle, who won the 1958 Nobel Peace Prize for having demonstrated how genes control the basic chemistry of the living cell; and Howard Hanson, a composer/musician who headed the Eastman School of Music for forty years and won the 1946 George Foster Peabody award for musical achievement.

Learn more about these men and the settlement of the area for free at the **Saunders County Historical Complex,** 240 North Walnut. This complex includes a museum building, a depot, a log house, a schoolhouse, a farm machinery building, a caboose, and a church. All the buildings are furnished with period pieces. For those of you with an aversion to ironing, there's a really scary collection of irons through the ages. On the front of the building is a 29,490-pound rock, which at one time was part of the Twin Rocks Marker on the **Ox-Bow Trail.** The Ox-Bow Trail was an important "feeder" trail to the Oregon Trail. From April through September the hours are Tuesday through Saturday, 10:00 A.M. to 4:00 P.M.; and Sunday, 1:30 to 4:30 P.M. From October through March hours are Tuesday through Friday, 10:00 A.M. to 4:00 P.M. The telephone number is (402) 443–3090.

LAND OF THE PIONEERS

Stop by for some famous Wahoo Wieners at the *OK Market* at 542 North Linden Street. (Wahoo is famous now for another reason: It was made the new "home office" of the David Letterman Show in May 1996.) The OK Market has six different kinds of Wahoo Wieners and dozens of different types of made-on-the-premises sausages, from garlic link baloney, Swedish potato sausage, and smoked bratwurst to *jaternice* (a blend of pork meats and bread) and *jelita* (a primary ingredient is blood). The 1917 building itself is quite remarkable. It has been deliberately maintained to look as though you've walked into the year 1926. The hours are Monday through Friday, 8:00 A.M. to noon and 1:00 to 5:30 P.M.; and Saturday, 8:00 A.M. to noon. Call (402) 443–3015.

Stop in next door at the *Wahoo Bakery*, 544 North Linden Street, where owners Jim and Maralee Taylor justifiably pride themselves on their Taylor Made Pastries for all Occasions. They have mouthwatering baked goods such as white rye bread, horn rolls (that's "rohlicky" if you speak Czech), and to-die-for *kolaches*. A *kolache* is a sweet bun with an indented top, loaded with fruit (even prunes!), poppy seeds, or cream cheese. Buy a lot—they're addictive. The bakery is open Monday through Friday from 6:15 A.M. to 4:00 P.M. and Saturday from 6:15 A.M. to 2:00 P.M. The number is (402) 443–3387.

No stop in Wahoo would be complete without a meal at the *Wigwam Cafe* at 146 East Fifth Street. This charming cafe is another chance to step into the past. Ceiling fans, exposed brick walls, booth seating, and low countertops provide an inviting setting for a great meal. The name of the cafe comes from a collection of Native American figurines. The food is pure-and-simple country cooking, from burgers to meat loaf to fried chicken and fish. Occasionally the owners, Clayton and Silvia Wade, make something different, such as Mexican food or specialties from Silvia's native Romania. Try the homemade pie. None of the meals are priced over

---

AUTHOR'S FAVORITE ANNUAL EVENTS IN SOUTHEAST NEBRASKA
(Call ahead to verify dates; all area codes are 402)

Annual Arbor Day Celebration, Nebraska City, last weekend in April, 873–3000

Renaissance Festival, near Raymond, third weekend in May, 783–5255

Rock Creek Trail Days, Fairbury, first weekend in June, 729–5777

Homestead Days, Beatrice, last weekend in June, 223–3514

July Jamm Music Festival, Lincoln, last full weekend in July, 434–5335

Czech Festival, Wilber, first full weekend in August, (888) 494–5237

Capital City Ribfest, Lincoln, third weekend in August, 441–8744

Applejack Festival, Nebraska City, third weekend in September, 873–3000

Flea Market and Arts-and-Crafts Show, Brownville, last weekend in September, 825–4751

Germanfest, Syracuse, last weekend in September, 269–3298

Star City Parade and Festival, Lincoln, second weekend in December, 434–5335

$7.00. The Wigwam Cafe is open Monday and Wednesday through Friday from 6:00 A.M. to 4:00 P.M., Saturday from 6:00 A.M. to 2:00 P.M., and Sunday from 8:00 A.M. to 2:00 P.M. You can phone them at (402) 443–5575.

As you drive by the **Saunders County Courthouse** on Highway 77, take note of a mounted torpedo surrounded by small American flags. It is displayed in memory of the men who died in the submarine USS *Wahoo,* which was sunk by the Japanese in 1943 after sinking twenty enemy ships. A plaque lists the names of the crew members who are still noted as "on patrol."

Lancaster County

The **Rogers House Bed & Breakfast,** an elegant three-story brick home at 2145 B Street in **Lincoln,** was built in 1914 in one of Lincoln's oldest neighborhoods as a retirement home for a prominent banker. In 1984 it became Lincoln's first B&B and the second B&B in the state. Owner Nora Houtsma's attention to detail makes a stay at this enchanting, light-filled B&B very pleasant indeed. Each of the eight rooms is decorated with antiques, and each has a private bath (four have claw-foot bathtubs and antique pedestal sinks). Windows of leaded and beveled glass, French doors, polished hardwood floors, three sunrooms, and a library round out the amenities. The **Ricketts Folsom House,** next door at 2125 B Street, is also owned by Ms. Houtsma. Its four rooms are equally as welcoming as those in the Rogers House and were renovated with the business traveler in mind; these rooms are wired for phones and lap-top computers. Both the Rogers House and the Ricketts Folsom House offer a full breakfast, which can be served wherever guests prefer: in their room, in the dining room, or in the sunrooms. Room rates range from $68 to $150 for the one third-floor room with a Jacuzzi. Children ages ten or older are welcome. Open daily except for Christmas Eve and Christmas Day. Call (402) 476–6961 for reservations. The Web site is www.rogershouseinn.com.

The **Museum of the Odd,** located in a two-story pink home at 701 Y Street, couldn't be more aptly named. Owner, curator, and artist Charlie Johnson has amassed an astonishing collection of oddities, which covers nearly every square inch of his residence, including the floors, walls, and sometimes ceilings. The mind tends to reel with delight when presented with shelves of cartoon-character bubble-bath containers, plastic banks, toy trains, rubber animals, pulp magazines, religious icons, children's books, baseball cards, board games, Halloween

Rogers House Bed & Breakfast

and Day of the Dead trinkets, sci-fi magazines and figurines, Mardi Gras beads, and a seemingly endless explosion of ordinary items that assume oddity due to their sheer number and presentation. One visitor described the Museum of the Odd as a massive collection of "shrapnel from the twentieth century's pop-culture explosion." Be sure to call ahead to make sure Charlie will be home to admit you to his shrine to oddity. The phone number is (402) 476–6735. There's no admission charge, but donations are appreciated.

Visitors to the **Bluestem Bookstore,** at 712 O Street in Lincoln, are likely to be greeted by the resident cat, Thurber. The seventeen-year-old feline is reaching "a dignified middle age," according to owners Scott and Pat Wendt, and he is routinely named the Employee of the Month. If asked politely, Thurber may even sleepily share one of the cozy overstuffed chairs that encourage people to tarry and read. Housed in a former beer warehouse in the historic Haymarket District, the bookstore contains more than 30,000 used, rare, scholarly, and out-of-print books. Specialty areas include western Americana, military history, aviation (Charles "Lucky Lindy" Lindbergh did learn to fly in Lincoln, after all!), literature, Nebraska history, and Nebraska authors. There are also substantial collections of science fiction, poetry, theater, and children's books. Often there are several regulars in the store engaged in a lively conversation with the Wendts. Hours are 10:00 A.M. to 5:00 P.M. Monday through Saturday. The number is (402) 435–7120.

After your visit to Bluestem Bookstore, take some time to stop at other interesting places along the brick-lined streets of Lincoln's *Haymarket District.* In addition to the usual brewpubs, restaurants, galleries, and antiques stores, there's a place to buy treats for your pets and a store filled with beautiful bed linens. Stop by *Conner's Architectural Antiques* (appropriately dusty and jam-packed with salvaged doors, windows, lamps, wooden columns, furnace grates, and tin ceilings) at 701 P Street. Buy Nebraska-made products at *From Nebraska,* at 140 North Eighth Street. *The Oven,* 201 North Eighth Street, serves Indian food in one of the most simply attractive restaurants in town. Stop in for coffee at *The Mill,* 800 P Street, and visit with artists at the *Burkholder Artists Cooperative,* 719 P Street. Several art cooperatives and galleries in the Haymarket District hold "First Friday" open houses in the evenings on the first Friday of the month.

Although the *Nebraska State Capitol,* Fifteenth and K Streets, is hardly off the beaten path, it is decidedly worth a visit and a free tour. It's not hard to find; in fact, at 400 feet it's the tallest building in Lincoln and is visible from up to 30 miles away. This stunning architectural masterpiece was designated the "fourth architectural wonder of the world of all time" by the American Institute of Architecture in 1948. Designed by Bertram Goodhue, the capitol is filled with incredible mosaics, murals, heavy carved doors, and a multitude of minute details that add up to a very beautiful building. (You can even get married there; the daughter of former Governor Ben Nelson wed there in October 1998.) Every piece of art

It's in the Cards

*W*ay Home Music and Books, located at 3231 South Thirteenth Street in Lincoln, is a cool place to score a lot of things you would not likely find at a typical mall-type bookstore. Books, magazines, tapes, and CDs include such topics as astrology, religion, women's issues, Native American culture, gay and lesbian issues, UFOs, relationships, and health. Pick up some tarot or medicine cards or some runes. The Way Home also has a great selection of candles, crystals, incense, rocks, and jewelry.

Depending upon the day you visit (closed Monday), there may be a resident psychic, channeler, or tarot-card reader available for a private session. Hours are Tuesday through Friday, 10:00 A.M. to 7:00 P.M.; Saturday, 10:00 A.M. to 6:00 P.M.; and Sunday, noon to 5:00 P.M. Co-owner Scott Colborn also has a wonderful, spine-tingling show on KZUM radio called Exploring Unexplained Phenomena. *For more information about the store or the radio show, call (402) 421–1701 or e-mail kcolborn@inetnebr.com.*

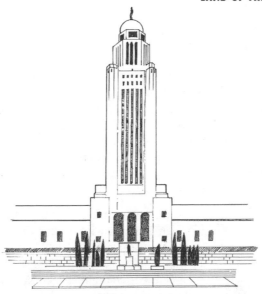

Nebraska State Capitol Building

inside and out is a symbolic reminder of events in the story of Nebraska and the story of humanity. The statue atop the capitol, *The Sower,* which was sculpted by Lee Lowrie, symbolizes the sowing of seeds of life for better living in the future. (Locals have an exceedingly irreverent and suggestive nickname for the capitol building; find someone with a sense of humor to ask what it is.) The statue of a pensive-looking Abraham Lincoln, facing west outside of the capitol, was done by Daniel Chester French, sculptor of the Lincoln Memorial in Washington, D.C. Don't fail to view the plains from the capitol's fourteenth-floor observation deck. Hours are Monday through Friday, 8:00 A.M. to 5:00 P.M.; Saturday and holidays, 10:00 A.M. to 5:00 P.M.; and Sunday, 1:00 to 5:00 P.M. For more information call (402) 471–0448. The Web site is www.capitol.org.

One of Lincoln's smallest bars has a big reputation in the world of blues music. Measuring only 20 feet by 90 feet, the *Zoo Bar*'s walls are lined with photographs of bands that make this downtown Lincoln bar a regular stop on their tours. Nationally and internationally famous blues acts such as Albert Collins, Luther Allison, Kinky Friedman, Marcia Ball, Gatemouth Brown, Jay McShann, Lonnie Mack, and far too many more acts to mention have all played the Zoo to wildly enthusiastic crowds. Any given night will see a capacity audience of 150 people. If the band is hot, be prepared to stand in line, but think of it as an opportunity to make some new Lincoln friends. The Zoo is often visited by famous fans of the blues when they are in town, including Patrick Swayze, Wesley Snipes, and Kris Kristofferson. Former Nebraska Senator Bob Kerrey has also been known to stop in. In 1993, the Zoo Bar received the W. C. Handy Award for Best Blues Bar in the Nation from the Blues Foundation in Nashville. Although blues is the standard fare, the Zoo also books jazz, bluegrass, reggae, and rock and roll. The address is 136 North Fourteenth Street. Hours are Tuesday to Friday, 3:00 P.M. to 1:00 A.M.; Saturday, 2:00 P.M. to 1:00 A.M.; Sunday, on occasion, 5:00 to 10:00 P.M. Call (402) 435–8754 for more information. The Zoo Bar is part of the "Beermuda Triangle" in downtown Lincoln, consisting of the Zoo Bar, O'Rourke's, Duffy's, and Barrymore's (okay, it's not three bars, it's four).

Barrymore's Lounge, with an alley entrance between O and P Streets and Thirteenth and Fourteenth Streets, is in back of the old Stuart Theater. The door is original, the same one used by Mickey Rooney and Helen Hayes during the building's former incarnation as a theater. The lounge is complete with a light board, hanging backdrops that reach ten stories to the ceiling, and dressing rooms. There's a genteel feel here, and it's a popular place for après-performance gatherings from the nearby world-class Lied Center for the Performing Arts. The phone number is (402) 476–6494.

If you're old enough to remember strapping on a pair of roller skates, or if you're a fan of in-line skating, the *National Museum of Roller Skating* in Lincoln will hold some fascination for you. See the 1819 French Petitbled, the first roller skate ever patented, and the original modern

Ghosts of Lincoln

G houlies, ghosties, and long-legged beasties. Lincoln does not lack for stories of phantoms.

The C. C. White Building on the Wesleyan University Campus is said to be visited by the ghost of Miss Urania Clara Mills, an elderly music teacher who died in 1940. The apparition is clad in an ankle-length brown skirt, and she wears her hair in a bun. The Capitol Building is also haunted by the spirits of two men: one who fell to his death in 1967 while stringing

Christmas lights, and another who fell from a spiral staircase, which is now closed to the public. It is said that the capitol was built on a slight rise that was sacred to the Indians, so native spirits still inhabit the site. While the ghosts may be scary, some swear the single most bone-chilling thing about the capitol is opening day of the legislative session, when lobbyists, favor seekers, and bootlickers swarm about the senators in a feeding frenzy.

roller skate patented by James L. Plimpton in 1863. The museum has the world's largest collection of roller skates and roller-skating memorabilia, both archival and modern, ranging from wheels to toys to posters, photographs, trophies, and medals. There are displays on roller disco, vaudeville and trick skaters, and skating animals. Tara Lipinski, 1998 Olympic gold medalist, loaned a pair of her roller skates and a fetching outfit. Also featured are roller-skating costumes bedecked with fringe and sequins. Ask curator Deborah Wallis to tell you the story of the English guy, who a long time ago wore a pair of old skates to a fancy costume ball and smashed into something expensive and extremely breakable; other people's embarrassment is always amusing. Located at 4730 South Street, the museum is open Monday through Friday, 9:00 A.M. to 5:00 P.M.; closed on holidays but open on some weekends in the summer. Admission is free; donations are welcome. Call (402) 483–7551, ext. 16, or visit the museum's Web site at www.rollerskatingmuseum.com.

Pioneers Park, at South Coddington and West Van Dorn in the southwestern part of Lincoln, offers a quiet retreat to residents and tourists alike. There are duck ponds, thousands of pine trees planted by the WPA, hiking trails, a toboggan run, playgrounds, a challenging eighteen-hole golf course, picnic areas, and an amphitheater for summertime performances.

Ya Gotta Have Art

*T*he **Sheldon Memorial Art Gallery and Sculpture Garden,** *on the grounds of the University of Nebraska at Twelfth and R Streets in Lincoln, is one of those places where you can feed your mind and your soul. The emphasis of the permanent collection is on twentieth-century American art, and there's always a great temporary collection on display. However, it's a great place to visit no matter what the current exhibitions are. The building is a quiet place, airy and light-filled, designed by Philip Johnson. But the best part is the sculpture garden, which is a sunken garden with little concrete seats, ponds, fountains, pretty potted plants,* *and, of course, some mighty fine sculpture. Even though the garden is just a few feet away from busy sidewalk traffic, somehow it remains a peaceful, sheltered setting day or night. At night you'll detect some young-and-in-love smoochers in the shadows, and during the day you can watch the sun cast shadows on the sculpture—something I often did to escape from piles of books and papers during my grad-school days. Now I'm mostly at the Sheldon on weekends to see independent and foreign films at the Mary Reipma Ross Theater. Jazz aficionados will appreciate the Jazz in June held every Tuesday evening in the Sculpture Garden.*

Several sculptures add grace to the park. They include a huge bronze buffalo, four large sandstone columns that at one time were a part of the former Federal Treasury Building in Washington, D.C., and a bigger-than-life-size statue of Chief Red Cloud, which was approved by Native American leaders as being truly representative of the Sioux tribes. Within Pioneers Park is the 136-acre **Pioneers Park Nature Center,** with 6 miles of hiking trails through native short-grass, tallgrass, and lowland prairie, wetlands, a riparian forest, wildflower areas, and herb gardens. There are two buildings with natural-history and live-animal exhibits, which are beautifully landscaped with plants that attract birds and butterflies. Hours at the nature center are June through August, Monday through Saturday, 8:30 A.M. to 8:30 P.M., and Sunday, noon to 8:30 P.M.; September through May, Monday through Saturday, 8:30 A.M. to 5:00 P.M., and Sunday, noon to 5:00 P.M. Call (402) 441–7895 for further details.

If you've got a sense of the macabre, you might consider stopping at the 190-acre **Wyuka Cemetery.** This Lincoln site is where the first post–World War II serial killer is buried. For five days in 1958, nineteen-year-old Charlie Starkweather went on a killing spree with his fourteen-year-old girlfriend, Caril Ann Fugate, which left ten people dead in Lincoln and Lancaster County. Terror-stricken residents of the area seldom left their homes for those five days, and the Lincoln paper published its last extra edition during the siege. Starkweather was captured and executed; Fugate spent twenty-five years in prison. Bruce Springsteen's album *Nebraska* includes a song based on this bloodbath, and the movie *Badlands,* with Martin Sheen and Sissy Spacek, is similarly based on this tragic episode in Lincoln's history. The address at Wyuka Cemetery is 3600 O Street. (O Street, by the way, is considered to be the longest, straightest main street in the world. Highway 34, which is O Street in Lincoln, runs for approximately 50 miles east to Union, Nebraska. O Street has been immortalized in verse by Allen Ginsberg, who wrote the poem "Zero Street" while visiting his friend, the novelist Karl Shapiro, who taught at the University of Nebraska.)

If you like dolls, the **Gladys Lux Historical Gallery** will be your cup of tea. The collection, housed at the University Place Art Center, 2601 North Forty-eighth Street, has more than 1,600 dolls dating from 1785. There are bisque dolls from the 1840s, wooden dolls, wax dolls, American Indian dolls, Barbie and Madame Alexander and Kewpie dolls . . . and that's just part of the collection. There's a whole slew of doll accessories. Hours are Tuesday and Thursday, 10:00 A.M. to noon; and Saturday, 1:00 to 5:00 P.M. Admission is free. The phone number is (402) 466–8692. The Web site is www.universityplaceart.com.

Not far away is another unusual and wonderful collection. The *International Quilt Study Center* houses the largest publicly owned quilt collection in the world. Several hundred quilts range from traditional to quite modern; they date from the 1700s to contemporary. These rare quilts on display are rotated every six months, so it's unlikely you'll ever see the same quilt twice.

The center is located in the University of Nebraska-Lincoln Home Economics Building on Thirty-fifth Street just north of the East Campus Loop off Holdrege Street. Hours are Monday through Saturday, 9:30 A.M. to 4:30 P.M.; and Sunday, 1:30 to 4:30 P.M. Admission is free. Call (402) 472–6549 for more details. The Web address is www.quiltstudy.unl.edu.

For people who'd like to see what the countryside looked like before it was altered by humankind, a visit to *Nine-Mile Prairie* near Lincoln is in order. Located on West Fletcher Avenue, off Northwest Forty-eighth Street, this 230-acre area is one of the largest unplowed, virgin tallgrass prairies left in Nebraska. Approximately 350 kinds of plants are known to grow on the prairie; most are native and some are quite rare. More than eighty kinds of birds have been sighted in the Nine-Mile Prairie. Animals such as deer, badgers, squirrels, and mice inhabit the prairie, as do a variety of insects. When you go, remember not to pick or collect the plants, not to litter, and not to smoke. Information about the prairie and its uses and care can be obtained by calling (402) 472–2971.

Peace, Love, and Understanding

*P*rairie Peace Park, *a monument to global understanding, is located just north of Interstate 80 at exit 388, west of Lincoln. For those with a sense of the ironic, it's also only a few dozen miles down the road from the new Strategic Air and Space Museum, off exit 426 and between Omaha and Lincoln. Some might say that the museum is a monument to war, while others might say its exhibits are what kept the* United States from falling under the Communist domino effect. You decide. In any case, Prairie Peace Park has indoor and outdoor sculptures, murals, paintings, and mazes to "promote cultural diversity and understanding." Prairie Peace Park charges admission; call (402) 466–6622 for more information. The Web site is www.igc.apc. org/Peace Park.

Another natural prairie (this one is 15 miles southwest of Lincoln or 3.1 miles south of Denton) is the *Spring Creek Prairie.* Its 610 acres include one of the largest tallgrass prairie tracts in the state; only 2 percent of the native tallgrass prairie that existed in the nineteenth century remains extant. This former farm, now owned by the Audubon Society, was spared the plow because its rock-strewn soils and steep hills of an ancient glacial moraine were suited less for farming and more for grazing. A stroll across the land will reveal wetlands, natural springs, creeks, ponds, and woodland. Wildlife may include deer, red foxes, coyotes, badgers, beavers, and muskrats. Spring Creek is also home to several species of birds whose population has been declining; these include dickcissel, field sparrow, greater prairie chicken, Bell's vireo, and red-headed woodpecker. All this is within 75 miles of Nebraska's two largest cities and about half the state's population. You'll hardly be the first tourists; arrowheads are not uncommon, and, in places, you'll be walking in Oregon Trail ruts. For more information call (402) 797–2301.

The *Princeton Tavern,* 7 miles south of Lincoln on Highway 77, offers great Mexican food on weekends in a thoroughly American Midwest setting. The decor is knotty-pine walls, with a new linoleum floor. On Friday, Saturday, and Sunday nights, the tavern is filled with customers who come from miles around for tacos, enchiladas, burritos,

Fall for Nebraska

*T*he fall foliage of Nebraska is, admittedly, not nearly as famous as the fall foliage in New England. But the fall colors along the heavily treed Missouri River in southeast Nebraska are very nice indeed. And a bonus: The roads, restaurants, and hotels won't be overly crowded with tourists from around the world. On any given byway it'll likely be just you and a whole lot of pretty scenery. And you won't be greeted by taciturn locals who say, "Aye-yup, you can't get there from here."

The intensity of the fall color is dictated by the amount of rainfall in the preceding months. Some years are downright spectacular, and other years are still well worth a visit. Find yourself a road anywhere just south of Nebraska City all the way down to Indian Cave State Park near the river, take your time, and enjoy your surroundings. The Southeast Nebraska Visitors Guide *includes a "Country Lanes Scenic and Fall Foliage Tour"* page with a map for your convenience. The guide also recommends this slow-paced tour in the early spring, when the redbud and plum trees are in bloom. Call the Nebraska Tourism Division at (877) NEBRASKA to get a free copy of the guide.

and nachos. The tavern serves regular bar-style food as well, such as burgers, wings, catfish, pork tenderloin, livers, and gizzards. Daily specials tend to fit the square-meal definition found in Jane and Michael Stern's cookbook *Square Meals:* It has to be *big*, and it has to be *good . . .* and you have to *want* it. Locals say the bank was robbed (when there was a bank; at present the town has a population of about thirty) by the James gang. But you won't get robbed; the highest price on the menu for more-than-you-can-eat Mexican food is $7.95. The telephone number is (402) 798–9950.

You can't leave Lancaster County before going to the **James Arthur Vineyards** near the community of Raymond. The vineyards cover 400 acres of rolling hills and prairie grasslands. The building itself is really quite nice—it's open and inviting with a huge wraparound porch. In warm weather you can sit on the porch or walk up a hill to gazebos. In cold weather you can sink into some comfy chairs inside by the fireplace. Buy some of the award-winning wine and some of the great cheese, meats, salmon, and trout at the gift shop, and you've got yourself a picnic. The food is very good, and the ambience is even better. To get to James Arthur from Lincoln, take Fourteenth Street north for 7 miles and turn west on Raymond Road for 2½ miles. The address is 2001 West Raymond Road, and the phone number is (402) 783–5255. The Web site is www.jamesarthurvineyards.com.

Otoe County

Nebraska City, one of the oldest communities in the state, was founded in the early 1850s by William Nuckolls as a trading post and a riverboat stop on the Missouri River. The city's attractions are as varied as its visitors. First is **Arbor Lodge State Historical Park and Arboretum,** a beautiful estate that was the home of J. Sterling Morton, founder of Arbor Day, which is now celebrated internationally. In 1854 a young Morton left Michigan with his new bride to take up residence in Nebraska Territory. They missed the trees of home and quickly planted trees, shrubs, and flowers around their home and added an apple orchard. A journalist by profession, Morton became the editor of Nebraska's first newspaper and used it as a way to spread the word across the territory about his tree-planting convictions. Morton's interest in trees stemmed from practical reasons: They were needed for fuel, lumber, fencing, and many other purposes. He felt that with enough trees, Nebraska could become the "Sylvan Queen of the Republic." Arbor Day became an official Nebraska holiday in 1872. Visitors to Arbor Lodge

State Historical Park and Aboretum today will find a magnificent Neo-colonial mansion of fifty-two rooms furnished in Victorian and Empire pieces, plus some great Stickley furniture. There's even a one-lane bowling alley. Stroll through the beautifully landscaped grounds, with a seventy-two-acre arboretum that contains 270 varieties of trees and shrubs, and a formal rose garden. The grounds are open year-round. The mansion is open daily from April through December. A Game and Parks permit is required, and a nominal admission fee is charged. Call (402) 873–7222 or visit the park's Web site at www.ngp.ngpc.state.ne. us/parks/arbor.html. Here's one more bit of Arbor Lodge trivia: J. Sterling Morton's son, Joy, founded the Morton Salt Company.

Just across the road west from Arbor Lodge State Historical Park and Aboretum is the *Arbor Day Farm,* 100 Arbor Avenue, a 235-acre working apple orchard and tree farm. This orchard is one of several in Nebraska City, which is a good reason for Nebraska City to be called the Apple Capital of Nebraska. There's something about the local soil that makes for arguably the best apples in the world. If you're in town in the fall, be sure to pick up some apple cider. You can buy apple pies and nature-related items at the gift shop. During apple season you can watch as apples are sorted and boxed. Pies are available seasonally. Hours are Monday through Saturday, 9:00 A.M. to 5:00 P.M.; and Sunday, noon to 5:00 P.M.; closed Christmas, Thanksgiving, and Easter. For

Unadilla, Punxsutawney West

*W*hether or not Punxsutawney Phil sees the shadow of his furry little head, the Otoe County community of **Unadilla** has a celebration on the first Saturday in February. In 1988 Unadilla was officially proclaimed the Groundhog Capitol of Nebraska. What's a name without a festival, you may well ask. The Groundhog Festival, held in the tiny downtown district, consists of a wild game feed and, weather permitting, a parade. The weather is a factor, one would assume, because it's probably not much fun riding in a convertible on frigid days when the wind comes sweeping down

the plains. Such an experience would give new meaning to "a smile frozen on her face."

Located 28 miles southeast of Lincoln on Highway 2, Unadilla was named after the community of the same name in New York. Unadilla is an Iroquois Indian word meaning "a place of meeting." The Groundhog Day Festival is not a bad place to meet some new friends. And while you're in town, take a hike at the nearby Deacon Prairie, where in warmer months you might espy a Western Fringe Prairie Orchid, which is on the endangered species list.

more information call (402) 873–9347. Visit the Web site at www.arbor day.org.

Mayhew Cabin and Historical Village Foundation, at 2012 Fourth Corso in Nebraska City, was once the westernmost branch of the Underground Railroad, which operated to help slaves reach free territory in the 1800s prior to the Civil War. The site was initially named after John Brown, who believed that slavery was a sin against Christianity and could only be resolved through armed conflict. His most famous raid took place in October 1859 at Harpers Ferry, West Virginia. He was convicted of treason and hanged three months later. It is believed that he made several visits to Nebraska City in the 1850s. Nebraska City's location on the edge of free territory and near the site of the Missouri River crossing made it an integral part of the Underground Railroad. The cabin on site was built in 1851 and has been authenticated by the Nebraska State Historical Society as one of the oldest buildings still standing in Nebraska. A hand-dug cave under the cabin was built under the ruse that it would be a root cellar for a new "vegetarian society." A tunnel from the cave leads to South Table Creek, where slaves could slip away down the creek bed. In addition to the cabin and cave, the historical village has several historical structures from the area. Owners Larry and Linda Shepard have restored much of the facility. Inside they have added "An Evening on Main Street," which portrays a stroll down an 1890s main street. Mayhew Cabin and Historical Village is open April 1 through October 31, Monday through Friday, 10:00 A.M. to 5:00 P.M. and weekends 10:00 A.M. to 6:00 P.M. Admission is $6.00 for adults and $5.00 for children age fourteen and under. The telephone number is (402) 873–3115.

The *Arbor Day Farm Lied Conference Center,* at 2700 Sylvan Road in Nebraska City, offers deluxe accommodations in a beautiful Adirondack-style lodge. It is situated on 260 acres of the Arbor Day Farm and serves as an environmental-education resource for the National Arbor Day Foundation. The lodge features 144 rooms on three levels, fine dining, a cocktail lounge, a lap-size heated pool, exercise equipment, a fitness center, bike rentals, golf, carriage rides, and hiking trails. The building's heating and cooling systems are powered by an ultramodern energy plant fueled by wood chips. The Lied Center's design was one of thirteen selected to appear in the American Institute of Architects' first annual Exhibition on Environmentally Conscious Architecture in 1991. The rooms are lovely, and prices vary throughout the year from $89 to $109 for a single room. Reservations are recommended. Ask about the special packages throughout the year. For more information or to make reservations, call (800) 546–LIED (5433) or (402) 873–8733. Visit the Web site at www.adflcc.com.

Another great place to stay in Nebraska City is the **Whispering Pines B&B,** at Twenty-first Street and Sixth Avenue (Steamwagon Road). The century-old, two-story brick house is surrounded by six and a half acres of trees, fish ponds, fountains, and paths. W. B. and Shirley Smulling have planted thousands of flowers for your enjoyment (and for the enjoyment of the deer; Shirley says they like tulips but not the narcissus or daffodils). The five bedrooms are furnished with antiques; two have private baths. Relax on the veranda, soak in the hot tub, play a game of horseshoes or croquet, or try to spot the wild foxes, which put in sporadic appearances. Breakfast is generally a baked egg strata, waffles with homemade preserves or syrup, apple pancakes with homemade apple cider sauce, and fresh fruit, which quite often are blackberries or raspberries picked right on the grounds. They are closed on Christmas Eve and Christmas Day and on New Year's Eve and New Year's Day. Rates range from $55 to $80. To make reservations, call (402) 873–5850. Their Web site address is www.bbonline.com/ne/whispering/.

Nebraska City also offers an abundance of outlet shopping. A **VF Factory Outlet** mall is on the south edge of town, at US 75 and Nebraska Highway 2. Downtown outlets include the **Pendleton Outlet Store,** the **Full-Size Fashion Outlet,** and the **Special Occasions Outlet.**

If you feel like dancing, do take the time to go to **Syracuse** and the old-fashioned dance hall called the **Elms Ballroom.** The hall draws large groups of dancers in the evening to enjoy the music of live bands, which play everything from fifties music to rock 'n roll. Syracuse is southeast of

Puppy Love

*T*he **Elms Ballroom,** *in Syracuse, is where the cutest boy in the world took me on our first date. We donned our respective motorcycle helmets and drove there through a sticky summer night on his Honda. I don't remember much of the evening, being awash in teenage love, but I do remember how sweet it was that entire families came to the dance—*

Grandpa and Grandma all the way down to toddlers. There are still quite a few places in Nebraska where weekend dances are a family affair, such as the Elms. Big band, polka, rock 'n' roll . . . every time I drive through Syracuse I think of that cute boy. The relationship wasn't destined for eternity, but it sure made that summer one to remember.

Lincoln on Highway 2. The telephone number is (402) 269–9914.

Johnson County

The bridge of Johnson County in **Cook** is the only covered bridge in the state; it links Windmill Memorial Park and Triangle Park. Stop for a picnic in this pleasant area and enjoy what Cook residents worked so hard to create. Cook, located on Highway 50 in northern Johnson County, has a lot of active town boosters, and the 42-foot-long covered bridge is a result of many volunteer hours and donated materials.

If the Johnson County Courthouse and town square in **Tecumseh,** at the junction of Highways 50 and 136, look familiar to you, it might be because they were featured as the location for the filming of *Amerika,* a popular television miniseries filmed in the 1980s. Go into any store or restaurant in town and ask about the filming; it's likely you'll be talking to one of the hundreds of area residents who appeared as extras.

OTHER ATTRACTIONS WORTH SEEING IN SOUTHEAST NEBRASKA

(All area codes are 402)

ASHLAND

Mahoney State Park,
28500 West Park Highway,
I–80 exit 426; 944–2523;
www.ngpc.state.ne.us/
Strategic Air and Space Museum, *I–80 exit 426;*
944–3100 or 800–358–5029;
www.sacmuseum.org
Wildlife Safari Park, *I–80 exit 426; 944–9453*
Quarry Oaks Golf Course,
16600 Quarry Oaks Road,
I–80 exit 426; 944–6000
(call ahead for a challenging game on a stunning course)

GREENWOOD

Bakers Candy Factory,
60 North Highway 6, I–80 exit 420; 789–2700

Nemaha County

You might have imagined there would be a Podunk, Nebraska, and indeed, there was. The times have changed, however, and so has the name of the town. The former Podunk is now **Brock** and is in northern Nemaha County on Highway 67.

Head about 12 miles northwest to **Auburn,** which has been called the antiques capital of southeast Nebraska. (According to a promotional brochure, it's also referred to as Nebraska's Oldest Tree City, U.S.A., and Home of the World's Largest Leaf.) This pleasant little town, with a population of 3,500, has six antiques stores. If you've been looking for that one-of-a-kind piece of china to complete your collection, a Roy Rogers doll, or a metal doorstop, this could very well be your lucky day. If you work up an appetite while antiques shopping, there's a very nice restaurant called **Arbor Manor** at 1617 Central Avenue. Four first-floor rooms in a 1908 Victorian home are the setting for some great steaks, which are cut up right in the kitchen. Camille Stanley, owner and manager, prepares wonderfully hearty soups such as a tomato-based broccoli and ham, cauliflower and crab, hamburger, and "whatever goodies" she has on hand. Summertime soups include gazpacho or fruit soups. Steak entrees range from $9.95 to $18.50; chicken and fish entrees are available for $7.50 to $12.95. Hours are Monday through Saturday, 5:00 to 9:00 P.M.; phone (402) 274–3663.

Coryell Park is an unexpected pleasure, located in the middle of farm fields. This privately owned park was the original homestead of Richard Coryell, and part of it was converted into a thirty-two-acre free park for public use in 1934. A sign, with a message from the Coryell family, states: IT IS THE WISH OF THE DONORS THAT THE PUBLIC MAY, WITHOUT MONEY AND WITHOUT PRICE, ENJOY ITS PRIVILEGES. WE ONLY ASK CIVILITY, DECENCY, AND GOOD ORDER FROM ALL, THAT ALL MAY ENJOY ITS BLESSINGS.

These blessings include enclosed picnic shelters, playgrounds, a basketball court, a social hall, a re-created homestead house, and an incredible stone chapel, which is often used for weddings. To get to Coryell Park, take Highway 136 until you're 7 miles west of Auburn, turn north, and go 3 miles. The park closes at sunset. Reservations for large groups can be made by calling (402) 856–2875.

Brownville, east of Auburn on Highway 136 on the Missouri River, might give Rome a run for its money; Brownville is also known as the City of Seven Hills. Brownville was settled in 1854 and became a major steamboat landing, river crossing, overland freighting terminus, and grain-milling center. It has more museums, historic homes and sites, galleries, and craft and antiques shops than you can shake a stick at. Of particular note is the *Captain Bailey House/Brownville Museum,* at Fourth and Main Streets. This seven-gabled, Gothic Revival house was built of bricks made in Brownville. The house is full of antiques, and it even comes with a ghost. When Mrs. Bailey was found dead of poisoned ice cream, suspicion fell on a woman who was said to be overly fond of Captain Bailey. When the newly spouseless Captain Bailey failed to return her affections, he was also found dead from poisoned food. Listen carefully and you may hear the rustling of petticoats or creaking footsteps. The Captain Bailey house is open on weekends early in May and September through mid-October from 1:00 to 5:00 P.M. and daily in June through August from 1:00 to 5:00 P.M. Admission is free. The number is (402) 825–6001.

Also on Main Street is the *Whiskey Run Creek Vineyards & Winery,* where you can stop for a toast in a century-old barn situated over a creek. Hours are 10:00 A.M. to 5:00 P.M. daily. The number is (402) 825–4601. Visit the Web site at www.whiskeyruncreek.com

The *Brownville Village Theater* was originally the Christian Church and now draws worshipers of live theater. The oldest in the state, this fourteen-week summer repertory theater is supported by Lincoln's Nebraska Wesleyan University. Performances begin the first Saturday in June. Each person is not only an actor but also serves as a technician, working on scenery, properties, costumes, light and sound, box office, makeup, and house management. The theater presents at least six shows, in alternating sequence, which draw audiences from hundreds of miles away. The Brownville Village Theater is 1 block south of Main Street at College Street. Reservations are highly encouraged. For more information, call (402) 825–4121 after June 1. Visit the Web site at www. ci.brownville.ne.us/bvt.

Brownville's connection to the river is preserved at the *Captain Meriwether Lewis Museum of River History,* a steam-powered, side-wheel vessel that helped channelize the unpredictable, wild, and often dangerous Missouri River. Visitors will see what role this massive dredge played in taming the Missouri and will also learn about the geology of the Missouri River basin. Giant steam engines and boilers show how the vessel worked; dining halls, sleeping quarters, and the pilothouse show where the fifty-two-man crew worked. Open daily from Memorial Day through Labor Day; weekends in April, May, and September. Hours are 12:30 to 5:00 P.M.; admission for guided tours is $2.00 for adults and 75 cents for children age fourteen and under. Call (402) 825–3341 for more information.

After all the sight-seeing you'll want to boost your energy level at the *Brownville Mill,* the oldest health food store in the state, at First and Main Streets. Choose from a huge variety of fresh health foods, hundreds of vitamins, nuts, honey, seeds, and trail-mix snacks. Brownville Mill is open year-round, Monday through Saturday, 9:00 A.M. to 5:00 P.M.; from May to December it's also open Sunday from 1:00 to 5:00 P.M. Owner Harold Davis still grinds flour, an activity that harkens back to Brownville's past as a milling center. Although Davis is deeply committed to historic preservation in Brownville, he's not immune to the joys of modern conveniences—he uses two small electric grindstones to make his flour. The telephone number is (800) 305–7990. The Web site is sky port. com/brownvillemills/.

Afer stocking up on healthy food and trail mix, you're ready for the 21-mile *Steamboat Trace Trail,* which starts south of Brownville and extends north through spectacular river-country scenery almost all the way to Nebraska City. Hike or bike, or like me, amble along the trail; I guarantee you'll agree it's quite lovely. For information call (402) 335–3325 or visit the Web site at www.ci.brownville.ne.us/trace.

Richardson County

One of the more interesting characters in Nebraska history was Joseph Deroin, the son of French trader Amable Deroin and an Otoe Indian woman. He claimed land on the Half-Breed Tract, which covers land in what is now Nemaha and Richardson County. Deroin established a trading post on the Missouri River and laid out the village of St. Deroin. He had three wives, has been described as "overbearing and tyrannical," and apparently came to view the village as his fiefdom. He was killed while trying to "collect" $6.00 for a pig from settler James Biddow. According to local legend, Deroin was buried astride his horse in the town cemetery. Another colorful graveyard legend holds that A. J. Ritter lost an arm while "fishing" with dynamite. His arm was buried before the rest of him, and sometimes, on certain nights, Mr. Ritter rises one-armed from his grave, searching for his lost arm. St. Deroin, at one time home to 300 people, was abandoned when the Missouri River channel shifted course and a cholera outbreak claimed many lives. By the 1920s all that remained was a one-room school. At present, St. Deroin is part of Indian Cave State Park and welcomes visitors to the school, a reconstructed log cabin, and a general store. Living-history demonstrations on weekends in summer and fall bring the village back to life.

The pristine *Indian Cave State Park,* 2 miles north and 5 miles east of

Bad Name, Good Idea

There was once a site near Auburn with a name that is currently very politically incorrect and insensitive. The 125,000-acre **Half-Breed Tract** *was set aside by the government in 1830, per the Prairie Du Chien Treaty, specifically for abandoned children born to fur traders and their Native American wives. As adults, these mixed-blood descendants often had difficulty in establishing a claim to tribal lands and thus were compensated with land between the Little Nemaha and Missouri Rivers. The owners were not required to live on the land, and much of it was ultimately sold to white settlers. A historical marker is located ¾ mile east of Auburn on US 136.*

Shubert, is named for a large sandstone cave, which has the only known Native American petroglyphs in Nebraska. The park has more than 3,000 acres of land along the Missouri River, of which more than 2,300 are heavily forested. It is particularly beautiful in autumn when the leaves turn. There are 20 miles of hiking trails, with Adirondack shelters for backpackers, year-round primitive camping, modern camping year-round, horseback trails, and Missouri River fishing. The park's visitors center is open Memorial Day weekend through October, 9:00 A.M. to 5:00 P.M. Living-history programs are scheduled on weekends. Riverboat tours are available over Labor Day weekend. Cross-country skiing and sledding are popular winter activities in the park. A park permit is required. Call (402) 883–2575 or visit the park's Web site at www.ngp.ngpc.state.ne.us/parks/icave.html.

East and south of Shubert is the very small town of *Barada* (population twenty-four), which was named after yet another colorful Nebraska figure. Antoine Barada was the son of a French nobleman who spotted the "most beautiful woman in the world" smiling at him from a window above a Paris street. He couldn't get her out of his mind and returned to the house only to discover that she was a Native American who had returned home to her "buffalo and campfires." He knew nothing of her but her name, Taeglena, but he sold his possessions and came to America to roam the huge stretches of the Louisiana Territory looking for her. For ten years he worked as a trapper and a hunter, all the while searching Native American villages for his beloved. One fateful day he heard her name said by an old woman outside a tepee; inside was the woman for whom he had given up everything. They married and had several children, including Antoine, who became famous for his extraordinary strength. He could snap a canoe paddle in half, was said to pound a post into the ground so hard it struck water and created a 50-foot fountain (well, okay, this may be more folklore than fact), lifted a barrel of flour weighing 1,500 or 1,800 pounds (sources differ), and won a wrestling match by pinching his opponent with his *toes* until the opponent gave up in pain. He worked with a fur-trading company and tried to strike it rich in California. He settled down in Barada on his parents' land and lived there with his wife until his death in 1885. He is buried in the Barada cemetery.

Does all this talk of superhuman physical strength make you hungry? Then your next stop should be *Rulo,* on Highway 159, and the *Camp Rulo River Club* for a delicious meal of deep-fat-fried catfish or carp. Watch the Missouri River roll by and imagine Native Americans in canoes or Lewis and Clark in keelboats floating past. Camp Rulo River Club is open Tuesday through Sunday, 11:00 A.M. to 9:00 P.M.; it is closed on Monday and may close early on winter nights. The catfish dinner is $9.50; the carp is $7.95. Both come with potatoes, soup, and a trip to the salad bar. The telephone number is (402) 245–4096.

Pawnee County

Pawnee County is an outdoor enthusiast's paradise, with 2,238 acres in wildlife-management areas. The area is famous for its game-bird population. You'll find pheasant, quail, dove, wild turkey, and prairie chicken. (Nebraska hosts the largest population of greater prairie chickens remaining in North America.) Deer and other small mammals are also easily observed. *Burchard Lake* (north and east of the community of *Burchard,* on Highway 4) offers year-round fishing, camping, picnic areas, and hiking around a 150-acre lake. Of special interest to birders is the curious "booming," or mating ritual, of the prairie chickens, who puff themselves up and drum on the ground. The booming occurs in February, March, and April. Blinds have been set up in the park so that visitors can watch this delightful spectacle without disturbing the birds. Take heed of the signs, which caution visitors not to bother the prairie chickens.

History enthusiasts will also find plenty of attractions in Pawnee County. The *Pawnee City Historical Society Museum,* located on the east edge of *Pawnee City* on Highway 8, has nineteen buildings that are chock-full of pioneer furnishing and memorabilia. Buildings include an 1881 school, reputed to be the country's smallest schoolhouse and which has a picture of George Washington, whose painted eyes seem to follow you around the room; an 1857 log cabin; and the home of David Butler, Nebraska's first governor. Don't miss the hand-built experimental tailwind airplane. One building contains more than 800 kinds of barbed wire, one of the largest barbed-wire collections in the Midwest. You may scoff at the idea of barbed wire, but barbed wire is one of the main reasons farm country is just that instead of ranch country. Pioneer farmers put up barbed wire to keep ranchers' livestock out of their crops. Barbed wire meant the end of large herds of free-roaming animals, signaled the end of lengthy cattle drives, and pretty much put a cease-and-desist order on the wild days of the Old West. The museum is open April through October, Tuesday through Friday, 9:00 A.M. to 2:00 P.M., Saturday, 9:00 A.M. to 4:00 P.M., and Sunday, 1:00 to 4:00 P.M.; November through March, Tuesday through Thursday, 8:00 A.M. to 4:00 P.M., or by appointment. Call (402) 852–3131. The Web site is www.roots web.com/~nepawnee. Donations are appreciated.

If you're looking for divine place to stay in Pawnee County, the **Convent House B&B,** at 311 East Hickory in **Steinauer,** is the answer to your prayers. This two-story, square brick house was home to Benedictine nuns before becoming a B&B in 1993. About the only reminder of the convent days is a Barbie doll, dressed like a nun, in the hallway. The rooms are small (nuns are not generally given to creature comforts) but very cozy. Hunters are welcome; there's a kennel out in the back. Guests can prepare meals in the kitchen if they choose. Innkeeper Irma Gyhra says that guests relish the

A note for film buffs: In 1997, the Swiss filmmaker Karl Saurer made a documentary about Swiss immigrants who settled in Steinauer. A note for linguists: Some people pronounce the name of the town as "Steener," while others say "Stinehour." Both are correct—go figure.

peace and quiet in this small community of ninety people. The rooms cost $52 and $65. The inn is open year-round, including holidays. Children are welcome, too. Call (402) 869–2276 for reservations. Just west of the B&B is **St. Anthony's Catholic Church.** The church has many stained-glass windows, including a stunning rose-petal window that is said to rival those of churches in Europe.

Gage County

*H*omestead National Monument of America, 4½ miles west of Beatrice on Nebraska Route 4, is a tribute to Daniel and Agnes Freeman, who were among the first applicants to file for 160 acres of free land under the Homestead Act of 1862. Daniel Freeman, a Union scout from Iowa, filed the first claim at the land office in Brownville, Nebraska, on January 1, 1863. The Freemans joined the post–Civil War rush of homesteaders, which was soon followed by a wave of European immigrants enticed to America by railroad companies eager to sell millions of acres of grant land and to provide farm-to-market transportation. At present, the fascinating story of the homesteaders unfolds for visitors to the monument with every facet of pioneer life, audiovisual programs, and special activities for children. A restored cabin and a one-room frontier schoolhouse are open to the public. A 2½-mile hiking trail takes you through lowland prairies and woods, upland prairie, along an original Osage orange hedgerow fence, and past the graves of the Freemans (they lived here until Daniel's death in 1908). Homestead has the second-oldest tallgrass prairie restoration project in the United States. Here's an interesting fact for film buffs: A former superintendent, Constantine Dillon, made the cult-film classic *Attack of the Killer Tomatoes.* The park is open weekdays from 8:30 A.M. to 5:00 P.M. and weekends from 9:00 A.M. to 5:00 P.M. It is closed on Thanksgiving, Christmas, and New Year's. For more information call (402) 223–3514 or visit the Web site at www.nps.gov/home.

The *Gage County Historical Museum,* at Second and Court Streets in *Beatrice,* is housed in a brick 1906 Burlington Railroad depot. The Neoclassical Revival style of the depot was chosen to reflect the community's growth and affluence. (Beatrice was the initial home of the now internationally famous Beatrice Foods.) Its collections feature historic artifacts from several towns in Gage County and displays on rural life and the development of the railroad. Children like the caboose on the grounds. The annual Industry Days, held the last Sunday in April, features living-history demonstrations of steam- and gas-powered equipment. A special component of Industry Days is the exhibit of Dempster engines made in Beatrice. On permanent display is memorabilia of actor Robert Taylor, who grew up in the area. Open Memorial Day through Labor Day, Monday through Saturday 9:00 A.M. to noon and 1:00 to 5:00 P.M. and Sunday 1:30 to 5:00 P.M. The rest of the year it's open Tuesday through Friday 9:00 A.M. to noon and 1:00 to 5:00 P.M. and Sunday 1:30 to 5:00 P.M. Donations are welcome. For more information call (402) 228–1679.

For a thoroughly international experience in Beatrice, try a meal at the

Vote Me In!

*Y*ou can check out more than books at the **Beatrice Public Library,** 100 North Sixteenth Street. *You can check out the story of* **Clara Colby,** *one of the pivotal players in the national movement for women's suffrage, or right to vote. In 1872 Clara and Leonard Colby moved to "the little western town." Leonard started a law practice and promoted real estate ventures. His better half started a public library and community theater. In 1877 the early suffragette Elizabeth Cady Stanton came to Beatrice for a library lecture. A year later Susan B. Anthony, perhaps the most famous suffragette of all, attended the Gage County Fair.*

The die was cast; Clara Colby became a suffragette. By 1883 she was the editor and publisher of The Woman's Tribune, *now recognized as one of the primary women's-rights newspapers of the era. By the next year Clara's efforts were recognized by the National Woman Suffrage Association as its "official house organ" and began reaching a national audience for her Beatrice-based publication. American women were granted the constitutional right to vote in 1920 after decades of often acrimonious debate. Today the notion that women have the right to vote doesn't turn a single head.*

Black Crow Restaurant, at 405 Court Street. This beautiful restaurant offers fare that is a far cry from country cooking. Owner and pastry chef Ray Arter trained in Paris and worked at Andiamo's in New York City. He met his wife and co-owner, Kate Ratigan, while they were both working at a restaurant in Vail. On a recent day the menu featured rack of lamb with creamy Dijon sauce, pan-seared salmon picatta with capers, roast pork loin with mushrooms and red wine sauce, and creamy garlic polenta. Fresh oysters, fish, and mussels are not your typical small-town offering. The prices reflect the quality of the food and range from $6.50 to $19.95, but there are $4.95 lunch specials daily. The decor is elegant, but you need not be; the attire is casual. Ethnic meals range from German to Cajun, Polish, Russian, or Caribbean. The bar is well stocked with imported beer, fine wines, and specialty liquors. The Black Crow is open Tuesday through Saturday. Reservations are recommended. Lunch is served from 11:30 A.M. to 2:00 P.M.; dinner is from 5:30 to 10:00 P.M. The telephone number is (402) 228–7200.

Two miles southwest of the town of *Filley* is the *Filley Stone Barn.* This large barn was built by Elijah Filley in 1874, when he became so disgruntled with grasshoppers that he created a structure to keep the pesky critters out. Built of limestone and rock, the barn has four levels and a threshing floor strong enough to "hold a herd of elephants." The barn dance held to celebrate its completion was attended by people from as far away as 50 miles. The barn is open the second Saturday and Sunday in July and the third Sunday in October for special programs and demonstrations. For more information call (402) 228–1679.

Butler, Seward, and Polk Counties

If you come across three ladies in a broken-down old convertible in *Butler County,* think of the movie *To Wong Foo, Thanks for Everything, Julie Newmar,* which starred Patrick Swayze, Wesley Snipes, and John Leguizamo. This movie was filmed on location in *Loma,* a town so small it isn't even on the map. Loma used to be a thriving community with several businesses, but when the railroad stopped running, it dwindled in population. The only business, and one of the few buildings, in town is the *Bar M Corral.* Stop in for a drink, say hello to owner Betty Smith, and buy a "Loma goes Hollywood" T-shirt. Take the time to enjoy the beautiful view of the surrounding countryside; it's one of the reasons the production company chose to film here. Loma is north of Highway 66 between Valparaiso and Dwight; watch for the small road sign. The Bar M Corral is open from about 9:00 A.M. to 1:00 A.M.; closed Monday. Give them a call at (402) 545–2174.

Seward, a pretty little college town north of I–80 at exit 379, has eight city parks and is a great place to get off the road and stretch your legs. Seward is Nebraska's official Fourth of July City and hosts a massive celebration attended by more than 40,000 people annually. If you happen to stop at the closest I–80 rest area early on July 4, you might get "kidnapped" by local officials or the state patrol to be guests of honor for the day. It is getting more difficult, however, to find willing "kidnappees" since we live in such fast-paced and wicked times. Some families decline the offer, not willing to alter their travel schedule for a day, while others just will not believe there isn't some kind of quirky nastiness in store for them. If you are indeed the chosen, be trustful, because you'll get to ride in the parade, get your picture in the newspaper, and generally be treated like visiting royalty. Additionally, if your marriage is in trouble, a day in Seward would do you well; the Fourth of July celebration in 2000 honored 103 couples who'd been married for more than fifty years ... and those are just the ones who showed up.

The *Polk County* community of *Stromsburg* is known as the Swedish Capital of Nebraska. It hosts a colorful Swedish Days festival every year in June, which offers a sweet little carnival and a rowdy beer garden. In other words, something for everyone. Stromsburg is located about 20 miles north of the York exit on Interstate 80.

York and Fillmore Counties

Plan on spending some time eating in York and Fillmore Counties. In the town of *York* (take the Interstate 80 exit north at Highway 81), you'll find great food at *Chances R,* 124 West Fifth Street. Although it is a very pretty place with paneling, nice lighting, and lots of brass, you won't care what it looks like once your order has come. You'll be too busy enjoying your food! Order the chicken and judge for yourself if they do indeed have some of the best pan-fried chicken you've ever eaten. Chicken dinners are $10.95. Chances R also has a huge Sunday brunch; it's pretty reasonable at $13.95 and well worth any wait or "Oh sheesh, I ate too much" feeling you may experience. The restaurant is open Monday through Saturday from 6:00 A.M. to midnight and Sunday and holidays from 8:00 A.M. to 11:00 P.M. The telephone number is (402) 362–7755.

In *Fillmore County* be prepared for two of the best burgers in southeast Nebraska. The *Frosty Mug* in *Milligan* (population 328), on Highway 41, and *Jan's Strang Tavern* in *Strang* (population 42), at the junction of Highways 81 and 74, vie regionally for the "best burger" designation. The Frosty Mug, at 602 Main Street, is open Tuesday

Take a Bite of History

*A*t the turn of the twentieth century, a sizable group of Germans immigrated from Russia and settled in Nebraska. Their history dates from 1770, when Catherine the Great gave free land to German settlers willing to move to Russia. The deal was sweetened with exemption from taxation and military service, and the promise of freedom of language and religion for one hundred years. All good things must come to an end; burdened with high taxes and military duties, scattered groups of Germans in Russia were looking to relocate at the same time the American Midwest was open for settlement. (There's a museum in Lincoln, at 631 D Street, that tells their story.) One part of their cultural heritage that they brought with them was a recipe for traditional cabbage rolls, or runza. As you travel across the state, you'll likely spot franchised restaurants that are called, appropriately and simply enough, Runza Restaurants. Stop in and buy a couple, both traditional and with Swiss cheese. You'll be surprised how good some hamburger, cabbage, and onions baked into what looks like a small loaf of bread can be. When you get home you can make your own runza from this recipe printed in Event-Full Recipes of Nebraska by the Nebraska Events Association.

Cabbage Rolls

Make enough of a basic yeast roll recipe to yield about twelve rolls.

For filling:

1½ lbs. hamburger

3 medium onions

½ medium head cabbage

Crumble and cook hamburger in a skillet. It shouldn't be browned but should be thoroughly cooked. Finely chop cabbage and onions, as for slaw. Cook cabbage and onions in a small amount of water until tender. Drain fat from the meat and water from the vegetables; mix vegetables and meat together and season with salt and pepper to taste.

After the dough for the rolls has risen, knead it down with flour until smooth and elastic. Using half of the dough, pull off twelve egg-size pieces. Flatten each piece of dough into a 4-inch round and place on greased cookie sheets (six to a sheet; leave 2 inches between them). Put ½ cup of the filling on each round, leaving a ¼-inch edge. Using the remainder of the dough, make twelve more rounds, then cover the filled rounds with these and pinch the edges together. Cover with towels and let rise in a warm place for about an hour. Bake in a 375-degree oven for 20 to 25 minutes, or until nicely browned. (Switch cookie sheets halfway through baking time so that tips and bottoms brown evenly.) Note: Proportions of meat and vegetables are up to individual tastes, and amounts can be varied.

through Thursday, 8:00 A.M. to 11:00 P.M.; Friday, 8:00 A.M. to 1:00 A.M.; Saturday, 2:00 P.M. to 1:00 A.M.; and Sunday, 2:00 to 11:00 P.M. The telephone number at the Frosty Mug is (402) 629–4280. Jan's Strang Tavern, downtown on Main Street, is open Monday through Saturday from 7:00 A.M. to "whenever the last person leaves," which is generally at 1:00 A.M. The Strang Supreme Burger at Jan's has a special seasoning and comes topped with Canadian bacon, cheese, and mushrooms on a Kaiser roll, which will set you back a mere $3.65. The telephone number is (402) 759–4834.

Saline County

When you're in **Wilber,** you're in Czech country. Wilber is the National Czech Capital and was designated as such by an act of Congress. Wilber is located at the junction of Nebraska Highways 103 and 41. When you drive into town, you might feel as if you've driven into a small European village. Visitors are encouraged to "Czech" into the two-story brick **Hotel Wilber,** at Second and Wilson Streets. The most famous visitor to Wilber was Bobby Kennedy, who stopped on a whistle-stop tour during his presidential campaign. In the lobby, the original red-oak woodwork, pressed-tin ceiling, and old oak phone booth evoke images of a bygone era. There are ten rooms; rates range from $45 to $68. An old-world-style pub and a private beer garden await guests in this century-old B&B. Breakfast includes bacon and eggs, hash browns, pancakes, and waffles, plus the traditional Czech pastry *kolaches.* Call (402) 821–2020 for more information.

If your stay at the Hotel Wilber piques your curiosity about all things Czech, take the time to visit the Wilber **Czech Museum,** at 102 West Third Street. It contains an outstanding collection of Czech dolls, dishes, laces, and costumes, plus replicas of early immigrant homes and businesses. Visitors are likely to find several women working on quilts in the afternoon sun that streams through the windows. You can also buy a number of books, including a *Love Those Dumplings* cookbook and *Czechoslovak Wit and Wisdom.* You might want to pick up *A Poetic History of Wilber,* a 135-page poem written by Irma Anna Freeouf Ourecky, probably the coolest person in town. Donations are accepted. The museum is open daily all year, except on holidays, from 1:00 to 4:00 P.M. The number is (402) 821–2485. If you're in town on the first weekend of August, it'd be well worth your time to experience the **Czech Festival.** Parades, polka bands, Catholic masses, beer gardens, a carnival, and a plethora of brightly costumed Czech queens from across the nation are just part of the fun.

Jefferson County

Jefferson County's history includes all the drama and action of the Old West, with chapters on Kit Carson, John C. Fremont, the Oregon Trail, the Pony Express, and Wild Bill Hickok. **Rock Creek Station State Historical Park,** near **Fairbury** in rural Jefferson County, is where James Butler "Wild Bill" Hickok started his reputation as a ruthless gunslinger. One hot July day in 1861, for reasons that have never been determined, Wild Bill fatally shot David McCanles (the owner of Rock Creek Station) and wounded two others in cold blood. Legend has it he went on to kill dozens of people before his own death at age thirty-nine in Deadwood, South Dakota, holding the now-famous Dead Man's Hand of aces and eights during a poker game. Hickok's fame was assured by glorified, exaggerated written accounts of his derring-do in dime novels of the time. At present, Rock Creek Station is an excellent park that covers 350 acres of prairie hilltops, timber-studded creek bottoms, and rugged ravines. This is the first publicly owned site along the Oregon Trail where deep wagon ruts are clearly visible. A visitors center contains artifacts from the days of the Oregon Trail and the Pony Express. Rides in an ox-drawn covered wagon help you understand the slow and uncomfortable nature of the nineteenth century's mode of travel. The park is 6 miles east of Fairbury and 1 mile south, then ¼ mile east. The grounds are open year-round for day use. The visitors center is open weekends starting in mid-April and daily from May 1 to mid-September. A park permit is required. For more information call (402) 729–5777.

Another fascinating rural Jefferson County site, 8 miles north and west of Fairbury, is the **marked grave of George Winslow,** one of the rare marked Oregon Trail graves. Winslow is one of the estimated 350,000 people (or one out of seventeen of those persons who started westward) who died on the Oregon/California Trails before reaching their destination. According to Merrill J. Mattes' *The Great Platte River Road,* the most common cause of death by far was Asiatic cholera. Drownings when wagons or ferries tipped over were the second-most-common cause of death. Other significant causes of death were being crushed by wagon wheels (many died of head injuries since they slept under the wagons), sustaining fatal injuries while handling domestic animals (becoming snarled in harnesses), and stampedes. Another common cause of death was by accidental gunshot. George Winslow, who had hoped to take advantage of the discovery of gold in California, was a victim of cholera on June 7, 1849. The month before his death he wrote a letter to his wife in Massachusetts. It read, in part: "I do not worry about myself—then why do you for me? The reports of the gold region here are as encouraging as they are in Massachusetts. Just imagine yourself seeing me return with from $10,000 to $100,000. Your loving husband, George Winslow." A brown rock placed in the marker is the original stone placed on his grave by his brothers-in-law and uncle at the time of his death.

Endicott, east of Fairbury on Nebraska Highway 8, is home to *Endicott Clay Products,* a premiere brick manufacturing and sculpture company. Its brick products are featured throughout Nebraska and the nation. (When you visit Lincoln, you can see an example of its brickwork in a large mural done by Jay Tschetter in the historic Haymarket District. It is the *Iron Horse Legacy,* a three-dimensional depiction of a locomotive crossing the plains.) Call (402) 729–3323.

Still more pioneer history is evident in *Steele City,* population 101. Visitors may tour the restored 1880s bank, built from bricks kilned locally, which now houses a museum, a stone blacksmith and stone livery stable, windmills, and old machinery shops, which are open Sunday, 2:00 to 4:00 P.M., from Memorial Day weekend through the third Sunday in September. Don't miss the uniquely beautiful stone 1881 Baptist Church. Steele City is southeast of Fairbury on Nebraska Highway 8.

Down the road on Highway 8 is *Odell.* If you like to discover things, you might find an *Odell diamond.* The "diamonds" are actually curious quartz crystals, which are generally pink or clear, measure about $1/16$ inch thick, and are perfectly diamond shaped. Three and a half miles south of Odell, on Highway 8, is a state game preserve where, with a sharp eye and some luck, you'll pick up one of these geologic mementos. Many can still be found even though most of the diamond area was covered with water when a dam was built.

Thayer County

R oad-weary travelers can set themselves down on the *world's largest porch swing* in *Hebron.* Well, the swing is not actually on a porch, it's in the city park. But it is big, and it will seat more than twenty adults. After you've rested on the porch swing, explore Thayer County and its well-marked *Oregon Trail* route. Two miles north of Hebron, on Highway 81, is the largest stone marker on the Oregon Trail. As you follow the route, you'll see markers for the location of Thompson's Station, an early trading post, and foundations from the Kiowa Ranch, where early settlers gathered for protection from Native American raids. Remember, when you are on Highway 81 you are on the Pan American Highway, which extends from Winnipeg, Canada, to the southern tip of

Chile at Tierra Del Fuego. It is the longest stretch of continuous highway through the Americas.

Merrick and Hamilton Counties

entral City, in **Merrick County,** was at one time called Lone Tree because of a solitary large cottonwood that grew on the banks of the Platte River on the Ox Bow and California Trails. The tree died as hundreds of tourists either carved their names on it or carried off bits of it as souvenirs. Central City, 20 miles north of Interstate 80 on Highway 14, was the birthplace, in 1910, of acclaimed novelist and photographer Wright Morris. Morris won the Mark Twain Award, the Commonwealth Award for Distinguished Service in Literature, an honorary life membership in the Western Literature Association, and the Mari Sandoz Award for his writing. His photographs have been shown around the world.

Aurora, 4 miles north of Interstate 80 at Highway 14 in **Hamilton County,** has two fine museums that should not be missed. The **Plainsman Museum,** 210 Sixteenth Street, has a rotunda with eight larger-than-life murals that depict important events in the settling of the Plains. It has an original log cabin, a sod house, a Victorian home, and an early farm home. It has a collection of Native American artifacts and an interesting display about a white Civil War officer, Gen. Delavon Bates, who led a troop of black Union soldiers before settling in Aurora. The movie *Glory* is said to be based on his military service. The museum is open all year. Hours from April through October are Monday through Saturday, 9:00 A.M. to 5:00 P.M., and Sunday, 1:00 to 5:00 P.M.; and from November through March daily, 1:00 to 5:00 P.M., except major holidays. There's an admission fee. For more information visit the museum's Web site at www.plainsmanmuseum.org or call (402) 694–6531.

Connected to the Plainsman Museum is the **Edgerton Explorit Center,** at 208 Sixteenth Street, which is considered to be Nebraska's premiere hands-on science center, featuring great interactive displays for people of all ages. This museum is named in honor of hometown boy Dr. Harold Edgerton, who invented the strobe light. With the strobe light Dr. Edgerton is said to have "stopped time" with his now-famous photographs of a bullet piercing an apple and a single drop of milk splashing up to make a beautiful corona. Dr. Edgerton also worked with Jacques Cousteau on the *Calypso* with his sonar device that picked up remains of the Civil War gunship *Monitor* and other famous vessels thought lost forever. Hours are Monday through Saturday, 9:00

A.M. to 5:00 P.M.; Sunday, 1:00 to 5:00 P.M. Admission fee. Call (402) 694–4032 or (877) 694–4032 or visit the Web site at www.edgerton.org/.

Clay County

ou might say that *Clay County* is for the birds—for migrating waterfowl, to be more specific. Clay County is part of the Rain-water Basin, comprised of seventeen south-central counties in an area critical to migrating waterfowl. Sinklike depressions with claylike bottoms collect rain or runoff water to create natural marshes and lakes in this wetlands area. Most marshes or lakes cover from one to forty acres, but some are as large as 1,000 acres. By 1981 less than 10 percent of the original 4,000 wetlands remained intact; nine of every ten were destroyed either by draining or filling them to make the land more suitable to agriculture. The remaining wetlands, and the nearby Platte River, host one of the most spectacular congregations of migratory birds found on the entire planet. More than a half million sandhill cranes and nearly ten million ducks and geese pause here for several weeks, from late February through early April. Clay County has thirteen waterfowl-production areas, lagoons, and wildlife management areas. Two of the largest, offering breathtaking views of hundreds of thousands of ducks and geese, are the *Harvard Waterfowl Production Area,* east of the community of *Harvard,* and the *Massey Waterfowl Production Area,* south of *Clay Center.*

In eastern Clay County on Highway 6 in the community of *Sutton* is a cute little old house where you can get dressed up and pretend it's your last meal. *Aunt Emma's Tea and Gift House* serves an elegant eight-course meal, accompanied by violinists, made from recipes that were served on the *Titanic.* Edwardian etiquette should be observed at all times. Aunt Emma's also does murder-mystery dinners; don't miss the chance to partake in the likes of "Murder on the Grill" and "Pasta, Passion, and Pistols." The *Titanic* and murder-mystery evenings require reservations, but the rest of the time you can simply stop by 309 North Way Street for some nonsimple grub for lunch. Choose from Flowering Plum Cornish Hen, Chicken Lyonnaise, Steak Diane, Chicken Cordon Bleu, and several more entrees. Dinner prices range from $10.95 to $12.95. Lunches are served from 11:00 A.M. to 2:00 P.M. Monday through Saturday. They're closed on Monday in January, February, and March. The telephone number is (402) 773–5659.

If you eat meat, a stop at the *Roman L. Hruska Meat Animal Research Center* (3 miles west of Clay Center on Spur 18–D) might interest you.

This facility, run by the USDA, conducts studies on meat animals from "conception to consumption," including genetics and breeding, nutrition, meat science, and production for cattle, sheep, and swine. The center is open Monday through Friday, 8:00 A.M. to 4:30 P.M. Call (402) 762–4100 to arrange a free tour.

Your last stop in Clay County is the final resting place of Elizabeth Taylor and Tom Jones. Really. Elizabeth Taylor first gained local notoriety when her husband died, some say at her hands, which was never proven. Later she was said by community wags to be liberal with womanly favors to her cowhands, some of whom ultimately disappeared. What concerned her neighbors much more was the fact that their cattle often vanished as well. Taylor and her brother, Tom Jones, were thought by most right-thinking people of the time to be the culprits. However, some historians now assert she was simply a strong-willed woman trying to make her way in the world after her husband died of natural causes. She supposedly spurned the advances of men, who were perhaps more interested in her land and cattle than in her widowed self, to the consternation of males for miles around. In any case, Elizabeth and her brother would have been well advised to beware the Ides of March, for on March 15, 1885, a group of vigilantes hanged the notorious siblings from a bridge and left their swaying bodies to be discovered by a farmhand the next morning. The farmhand's nervous system took such a toll that he reputedly suffered from a speech affliction forever after. Eight of the men arrested were freed after a trial found a lack of evidence. Several others were advised as to when and how they might best leave the county. The siblings are buried in the cemetery at the ghost town **Spring Ranche.** Spring Ranche, which mushroomed into being as a supply center for Oregon Trail travelers, dwindled into ghost-town status after the West was settled. You can see the decaying hotel and the bank vault, which was too heavy to move away. The nearby depot was used until the railroad abandoned the route. To get to Spring Ranche, go west on Highway 41 from Clay Center about 9 miles and watch for signs indicating Spring Ranche south on a county road. For more information, call the Adams County Visitors Center at (402) 461–2370 or (800) 967–2189.

Nuckolls County

n August 1864 the Sioux and the Cheyenne raided 400 miles of immigrant trails and white settlements. Several sites in Nuckolls County were struck, including "The Narrows," whose name indicates that there was only room for one wagon at a time to pass between the bluffs and the river. More than fifty people were killed, hundreds of freight wagons were destroyed, and women and children were captured. The Indians held the area for several weeks before the U.S. Army regained control of the land for settlers. At present, visitors can follow the well-marked route of the immigrant trails and learn more about the attacks from historical markers in Nuckolls County. Stop in *Oak,* 5 miles south of Highway 4 on S65, and pick up more information at local businesses, or call (402) 364–2327 for information on narrated tours.

If you look for *Angus* on a map, you won't find it (it was 9 miles north of Nora on the Little Blue River), but at one time it was the home of an early-day automobile manufacturing site. The *Angus Automobile Company* began producing the Fuller Car in 1907. The company manufactured several models for three years before closing. A five-passenger touring car, which sold for $2,500, was the top-of-the-line model.

Superior, at the junction of Highways 14 and 8 in southern Nuckolls County, is the birthplace and final resting place of Evelyn Brodstone Vestey. Her story is the quintessential hometown-girl-does-good. The daughter of immigrant parents, and childhood friend of Pulitzer Prize winner Willa Cather, Evelyn graduated from high school at age fourteen, studied stenography and accounting after high school, and in 1895 moved to Chicago, where she earned $12 a week as a stenographer at Vestey Cold Storage. Ultimately, she became an executive of the company and earned $250,000, making her the highest-paid female executive in the world in the 1920s. She traveled internationally, establishing business contacts and settling labor disputes. As a romantic postscript to her career, she accepted Lord William Vestey's proposal of marriage and became Lady Vestey. Throughout her life she remained in close contact with family and friends in Superior. Even in her death she maintains contact with Superior; she's buried in the local cemetery and is, in all likelihood, the only member of British royalty buried in Nebraska. Each Memorial Day weekend the *Lady Vestey Victorian Festival* offers tours of many of the seventy Victorian homes in Superior. The festival also features a tour of a porcelain doll store, a Victorian fashion show, a high tea, and rousing croquet matches.

PLACES TO STAY IN SOUTHEAST NEBRASKA

(ALL AREA CODES ARE 402 EXCEPT WHERE NOTED OTHERWISE)

CRETE
The Parson's House,
638 Forest Avenue,
826–2634,
www.nabb1.com/
cre2634.htm

LINCOLN
Ricketts Folsom House,
2125 B Street,
476–6961

Rogers House B&B,
2145 B Street,
476–6961

NEBRASKA CITY
Arbor Day Farm Lied
Conference Center,
2700 Sylvan Road,
873–8733 or
(800) 546–5433

Whispering Pines B&B,
Twenty-first Street and
Sixth Avenue,
873–5850 or (888)
558–7014,
www.bbonline.com/ne/
whispering

PAWNEE CITY
My Blue Heaven B&B,
1041 Fifth Street,
852–3131,
www.innsite.com/
paw3131.htm

STEINAUER
Convent House B&B,
311 East Hickory,
869–2276,
www.bbonline.com/ne/
convent

WEEPING WATER
Lauritzen's B&B,
1002 East Eldora Avenue,
267–3295

WILBER
Hotel Wilber,
Second and Wilson Streets,
821–2020

PLACES TO EAT IN SOUTHEAST NEBRASKA

(ALL AREA CODES ARE 402)

BENNETT
Mamasita's (Mexican),
605 Monroe Street,
782–3000

EMERALD
Merle's Food and Drink
(American),
8250 West O Street,
474–6435

GRETNA
Linoma Beach
(pretty much everything—
huge menu),
17106 South 255th Street,
332–4500

LINCOLN
Arturo's Restaurante
(Mexican),
803 Q Street,
475–8226

Cornhusker Hotel
(Continental),
333 South Thirteenth
Street,
474–7474

Crane River Brewpub &
Cafe,
200 North Eleventh Street,
476–7766

El Toro (Mexican),
2600 South Forty-eighth
Street, Suite 17,
488–3939

Grateful Bread (bakery),
1625 South Seventeenth
Street,
474–0101

Imperial Palace (Chinese),
707 North Twenty-seventh
Street,
474–2688

Maggie's (vegetarian),
311 North Eighth Street,
525–1102

The Mill (coffeehouse),
800 P Street,
475–5522

P. O. Pears (burgers),
322 South Ninth Street,
476–8551

Rock 'N Roll Runza
(American, runzas),
210 North Fourteenth
Street,
474–2030

Thai House (Thai),
610 North Twenty-seventh
Street,
475–0558

Ted & Wally's (homemade ice cream),
701 P Street,
341–5827

Virginia's Travelers Cafe (diner),
3820 Cornhusker Highway,
464–9885

Wasabi (sushi),
239 North Fourteenth Street,
476–0006

YiaYia's (pizza),
1423 O Street,
477–9166

NEBRASKA CITY
Sunrise Cafe (American),
812 Central Avenue,
873–9100

PAWNEE CITY
Hallie's (American),
604 Ninth Street,
852–2445

PLATTSMOUTH
Mom's Cafe (American),
422 Main,
296–3000

PLEASANT DALE
Porky's (American),
102 Ash,
795–9915

HELPFUL SOUTHEAST NEBRASKA WEB SITES

BEATRICE
www.beatricechamber.com

BROWNVILLE
www.ci.brownville.ne.us

FAIRBURY
www.visitoregontrail.org

LINCOLN
www.lincoln.org

NEBRASKA CITY
www.nebraskacity.com

SUPERIOR
www.ci.superior.ne.us

WAHOO
www.wahoo.ne.us

WILBER
www.ci.wilber.ne.us

YORK
www.yorkvisitors.org

Lewis and Clark Land

Northeast Nebraska, with its rolling green hills, is defined by the Missouri River on the northern and eastern borders and extends to agricultural lands in the south and the Sandhills area on the west. Some of the earliest recorded historical events in the state occurred in northeast Nebraska. In 1720, a Spanish expedition under the command of Col. Pedro de Vallasur was attacked by Pawnee Indians along the Platte River. French explorers Paul and Peter Mallet crossed the area in 1739–40. Lewis and Clark explored this part of the Louisiana Purchase in 1804. Fur trader Manuel Lisa established a trading post in 1812 in the present-day Washington County for the St. Louis Missouri Fur Company. In 1820, the first army base west of the Missouri River, Fort Atkinson, was established to dissuade British interest and to foster settlement of the area. The Mormon Trail crosses northeast Nebraska north of the Platte River, and the old Lincoln Highway, the first transcontinental route for cars, roughly follows the path of Highway 34 across northeast Nebraska. Take advantage of the history as well as the interesting cities and small towns of this beautiful part of Nebraska.

Douglas County

Omaha is Nebraska's largest city, with a population of 357,777 within the city limits and nearly 700,000 in the metropolitan area. More than a million people live within a 50-mile radius of this dynamic and energetic city. The *Old Market,* east of downtown near the Missouri River, is a beautiful area of redeveloped warehouses on brick streets, which belie its Midwestern setting. Delighted visitors often exclaim that the Old Market could be in New York, or Chicago, or New Orleans, or even Europe. Boutiques, clothing stores, bookstores, an artists' cooperative and gallery, antiques stores, galleries, brewpubs, bars with live music, florists, coffee shops, record stores, and live theater are all available in the Old Market. Restaurant experiences run the gamut from exceedingly elegant to very casual, with prices set accordingly.

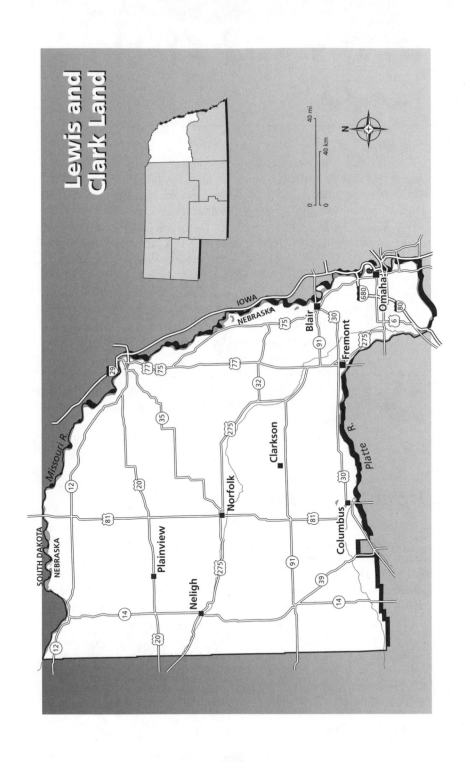

LEWIS AND CLARK LAND

AUTHOR'S FAVORITE ATTRACTIONS IN
NORTHEAST NEBRASKA

*(All area codes are 402
unless noted otherwise)*

***Ashfall Fossil Beds
State Historical Park,***
*2 miles west and 6 miles
north of Royal, 893–2000*

Cuthills Vineyards,
*3 miles west on H&N
Boulevard, Pierce,
329–6774*

***Fontenelle Forest Nature
Center,*** *1111 North Bellevue Boulevard, Bellevue,
731–3140*

Fremont Dinner Train,
*650 North H Street,
Fremont,
(800) 942–7245*

***John G. Neihardt Center
and State Historic Site,***
*Elm and Washington
Streets, Bancroft,
648–3388*

Louis E. May Museum,
*1643 North Nye Avenue,
Fremont,
721–4515*

Omaha is a veritable restaurant mecca. All over town you'll find steak houses, Italian, Creole, Greek, Persian, Southwestern, Mexican, French, Chinese, burger places, pizza places (try Zio's), and pasta places. You can't throw a stick without hitting a great restaurant. There's even a vegetarian restaurant right here in the heart of cattle country called McFoster's Natural Kind Cafe (Sunday brunch, live jazz, and always smoke-free) at 302 South Thirty-eighth Street (402–345–7477).

Because Omaha is the largest city in Nebraska, there are many attractions that are more than worth a visit. This book is for off-the-beaten path sites, but a few key attractions will be mentioned briefly. The *Henry Doorly Zoo,* 3701 South Tenth Street, is consistently ranked as among the very best zoos in the United States. If you need a testimonial, *Family Fun* magazine ranked the zoo as the best family spot in America, ahead of both Walt Disney World and Disneyland. The annual number of visitors, approximately 1.6 million, is as large as the entire population of the state! This incredible zoo covers 104 acres and has the world's largest enclosed rain forest, a free-flight aviary, a truly wonderful aquarium, where you walk through a glasslike tunnel as sharks and manta rays swim around you, an IMAX theater, and North America's largest cat complex. The recently opened Desert Dome has a daylight and nocturnal desert display. It's open daily from 9:30 A.M. to 5:00 P.M. but is closed on Thanksgiving, Christmas, and New Year's Day. Admission is $8.50 for adults, $7.00 for seniors, and $4.00 for children ages five through eleven. Admission to the IMAX is $6.75 for adults, $4.75 for children. Call (402) 733–8401 or visit their Web site at www.omahazoo.com/.

Another great attraction is the *Joslyn Art Museum* at 2200 Dodge Street. It has one of the nation's finest Western art collections (with a large collection of Swiss artist Karl Bodmer's watercolors and prints, which were made during his 1832–34 journey to the Missouri River frontier) plus classic and modern works. The collection is all housed in a beautiful Italian marble building. If you're there on the first Sunday of the month, take advantage of a great brunch with live music called

Bagels and Bach. The museum is open Tuesday through Saturday from 10:00 A.M. to 4:00 P.M. and Sunday from noon to 4:00 P.M. It is closed on Monday and major holidays. Admission is $6.00 for adults, $4.00 for seniors, college students, and young people ages five through seventeen. Browse Joslyn's Web site, www.joslyn.org, or call (402) 342–3300.

Girls and Boys Town, at 138th and West Dodge Road, is an interesting stop for travelers. Started in 1917 as a shelter for homeless boys by Father Edward J. Flanagan, Girls and Boys Town is now home to youths of both sexes: in August 2000 the residents voted to change the name to Girls and Boys Town. The fascinating history of Girls and Boys Town is told in the nicely designed Hall of History. Be sure to see Spencer Tracy's portrayal of Father Flanagan for which he won the Best Actor Academy Award in the 1938 movie *Boys Town.* The visitors center has a gift shop and cafeteria. The grounds are lovely, especially the rose garden, adjacent to Father Flanagan's house. Open daily from 7:30 A.M. to 4:30 P.M.; from May through August it's open until 5:30 P.M. There is no admission fee. Call (800) 545–5771 or (402) 498–1140; while surfing the 'net, visit www.boystown.org/.

Girls and Boys Town

LEWIS AND CLARK LAND

AUTHOR'S FAVORITE ANNUAL EVENTS IN
NORTHEAST NEBRASKA

If you like sports, remember that Omaha is home to the Lancers hockey team, the Racers basketball team, and the Golden Spikes baseball team. Omaha is also home to a delightful variety of cultural activities that include symphony, opera, ballet, community theater (the *Omaha Community Playhouse* is the largest in the country and is where Marlon Brando first trod the stage), dinner theater, and cutting-edge original productions from nationally acclaimed theaters. For more information on these and other attractions in Omaha, please contact the Omaha Convention and Visitors Bureau at (800) 937–6624, (402) 444–4660, or www. visitomaha.com.

Near the Old Market you'll find honest-to-goodness old-world cuisine and decor at the *Bohemian Cafe,* 1406 South Thirteenth Street. You can't miss it; it looks sort of like a chalet, and it's covered with colorful painted flowers. You'll think you're in Prague as you try tasty traditional Czech meals such as duck and dumplings, sausages, liver soup, and many other Central European specialties. They also have a selection of imported beer. Several years ago the Bohemian Cafe had a great radio advertising jingle that pretty much sums it up: Imagine polka music in the background with a male voice singing, "Dumplings and kraut today / At the Bohemian Cafe / Plenty of parking / Beer that is sparkling / See us for lunch, OK!" You'll likely see everyone in the family, from grandparents to babes in arms, at this popular restaurant. The hours are Sunday through Thursday, 11:00 A.M. to 9:00 P.M.; Friday and Saturday, 11:00 A.M. to 10:00 P.M. Credit cards are accepted. Reservations aren't necessary unless your party is larger than five. The telephone number is (402) 342–9838.

While you're on Thirteenth Street, you might want to stop in at the numerous antiques and second-hand stores in the neighborhood. You might want to stop in at one or two of the plenitudinous neighborhood bars, too, to make the acquaintance of some of the local residents.

(Call ahead to verify dates; all area codes are 402 unless noted otherwise)

Ethnic Festival, Norfolk, early June, (888) 371–2932

Czech Festival & Rodeo, Clarkson, last full weekend in June, 892–3556

Bluegrass Festival, Lyons, July 4th, 687–2640

John C. Fremont Days, Fremont, second weekend in July, 727–0547

Chicken Show, Wayne (an eggstravaganza eggstrordinaire), mid-July, 375–2240

Powwow, Winnebago, late July, 878–3100

Wine & Wings Festival, Cuthills Vineyard, Pierce, last weekend in August, 329–6774

Hartland Music and Arts Festival, Hartington, Labor Day weekend, 254–6380

Last Fling 'til Spring Car Show, West Point, third weekend of September, 372–3390

Lavitef Time, Norfolk, last weekend in September, 371–7845

Holiday Lights Festival, Omaha, late November through December, (866) 937–6624

El Museo Latino is a labor of love for executive director Magdelana García. After completing a master's degree in museum science, she was offered a job at the Guggenheim Museum in New York City but chose instead to return to Omaha (where she had moved with her family from Mexico City at the age of ten) to start one of the few Latino cultural museums in the Midwest. García and a dedicated crew of volunteers transformed a former printing business into gallery space in just thirty-four days in order to open on Cinco de Mayo in 1993. Since then they've moved to a larger space at 4701 South Twenty-fifth Street to allow for additional exhibitions, classrooms, and space for the resident dance troupe. Changing exhibitions in the gallery feature artwork created by people from other countries as well as works of local Latino artists. The museum is open Monday, Wednesday, and Friday from 10:00 A.M. to 5:00 P.M., Tuesday from 1:00 to 7:00 P.M., Thursday from 1:00 to 5:00 P.M., and Saturday from 2:00 to 5:00 P.M. Admission is $5.00 for adults and $3.50 for seniors and students. Call (402) 731–1137; visit www. elmuseolatino.org.

The *Great Plains Black History Museum,* at 2213 Lake Street in north Omaha, provides a look at the contributions homesteading African Americans made to the development of Omaha and the rest of the state. This fascinating museum has permanent and changing collections. There's also a nice display on African-American sports figures. Hours are Monday through Friday, 10:00 A.M. to 2:00 P.M. The admission is $2.00, and the phone number is (402) 345–2212.

Joe Tess Place, at 5424 South Twenty-fourth Street, has been around for years and is a local favorite for fresh carp and catfish, which are shipped in live from freshwater lakes in five states. Diners are greeted with a fountain that contains a giant albino catfish. The fish theme is carried out with stuffed fish on the paneled walls, fish posters near the bathrooms, and even neon fish on the beer signs. The food is as unpretentious as the decor; it's straight-ahead simple and good. Be forewarned that the fish you get here is not the fish you get from fast-food restaurants or the frozen-food section of a grocery store. This fish has a strong flavor and might come as a surprise to someone used to heavily processed fish. Give it a try, and chances are you'll be like Mikey in the old television commercial—you'll like it! Prices range from $1.95 for a Famous Fish sandwich to $7.50 for oysters when they're in season. Other choices are chowder, seafood salad, chicken, shrimp, and butterflied coho salmon. The jacket fries are great, and you can get a side order for only $1.00. Credit cards are accepted. Hours are Sunday through Thursday, 11:00 A.M. to 9:00 P.M.; and Friday and Saturday from 11:00 A.M. to 10:00 P.M. Joe Tess Place also features take-out orders

LEWIS AND CLARK LAND

and a fish market. The telephone number is (402) 731–7278.

While you're in south Omaha on Twenty-fourth Street, be sure to check out the international flavor of the area. There are lots of Mexican restaurants (*El Alamo,* at 4917 South Twenty-fourth Street, and the nearby *American G.I. Forum,* at 2002 N Street, are wonderful) and bakeries, a German restaurant, a Vietnamese restaurant, a Salvadoran/Mexican restaurant, and plenty of American-style restaurants.

The *General Crook House,* at Thirtieth and Fort Streets, provides an interesting stop for history aficionados and plant lovers alike. Brig. Gen. George Crook, who had his headquarters at Fort Omaha, lived in this large Victorian brick home from 1878 to 1882 while serving as commander of the Department of the Platte. General Crook distinguished himself in the Civil War and later became known as a famous Native American fighter. He became involved in the trial of Standing Bear, a Ponca chief who was arrested in Nebraska after illegally leaving Indian Territory (Oklahoma) while attempting to fulfill his oldest son's dying request: to be buried at home on traditional Ponca lands in northeast Nebraska. Although General Crook was named a defendant for the U.S. government, his sympathies were solidly on the side of Standing Bear and the twenty-nine other Poncas who were arrested with him. During the 1879 trial Standing Bear made the following emotional appeal: "My hand is not the color of yours. But if I pierce it, I shall feel pain. If you pierce your hand, you also feel pain. The blood that will flow from mine will be the same color as yours. I am a man. The same God made us both." The trial resulted in a court decision (astonishing for the times) that a Native American was indeed a "person" under the law, with the right of habeas corpus protection. At present General Crook's house is restored to its original poshness. The grounds are a monument to the Victorian-era

---

OTHER ATTRACTIONS WORTH SEEING IN NORTHEAST NEBRASKA

(All area codes are 402)

GENOA

Genoa Indian School, 107 North Walnut; 993–2330 or 993–2349. *This school once sprawled across 160 acres and had 600 students. It operated for fifty years and closed in 1934, but the shop building has been restored and is open to visitors.*

NIOBRARA

Niobrara State Park, 857–3373. *Enjoy scenic wonder and float trips on the Missouri River much as Lewis and Clark did.*

OMAHA

Durham Western Heritage Museum, 801 South Tenth Street; 444–5071 or www.dwhm.org

Omaha Children's Museum, 500 South Twentieth Street; 342–6164 or www.ocm.org

Freedom Park, 2497 Freedom Park Road; 345–1959 or www.omaha. org/freedom.htm *(Don't miss the USS Hazard minesweeper and the USS Marlin SST–2 submarine.)*

Bemis Center for Contemporary Arts, 724 South Twelfth Street; 341–7130 or www.bemiscenter.org

47

passion for gardening. The incredibly manicured Victorian Garden is the only one to be found in the area. In bloom most of the growing season, there are hundreds of exotic plants and flowers with names like rugosa rose, love-lies-bleeding, and elephant ears. The house is open Monday through Friday from 10:00 A.M. to 4:00 P.M. and Sunday from 1:00 to 4:00 P.M. Admission is $5.00 for adults, $3.00 for seniors and for children ages six to twelve. Call (402) 455–9990. The Web site is www.omahahistory.org/museum.htm.

Another important historical site is the **Mormon Pioneer Winter Quarters and Mormon Pioneer Cemetery,** at North Ridge Drive (Thirty-second Street) and State Street. This settlement, near the town of Florence in north Omaha, was home to up to 4,000 Mormons who wintered here to make preparations for their continued trip west after being forced from Nauvoo, Illinois, in 1846. More than 800 lots were laid out with log cabins, soddies, and dugout dwellings. Part of the water-powered gristmill they built still stands. More than 600 people, mostly infants and the elderly, died during the exceedingly harsh winter of 1846. They also died from a lack of fresh fruits and vegetables and from diseases of biblical proportions. The visitors center and cemetery recount the dramatic story of a strong-willed people who were determined at all costs to reach a promised land where they could freely practice their religion. The beautiful visitors center is open year-round from 9:00 A.M. to 9:00 P.M. If you're visiting around Christmas, do not miss the display of dozens of intricate gingerbread houses. There is no admission fee, and the telephone number is (402) 453–9372. Access the Web site at www.omaha.org/trails.

Malcolm Little, a baby boy born in Omaha in 1925, eventually became internationally known as Malcolm X, a leader in the fight for the racial equality of African Americans. The **Malcolm X Birthsite,** at 3448 Pinkney Street, consists of eleven acres of as-yet-to-be-developed ground, with a historic marker that commemorates his life and work. The site can be visited daily from dawn to dusk. There is no admission fee.

Another national leader born in Omaha was Leslie Lynch King, who would become the thirty-eighth President of the United States. Born in 1913, his parents divorced when he was two years old; his mother, Dorothy King, moved to Michigan and ultimately married Mr. Gerald Rudolf Ford, who adopted the boy and gave him his name. **President Gerald Ford's Birthsite,** at Thirty-second Avenue and Woolworth Avenue, is now a small park with the colorful Betty Ford Rose Garden, White House memorabilia, a replica of the house where President Ford was born (it was razed after being heavily damaged in a 1971 fire), and displays on Nebraska history. The telephone number is (402) 444–5692, which can be called on weekdays. Hours are 7:30 A.M. to dusk daily. Admission is free.

In west Omaha you'll find a "jewel" of a store. *Borsheim's,* in Regency Court at 120 Regency Parkway, is the largest single-unit retail jewelry store in the country, and also the one with the greatest volume. In addition to jewelry you'll find fine gifts—for yourself or that special someone—that include silver, crystal, china, watches, and decorative items. Borsheim's started small in 1870 and grew to its present position due to a well-deserved reputation for quality, selection, and good prices. It has customers from all over the United States, North and South America, Europe, Australia, Africa, and Asia. It is now owned by Berkshire Hathaway Corporation, which is headed by investment wizard and Omaha resident Warren Buffet, the second-richest man in America. The richest man in America, Bill Gates of Microsoft fame, bought his wife's engagement ring from Borsheim's. The hours are Monday and Thursday, 10:00 A.M. to 8:00 P.M.; Tuesday, Wednesday, and Friday, 10:00 A.M. to 6:00 P.M.; and Saturday, 10:00 A.M. to 5:30 P.M. Call (402) 391–0400 or (800) 642–4438 for a complimentary catalog.

If you're an outdoors kind of person, or if you want to stretch your legs on some great forested trails (who said Nebraska doesn't have trees?), consider a stop at the *Neale Woods Nature Center,* 14323 Edith Marie Avenue. The Neale Woods Nature Center is a 554-acre environmental oasis of hilltop forests, native prairies, and riverside woodlands along the Missouri River. There are 9 miles of trails, live animal exhibits, displays on plant and animal life, and a butterfly garden. Nebraska's largest observatory, with eight telescopes, provides stargazing and astronomy programs. Hours are Monday through Saturday from 8:00 A.M. to 5:00 P.M. and Sunday from noon to 5:00 P.M. Admission is $7.00 for adults, $6.00 for seniors, and $5.00 for children ages three to eleven. The telephone number is (402) 731–3140.

About twenty minutes west of Omaha is *Waterloo,* located on Highway 275. There you will find the gracious and inviting *J. C. Robinson House B&B* at 102 East Lincoln Avenue. This twenty-one-room mansion, built in 1905, is on the National Register of Historic Places. It has most of the original appointments, including hardwood floors, hand-carved paneling, stained and leaded glass, tiled fireplaces, and pocket doors between the living and entertainment areas. The house is genuinely wonderful, but one of the best features is the owner, Bill Clarke, who runs the B&B

J. C. Robinson House B&B

with his wife, Linda. Clarke is a retired military officer with great stories to tell, and the house is accented with items that the Clarkes collected from their overseas duties and which complement the antique furnishings. Clarke also has an interesting clock collection, which dates from 1735. Only four rooms are available because the owners want to give guests the kind of individual attention one might expect in such a home. The Silk Purse Room, accented with Linda's pig collection, reflects the Clarkes' sense of humor and whimsy. Room rates range from $65 for a single to $85 for a double in the stately master bedroom. The Clarkes pride themselves on their country breakfasts, but lighter meals for calorie-conscious guests are no problem. Pet boarding can be arranged. If you like animals, the Clarkes have two friendly Siberian huskies and three huge Maine Coon cats. If you don't like animals, they can be kept well away from you. Call for reservations at (402) 779–2704 or (800) 779–2705. The fax number is (402) 779–3235.

For a small community of just under 500, Waterloo has a wealth of dining possibilities. Within minutes of one another there's the Mexican restaurant of *Ell Bee's, Farmer Brown's Steak House,* and *Harr's Family Restaurant.* Between breakfast at the B&B and any of these restaurants, you won't find yourself hungry for long in Waterloo.

Sarpy County

ellevue, south of Omaha, Nebraska's oldest community, started in 1822 when the Missouri Fur Company established a permanent post here. It got its name from Manuel Lisa, a Spanish explorer who liked the scenery and dubbed it "Belle View." Other early visitors were Karl

Bodmer (the Swiss artist whose work is on display at Joslyn Art Museum in Omaha), explorers Maj. Steven Long and Gen. John C. Fremont, and Kit Carson. Free and guided weekday tours of several historic sites, including a log cabin built in the 1830s (making it one of the oldest intact structures in Nebraska), a railroad depot, Fontenelle Bank (built in 1857 and the state's oldest public building), the Presbyterian Church, and an early cemetery with the grave of Big Elk, the last full-blooded chief of the Omaha tribe, can be arranged by calling the Sarpy County Tourism Office at (402) 293–3080. They like it if you can call ahead of time.

The *Fontenelle Forest Nature Center,* at 1111 North Bellevue Boulevard, provides another chance to experience nature. It has 17 miles of hiking trails (1 mile of which is an equal-access boardwalk) on 1,300 acres and serves as a wildlife and environmental sanctuary that provides lots of glimpses of woodland creatures. The center, with 26,000 feet of exhibits, is open daily from 8:00 A.M. to 5:00 P.M. The admission fee is $7.00 for adults, $6.00 for seniors, and $5.00 for children ages three through eleven. Call (402) 731–3140 for more information.

Washington County

ashington County is the location of the first U.S. military post west of the Missouri River. *Fort Atkinson,* now a state historical park, was built in 1820 on the recommendation of reports from the Lewis and Clark expedition. *Fort Atkinson State Park* is located just off Highway 75 in the town of *Fort Calhoun.* Fort Atkinson was built to keep Canadians and the French and Spanish out of the territory, to protect the early fur trade and river traffic, and to foster relations with Native Americans. Perhaps this last function did not manifest itself; when the soldiers left in 1827, the Native Americans burned the fort to the ground, and nearly thirty years later the early settlers of Fort Calhoun salvaged what little they could for building materials. At its peak Fort Atkinson had a school (the first in Nebraska) and a library, a kiln, a brickyard, and a sawmill. Farming also produced food for the 1,000 soldiers and their families. The crops and vegetables produced came as somewhat of a surprise—after all, this was supposed to be the Great American Desert. In any case, nothing was left but a field until local citizens rallied to have the site saved in the 1960s, and the Nebraska Game and Parks Commission joined the effort. Archaeological digs, conducted in the 1970s by the Nebraska Historical Society, led to the discovery of the location of the original buildings. The present buildings are located on the same spot and look just as the originals once did. Fort

Atkinson State Historical Park makes history come alive—the visitors center has displays and interpretive materials, and periodic living-history demonstrations are held throughout the summer. Park grounds are open year-round, and the visitors center is open daily from 9:00 A.M. to 5:00 P.M. during the summer and on weekends in September and October from 10:00 A.M. to 5:00 P.M. A park entry permit is available on site. For details call (402) 468–5611 or log onto the Web site at www.ngp.ngpc.state.ne.us/parks/ftatkin.html.

North of Fort Atkinson State Historical Park is the *DeSoto National Wildlife Refuge,* east of Blair across the Missouri River on Highway 30. The refuge encompasses land in both Nebraska and Iowa. In spring and fall the refuge is host to thousands of migratory ducks and geese. Bald eagles are not uncommon. In the fall, between 300,000 and 600,000 snow geese and blue geese make a stop on their southward migration between their Hudson Bay nesting grounds in Canada and their Gulf Coast homes. (Where do you think the term "snowbird," for people who head south from cold climes for the winter, came from?) Glass-enclosed viewing provides comfy seating for wildlife observers. If you prefer, you can get out and hike or drive around the grounds. The visitors center has informative wildlife displays and videos, and it also has a beautifully designed museum with artifacts from the steamboat *Bertrand,* which sank in the Missouri River in 1865 on its way to supply mining camps in the Montana Territory. It was discovered in 1968, and most of the salvaged items, which were encased and preserved in Missouri mud, are on display. The 200,000 reclaimed objects—everything from canned goods to liquor, clothes, shoes, buttons, cooking utensils, cutlery, dishes, and mining equipment—are showcased in this wonderful museum. The entry fee is $3.00 per vehicle unless you have a duck stamp or someone in your car has a federal recreation passport. The refuge is open daily except for Christmas, New Year's Day, and Thanksgiving. For more information call the visitors center between 9:00 A.M. and 4:30 P.M. at (712) 642–4121.

Blair, west of the DeSoto National Wildlife Refuge on Highways 91 and 75, is the site of the *Tower of the Four Winds* in Black Elk/Neihardt Park, which overlooks the Dana College campus. Built to promote world peace, brotherhood, and humanity, the tower portrays the message of Black Elk, an Oglala Sioux holy man and visionary. He is said to have envisioned a radiant person with outstretched arms in a blessing to all people in front of the tree of life. The 45-foot tower, made from native rock and covered with a 50,000-piece mosaic, represents the messiah-like figure of Black Elk's vision. (See the listing for Bancroft in Cuming County for additional information about Black Elk and John Neihardt.)

Dodge County

remont, located at the junction of Highways 77 and 30, is an attractive community of approximately 24,000 situated near the Platte River. It was named for Gen. John C. Fremont, an early explorer of the West who earned the nickname of the "Great Pathfinder." If you prefer your path to end at an antiques store, the downtown area is thick with them. Spend some time doing your own exploring, and you'll see why Fremont is becoming known as the antiques capital of eastern Nebraska. Seven antiques stores represent nearly one hundred dealers and include *Antique Alley* (402–727–9542), with twenty dealers at 105 East Sixth; *C&E Antique Mall* (402–721–2102), specializing in elegant glass at 530 North Main; *Dime Store Days* (402–727–0580), with forty dealers at 109 East Sixth; *Park Avenue Antiques* (402–721–1157), with twenty-five dealers, at Fifth and Park; and *Yankee Peddlers West* (402–721–7800), with antiques, arts, and books, at 141 East Sixth.

After you find your antique treasures, celebrate your shopping prowess with an old-fashioned high tea or a great lunch at *Carey's Cottage,* on 732 North Park Avenue near the downtown area. Owner Helen Carey Krause was looking for a creative business venture to fill her time after the youngest of her four sons left home in 1993. She purchased a sweet little cottage, for which the word *quaint* is the very best description, and transformed it into a restaurant that draws customers to Fremont from all over Nebraska. Antique dishes, linens, and furnishings add a nice touch to the atmosphere of the Irish cottage. The extensive menu includes salads, homemade soups, quiche, apricot chicken, and sandwiches. The scones and the dessert offerings are legendary and are made fresh daily, as are all the items on the menu. Lunch is served Monday through Saturday from 11:00 A.M. to 2:00 P.M.; the price for big servings is $7.95. Afternoon teas are served from 2:00 to 4:00 P.M. If you think this is food for ladies only, think again. The servings are ample, and guests of the male gender will not be disappointed. Walk-ins are welcome, but reservations are preferred. Even if you do have to wait a while, it's worth it. In good weather there's a pleasant area for outdoor seating in the back. No credit cards are accepted, just cash or personal checks. Call (800) 680–7640 or (402) 721–7640.

You know how fussy babies sometimes are soothed into serenity by the sensation of being rocked gently in a moving car? The *Fremont Dinner Train* has that same effect on adults. It's hard to stay stressed when you're being served a fabulous five-course meal as you watch the scenic Elkhorn River valley roll by outside the window of a 1940s-era train car. (Maj. Stephen Long, the explorer who declared the land that you see from the train window to be part of the Great American Desert, crossed the Elkhorn River in 1820, just a few miles from the current railroad line.) Meals always include prime rib, with fowl, fish, or seafood alternatives. Evening rides are elegant and romantic, with big-band music playing in the background. Afternoon rides are more casual. Periodic special events on the train range from murder mysteries to USO shows, wine tastings, a Germanfest, and special holiday activities. The cost per adult is $45.95, not including tax or gratuity. Sunday afternoon trips are $39.95. Credit cards are welcome. There is a cash bar on the train as well. The office for the Fremont Dinner Train is at 650 North H Street; the train boards at 1835 North Somers Street. Call (800) 942–7245 for the required reservations. The Web site is www. dinnertrain.net.

For a different type of motorized experience, go twenty minutes northwest of Fremont, off Highway 275 near **Scribner,** to find the **Nebraska Motorplex,** south on Raceway Road (there are a couple miles of gravel road). The address is apt; drag racing is the fastest motor sport on the face of the earth, according to manager Steve Clarke. And some of the fastest cars in the world race on this 7,000-foot former airstrip for B-24s and B-25s, which is now surrounded by cornfields. This fifty-acre area, referred to as a Nebraska "field of dreams," is a wonderfully unlikely setting for cars that can reach up to 300 mph in five seconds from a standing start during the Mid-America Nationals, an event sanctioned by the International Hot Rod Association. Shirley Muldowney raced here in her pink Top Fuel Car. Stop in on weekends between mid-April and late October. Weekly programs draw an average of 240 drag racers and 2,000 fans. Gates open on Friday at 6:30 P.M., Saturday at 1:00 P.M., and Sunday at 7:30 A.M., with eliminations beginning at 1:30 P.M. Tickets are generally $6.00; national races cost more, depending on the event. Call (402) 492–8150 for a complete schedule of events.

Before leaving Dodge County, take Highway 91 west from just north of Scribner to **Dodge,** the Baseball Capital of Nebraska. But you won't find much evidence of baseball unless it's a summer night and the home team is challenging what will likely be the loser. This community of nearly 700 is becoming much more famous for **Vogies Quilts and Treasures,** a little store downtown at 153 Oak Street that has about a million miles of quilting fabrics. *Quilt Sampler* magazine includes Vogies as among the top ten quilt shops in America. More than 2,000 bolts of colorful fabric and numerous shelves of quilting supplies irresistibly lure quilters and crafters like bees to flowers. There are hundreds of quilting books and patterns, plus stencils and notions. If you get the notion to stop here, you won't be able to leave without some treasure of your own—even if you can't thread a needle. I succumbed to the lure of embroidery transfers for old-fashioned day-of-the-week tea towels; I'll finish them in a year or three. In addition to the quilting supplies there's a nice giftware department featuring "Country to Contemporary" items for nearly everyone on your gift list. Call ahead to arrange a tour. Hours are Monday through Saturday from 9:00 A.M. to 5:30 P.M.; (402) 693–2230. The Web site is www.fabshophop.com.

Make your next Dodge stop the *Bank-Quit,* a great restaurant with perhaps the cleverest name in all of Nebraska. It's housed in a former bank building, which sat empty for about sixty years after the Great Depression closed many banks. Owner Snooks Muller (if you're old enough to remember the Baby Snooks radio show, yes, that is where she got her nickname) says the most popular item is her homemade coconut cream pie. It's $1.50 a slice, but according to Snooks it's big enough that most people split it. She's not entirely sure where she got the recipe, but she thinks it was from her mom, who was herself "a pretty good cook." There's a tea in the afternoon, but the cappuccino seems to be more popular than the tea. You pay your bill, of course, at a teller window. And before you leave, go into the vault to check out the antiques and crafts. The Bank-Quit is open Monday through Saturday, 7:00 A.M. to 3:00 P.M. The telephone number is (402) 693–4165.

Burt and Thurston Counties

If you have a chance to stay overnight in *Burt County,* the *Benson B&B* in Oakland is the place to go. *Oakland,* on Highways 77 and 32, is a pretty little town of about 1,300 people with a decidedly Swedish heritage. Many homes display the traditional Swedish *dahla* horses, and the downtown area has businesses and street signs replete with Swedish touches. The Benson B&B, downtown at 402 North Oakland Avenue, is a former rooming house for railroad workers that was built in 1905. It has been painstakingly restored to provide you with an exceptional stay. The three rooms are decorated nicely, and you'll be provided with a robe, shampoo, conditioner, lotion, a shower cap, and even Nebraska-made chocolates in your room. Owners Norma and Stan Anderson kept all the original yellow-pine woodwork and transoms above the doors intact while adding touches like an oversize whirlpool tub and a television in the bathroom. The B&B, located upstairs from a craft shop and beauty shop, is light and airy. Guests are given full run of the place, including the sitting rooms and the family room, which has

The Answer Is Out There

Watch the nighttime summer sky. Do you feel like someone, or something, is watching back? In August 1977 a man claimed he was abducted by aliens in a UFO right outside of Pender in Thurston County. After the ship landed he lost his memory, but he does recall being in a white room with black-and-white patterns on the floor, walls, and ceiling. He claims a telepathic voice asked about science, religion, and math. Truth or fiction? You decide. But one time, on a road not far from here, I saw several manta rays flying along next to the car. Really.

more than 200 family-oriented videotapes. You can also watch life in a small town from the cheerful garden room. Norma serves up big, hot, and hearty breakfasts on antique china and crystal in the dining room. Children age thirteen or older are welcome. Room rates are $53 to $60; Discover cards are accepted. For reservations call (402) 685–6051. The Web address is www.flinthills.com/~atway/ne/benson/html.

While you're in Oakland, take a *Troll Stroll* in the park along a path lined with wooden trolls or visit the *Swedish Heritage Center,* at 301 North Charde Avenue. Swedish crystal, linens, and needlework brought by pioneers are among the articles on display.

Thurston County is rich in Native American culture and history. It is the site of the *Omaha Indian Reservation* and the *Winnebago Indian Reservation.* The Omaha Tribe of Nebraska hosts an annual powwow in *Macy,* on Highway 75, during the first full moon in August. It is the oldest continuous harvest celebration in the state (the first recorded one was held in 1805). The powwow begins on Thursday and ends on Sunday. For more information on the Omaha Tribe of Nebraska, call (402) 837–5391.

Overlooking the Missouri River near Macy is *Blackbird Hill,* the burial site of the Omaha Chief Blackbird. Nearby is *Robber's Cave,* in a sandstone bluff, which, legend holds, was the hideout for river bandits and the notorious James gang. The Winnebago Tribe of Nebraska hosts an annual

River Lair

*R*obber's Cave *used to be bigger, but time and erosion have turned it into just a small cutout in the sandy banks of the Missouri. It is said to be where river pirates ambushed trading vessels, stealing furs and supplies. It is also said to have once been a hideout of Jesse and Frank James after fleeing*

the disastrous raid on a Northfield, Minnesota, bank. To get there, take Highway 75 Southeast of Winnebago for 4 miles, then turn east 1½ miles on County Road 852. The trail to the river and the cave is there, which can be muddy. The trail is on private tribal land, but locals fish there.

powwow in Veterans Park in **Winnebago,** on Highway 77, on the last full weekend in July for four full days. For more information about the Winnebago Tribe of Nebraska, call (402) 878–2272. There is an admission charge for both powwows.

The community of **Walthill,** on Highway 77, has a very interesting museum at the **Dr. Susan La-Flesche Picotte Center.** Dr. Picotte was the nation's first Native American woman to become a medical doctor. The daughter of a chief who believed that learning the ways of the whites was a means of survival, Dr. Picotte was educated in the East and came home to dedicate her life to working among her people in the early 1900s. She practiced medicine in the hospital that now is a museum on the National Register of Historic Places as well as a National Historic Landmark. Each September the Susan LaFlesche Picotte Day is held to honor her work, with speakers, cultural activities, and exhibits. The Picotte Center is available for tours. Call (402) 846–5428 to arrange one; they're free.

Lovers' Leap

Visit **Blackbird Hill** and you may see a ghost or two. Legend has it that two men loved the same woman. The preferred man went hunting, and those who went with him returned to say that he accidentally drowned in the Missouri. The woman married the other man. Some years went by, and one day the presumed-drowned man returned. The husband feared his wife would leave him, so he cut her throat and leapt from Blackbird Hill. Some say the area where she bled to death never grew grass again. As for the worried husband, can you hear that plaintive and oh-so-faint ghostly moaning?

Tomb with a View

*B*lackbird Hill is the final resting place of Omaha Chief Blackbird. An outstanding warrior and even greater negotiator with early French and Spanish traders, he became a rich man from the fur trade, as did many in his tribe. However, his dealings with the white man also earned him a few enemies. It is said that he was taught by traders how to use arsenic and thus was able to rule through intimidation—after "predicting" terrible deaths for his enemies. He died, ironically enough, from a white man's disease when a smallpox epidemic swept through the tribe in the early 1800s. As he lay dying, he asked that his body be placed upon his favorite horse and that together they be buried on a bluff to enable them to view a 30-mile stretch of the Missouri River. Lewis and Clark passed by in 1804 and mentioned this site in their journals. In 1832 the painter George Catlin climbed up and took it upon himself to root around, whereupon he found a human skull presumed to be that of Chief Blackbird. The skull is now at the Smithsonian. Blackbird Hill is off Highway 75 between Decatur (the second-oldest town in the state) and Macy. Watch for signs leading east to the Missouri River and Blackbird Hill.

Dakota and Dixon Counties

The *O'Conner House Museum Complex,* 2 miles east of *Homer* off Highway 77 on a gravel road in *Dakota County,* makes a pleasant stop in northeast Nebraska. The O'Conner House is a luxurious fourteen-room mansion that took ten years to complete between 1865 and 1875. It has a curved staircase, a large Italian marble fireplace, eight bedrooms on the second floor, and servants' quarters in the basement. The O'Conner House has a special summer social in July, elaborate decorations in each room for the Christmas Tour, and Open House on the second and third weekends in November. The one-room Combs School, located next to the mansion, is where modern kids are taught readin', 'ritin', and 'rithmetic, and it is where a typical pioneer school day is re-created, which is authentic down to lunch from a syrup-pail bucket. West of the school is the Museum-Machinery Building, which houses antique farm machinery and office equipment. All the sites are open for visitors each Sunday from 2:00 to 4:00 P.M. in June, July, and August. Donations are accepted. Living-history classes are offered at the Combs School in May. Donations are accepted. For more information contact the Dakota County Historical Society at (402) 698–2161.

Wakefield has a great theater company. And if you're in town when the *Little Red Hen Theatre* has a production, do make time to enjoy the show. Three major plays are produced each year, and fine-arts activities are offered year-round at 316 Main Street. The telephone numbers for the Little Red Hen Theatre are (402) 287–2818 and (800) 287–3412.

Smoke on the Water

There is a volcano in Nebraska. Or at least there was at one time what seemed to be a volcano. The Ionia Volcano was located north of Newcastle in Dixon County. Five miles north of town is the site that Lewis and Clark recorded in their journals as a volcano, complete with fire and smoke, on a river bluff. This apparent volcanic activity is now believed to have been a decomposition of iron pyrite beds when they came into steamy contact with the river. The volcano was a cause of concern and consternation among early settlers. In 1878 the bluff was washed away, as were all reports of fire and smoke. A historical marker in Newcastle's Pfister Park explains the volcano and provides directions to the site. If you drive there, you won't see a very impressive volcano anymore, but there is a very impressive view from the bluff, where you can see three states: Nebraska, South Dakota, and Iowa.

To get to **Dixon,** your next stop, from Wakefield, you'll need to do a little backtracking. Go south 2 miles on Highway 16, turn west on Highway 35, go 8 miles to Highway 15, and then turn north for another 11 miles. Hungry now? Then stop for burgers and pizza at **Euni's Place** at Second and Conway. Owner Euni Diediker says that you can't miss it, since there are only two businesses in the entire town—hers and the grain elevator. Eight-ounce burgers are $2.25; cheeseburgers are $2.50. On busy Sunday evenings you might have to wait a bit for one of her famous pizzas. Choose from hamburger, sausage, pepperoni, combo, or supreme. The most you'll have to pay is $14.50 for the largest, and it's a whopper that can serve twelve people. The average American consumes approximately forty-six slices of pizza a year; make it a point to have several of them at Euni's. When asked why people come from hundreds of miles away to eat her pizzas, Euni simply says, "Because they're good." They must be, since her little pizza oven has been known to crank out nearly fifty pizzas in one night. She's closed on Monday, but open for lunch and dinner the rest of the week. Euni's original restaurant burned down in 1987, and not long after that the only gas station burned, too. So make sure you're not running on empty. The gas station has not been rebuilt. Euni's telephone number is (402) 584–9309.

Now you'll find yourself not only stuffed with pizza, but in a quandary. This is because you'll want to eat again just a few miles away at **Bob's Bar** in **Martinsburg.** Martinsburg is northeast of Dixon on Highways 9 and 16. The claim to fame at Bob's Bar is a huge hamburger, weighing in at nearly a pound. You needn't ask "Where's the beef?" but you might well be tempted to ask "Where's the plate?" since it will have pretty much disappeared under the burger. Like Euni's, people come from miles around for the food, although the waitress claims there's no secret to the burger's preparation. "We just cook it," she said. One suspects she might be related to modest-about-the-food Euni. But it's obvious from the number of patrons that there's something indefinably magic going on in the kitchen of this old two-story building. Burgers are $2.55; cheeseburgers are $2.65. Bob's is open every single day from 7:30 A.M. to 1:00 A.M. The number is (402) 945–2995.

Dixon County offers outdoor activities at **Ponca State Park,** on the Missouri near the community of **Ponca** (take 26E 2 miles north out of town). The park overlooks the only unchannelized section of the Missouri, giving a glimpse of the untamed river before dams changed its wild ways forever. Whether you rent a fully equipped cabin with a screened-in porch or rough it at a campsite, you'll find the park, with its 859 acres, to be a stupendously pretty place to hike wooded trails, ride a horse to the Three-State Overlook, swim in the pool, or have a picnic. A park permit is necessary and can be purchased on site. It costs $14 and is good for all game and park facilities statewide. The telephone number is (402) 755–2284. The Web address is www.ngpc.state.ne.us/parks.

Knox County

In south-central Knox County (3 miles north of Highway 59) is tiny *Winnetoon,* inhabited with fifty-nine people, a couple of dogs, and one stripper. The stripper is the lady who strips and refinishes antique furniture at the *Winnetoon Mini-Mall.* The mini-mall sells antiques of all kinds, handcrafted items, and a surprisingly good selection of natural-food items. You'll also be able to see and buy the work of the lanky Joe Serres, the "Carvin' Cowboy" who creates his work with a chain saw. Serres, delightfully modest and unassuming, has a wizardry for wielding a chain saw that results in wonderfully whimsical folk art such as totem poles, animals, and other figures. Check out the Privy Path with its outhouse collection. The mall is open year-round, Monday through Friday from 8:00 A.M. to 4:00 P.M., Friday from 6:00 to 9:00 P.M., and Saturday from 8:00 A.M. to 4:00 P.M.—or by "chance or appointment." The telephone number is (402) 847–3368.

Your next stop is west of the town of *Niobrara.* Near there you'll see the buffalo, and the elk, roam at the *Kreycik Riverview Elk Farm.* More and more farmers and ranchers in Nebraska are diversifying from traditional crops and livestock, and the Kreyciks are no exception. They have developed a passion for elk and buffalo, the alternative "crop," plus a great tourist attraction. From mid-May through September you can take a covered-wagon ride through three different pastures: one with buffalo, one with elk cows, and one with elk bulls. If you go in August you can hear the bull elk's bugle, a strangely high-pitched call that the girl elks must like a whole bunch. Lots of people go to the mountains to hear the elks bugle—they needn't bother, since we've got it right here in Nebraska. The rides are on Friday and Saturday at 10:00 A.M., 2:00 P.M., and 4:00 P.M. Sunday rides are offered at 2:00 and 4:00 P.M. The rides cost $5.00 plus tax. Call (402) 857–3850 to make arrangements. No tours are given on Memorial Day, the Fourth of July, or Labor Day. If you hunt, the Kreyciks also offer elk hunting in the fall. If you're not a hunter, the gift shop sells frozen elk meat. To get to there from Highway 12, go south on the oiled road across from the Niobrara State Park (there's a sign). Follow the oiled road until it ends, at which point you'll be heading west. Continue west until you see a cemetery on a hill (there's another sign), and follow that road south down the hill to the Kreyciks'.

Niobrara, at the junction of Highways 12 and 14, has two places of interest for those with an appreciation of Native American art and history. The *Northern Plains Art Gallery* at 89156 Highway 14 has handmade arts and crafts representing several northern Plains tribes. The gallery is open Monday through Saturday, 10:00 A.M. to 6:00 P.M. and Sunday, noon to 6:00 P.M. The phone number is (402) 857–3447. The *Ponca Tribe Museum* contains artifacts from the tribe's history such as photo archives plus artwork and a gift shop. The museum is open Monday through Friday from 7:30 A.M. to 4:00 P.M. It's on Main Street just across from the Green's Cafe; there's no street address posted, but don't worry, Niobrara is small and you'll find it. The number is (402) 857–3519. By the way, did you know that Europeans and Canadians refer to Native Americans as First Nations or First Peoples?

Here's another interesting thing about the community of Niobrara. The whole dang town has been relocated and rebuilt—twice. In 1881 catastrophic floods covered the town three times; the soggy townspeople wisely decided to pick up their homes and businesses to move to higher ground. Things were dry for decades until the late 1950s, when the construction of the Gavins Point Dam created the Lewis and Clark Lake, which in turn raised the groundwater level, which in turn flooded basements with consistent and dismaying regularity. The community voted to relocate yet again in the 1970s. The federal government paid for this move to the tune of $14.5 million. Compare this to the cost of $40,000 for the 1881 move. One can only conclude that death and taxes are not the only things certain in life; the cost of living going up seems fairly certain to me.

From Niobrara go east on Highway 12 and you'll come to the *Santee Sioux Indian Reservation,* which has been home to the Santee Sioux since 1868. A few years back, the Santee started a very small casino, but the powers that be in Nebraska took great exception to this; the money was impounded, and the casino closed briefly. The Santee Sioux are currently operating the casino while pursuing various legal strategies. The annual powwow is traditionally held the last weekend in June in the community of Santee on S54D, off Highway 12. For more information call (402) 857–2302.

Continue east on Highway 12, and you'll come to *Crofton.* This town is known as the "friendliest little town by a dam site" because of its proximity to *Lewis and Clark Lake* and *Gavins Point Dam.* The *Crofton Lakeview Golf Course* was named as one of the sixty-five "golfiest" spots in America by *Golf* magazine in 1995, and the magazine said the course "epitomizes the spirit of golf."

When you're in Crofton, plan on spending the night at the *Historic Argo Hotel* at 211 West Kansas Street. At first glance, the sturdy brick building, built in 1912, looks fairly institutional. However, once you step inside you're engulfed in a warm, spacious lobby with a tin ceiling, wood accents, and lots of windows. This historic hotel has been extensively refurbished; all seventeen rooms have brass beds, ceiling fans, central air, cable TV, and telephones. The honeymoon suite has a four-poster bed and a bath with a Jacuzzi. The rooms come with a dinner package (there's a remarkable restaurant in the hotel) if you like, or you can just have a continental breakfast. The top rate, for the honeymoon suite with dinner and champagne, is $135; a suite with dinner for two is $69.95 and includes breakfast. Double or single occupancy without dinner is $45.00. Elegant eight-course meals can be followed by a cigar from the well-stocked humidor in the "smoking room" (bar). Each of the four bathrooms have both a claw-foot tub and a modern shower. There's talk of a resident ghost, but it has been rumored to appear only in the basement—where you won't be. The places you will want to visit are the attractive, well-stocked bar in the back and the dance floor in the front. Live dinner music is featured every night. On Sunday through Thursday evenings you'll have the delightful experience of hearing the piano as played by Hermenia Bogner (the "Hat Lady"), mother of the owners. Mrs. Bogner is also an accomplished artist; twenty-five of her acrylics hang in the hotel. To make a reservation for dinner (the hotel is especially busy in the summer) or to book a room, call (800) 607-2746 or (402) 388-2400. See the Web site at www.theargohotel.com.

Cuming and Stanton Counties

ancroft, on Highways 51 and 16 in *Cuming County,* is a place where you can learn about Nebraska's Poet Laureate, John G. Neihardt, at the *John G. Neihardt Center.* Neihardt is most famous for his book *Black Elk Speaks,* which has been translated into dozens of languages and recounts the visions of his friend, the Oglala holy man and visionary Black Elk. A prolific writer and prodigious scholar, Neihardt finished his first book at the age of sixteen. He wrote nearly thirty books of poetry, fiction, and philosophy. After teaching in country schools, Neihardt moved to Bancroft in 1900, where he worked as a trader with the Omaha tribe and became an authority on its traditions and customs. The center, at the corner of Elm and Washington Streets, has a Sacred Hoop Prayer Garden, a little building where Neihardt wrote, and a modern visitors center with interesting exhibits and films about his life and work. The hours are Monday through Saturday from 9:00 A.M. to 5:00 P.M. and Sunday from 1:30 to 5:00 P.M. Donations are accepted. Call (402) 648–3388 or (888) 777–4667.

From Bancroft you'll be heading west now into *Stanton County* and one of the best meals in the state. You're going to the little community of *Stanton* (population 1,549), at the junction of Highways 57 and 24, and the *Uptown Brewery* at 801 Tenth Street. There are not enough superlative words to describe this place. The restaurant is the winner of several international food awards and dozens of area awards, and it is the only Nebraska restaurant outside of Omaha or Lincoln to have a three-diamond rating from the Automobile Association of America. Owners Rosalind Lamson and Adam Staib use only fresh and natural foods; nothing is canned, precooked, or processed, and you won't find sugar, refined salt, or lard on the premises. You may think this would lead to a boring menu, but you'd be dead wrong. The food is wonderful beyond belief. You could start with appetizers like Herring a la Russe, venison sausage, or caviar. A friend who lived in Japan said the Uptown has the best tempura ever. For entrees there's the Chilean sea bass, filet mignon, mesquite pork steak, prime rib, scallops Coquille Saint-Jacques, roast duck Grand Marnier . . . and that's just the beginning. There are also soups (my favorite is the Normandy tomato bisque) and pastas to die for. The desserts render me senseless with pleasure. Roz and Adam add items to the menu, seemingly daily, depending on where and when they can find the best and freshest, most natural foods available. There's always a vegetarian selection. Meals can range from about $8.00 on up to about $20.00. For drinks there's 115 wines and champagne. Ten beers, including Guinness, are on tap. The Uptown Brewery is in a renovated 1906 building that has had incarnations as a barrel house, warehouse, feed store, package store, and other restaurants. Don't worry about being underdressed; blue jeans and T-shirts are fine, but do get all decked out if you've a special occasion to celebrate. Lunches are served from 11:00 A.M. to 3:00 P.M. daily, Sunday brunches are from 11:00 A.M. to 2:00 P.M., and dinners are from 5:00 P.M. until closing. Reservations are not necessary. The phone number is (402) 439–5100.

Golfers will enjoy the nine-hole *Elkhorn Acres* golf course in Stantan. Two miles northwest of Stanton is one of the largest lakes in northeast Nebraska at the *Maskethine Recreation Area.* The lake is surrounded by a 300-acre wildlife-management area and includes an arboretum.

The area is open to seasonal hunting, fishing, swimming, boating, and camping.

Pamper yourself in **Beemer** (Highway 275 and L2OA), at **Carolyn's Hair Studio and Day Spa.** Get a Day of Bliss, with a Swedish massage, manicure and pedicure, a light lunch catered by Marilyn's, a touch of sun, a paraffin dip, ear coning, a whirlpool, a facial, and a finishing touch of a hairdo. Other pamperings include a Sampler Package or Indulgence, with many of the items listed above. A scalp massage and waxing are available, too, as are goodies like herbal teas, cheeses, nuts, chocolates, mineral water, coffee, and espresso. Call ahead at (402) 528–3836 to make arrangements.

Beemer is also a great place to whip your golf game into shape. The **Indian Trails Country Club golf course,** at 1128 River Road, is locally popular and draws visitors from far away as well. Try not to get distracted by the panoramic view of the wooded Elkhorn Valley. The greens are crowned, slick, and have subtle breaks. According to *Golfing Nebraska,* "An unusual hazard comes into play on the 10. If you go over the green you're in the graveyard." Green fees for eighteen holes range from $12 to $16 with an extra charge for the cart. The phone number is (402) 528–3404.

Pierce County

Just west of **Pierce** (Highways 13 and 98), you'll come to **Cuthills Vineyards,** Nebraska's first winery. (There's a second winery near Raymond called James Arthur Vineyard.) Cuthills is 3 miles west of Pierce and north of Willow Creek State Recreation Area. The prizewinning wine is produced by vineyard manager and wine maker Ed Swanson, who named the vineyard after the "cuthills" formed by glaciers that at one time scoured the area. A picturesque 1920s barn has been completely renovated to house the wine-making equipment (the grapes are crushed mechanically, so rid yourself of the notion of barefoot stompers) and a beautiful shop, where you can taste and buy the wine. After just a few years of production, Swanson now produces 25,000 bottles of wine. The wine pairs well with food, and its reputation is growing as quickly as the grape vines. Swanson currently produces semidry, semisweet, and sweet wine. A tasty mead (ask Ed's wife, Holly, to tell you the tradition of mead as a gift for newlyweds and the genesis of the word *honeymoon*) has been added to the line, as well as dry and sparkling wines. The shop also has great items like smoked salmon, grape wreaths, wooden wine boxes, wine glasses, wine biscuits, mustards, grape seed oil (tasty and good for you), corkscrews, baskets, T-shirts, candles, fudge sauces with wine, and more. A self-guided walking tour of the vineyards can be enjoyed at your leisure. Baco, the dog (named after a grape variety), will likely greet your arrival with tail-thumping but well-restrained glee. Cuthills Vineyards is open from January through April, Friday through Sunday, 1:00 to 5:00 P.M.; and May through December, Wednesday through Saturday, 11:00 A.M. to 6:00 P.M., and Sunday 1:00 to 6:00 P.M. They are closed on all holidays. The telephone number is (402) 329–6774. The Web site is www.cuthills.com.

If you sample a little too much wine, or even if you don't, head for the cozy new *Willow Rose B&B.* This large, two-story frame house is fashioned like a 1950s Southern mansion. Hang out on the deck to watch the creek flow by or soak in the gazebo hot tub. If you travel with ice skates in the winter, go for a brisk turn on the pond. The B&B is $\frac{1}{2}$ mile west and $\frac{1}{2}$ mile south of Pierce near the Willow Creek State Recreation Area. For reservations call (402) 329–4114.

Northwest of Pierce on Highways 13 and 20 is *Plainview, Nebraska's Klown Kapital,* so named because of the popular *Klown Band* that plays during the Klown Karnival in July. The *Klown Museum* is housed in the Chamber of Commerce office in a nicely renovated gas station on Highway 20. No klowning, the *Rose Garden Inn,* at 305 North Third Street, is a picturesque B&B. There are three guest rooms in this century-old Victorian home with a wraparound porch and curved-glass front window. Tickle the ivories on the baby grand piano in the parlor or stroll in the yard or rose garden, which are surrounded by a white picket fence. Owners Bob and Carolyn Smith offer a periodic Mystery Weekend, when guests are involved in what can be compared to a giant game of Clue® as they figure out who did the dastardly deed of murder most foul. Rooms with a private bath are $59.50; rooms with a shared bath are $47.50. Credit cards are accepted. Call (402) 582–4708 for reservations.

Antelope County

When you see the *Plantation House B&B* in Elgin ($\frac{4}{10}$ mile east and $\frac{1}{2}$ block south of Highways 70 and 14), you might wonder if you're in Nebraska or Georgia. The B&B is a huge twenty-five-room, Southern-style mansion that offers genuine Midwestern hospitality. Five rooms, all with private baths, are wonderfully appointed and can be yours from $55 to $75. Or you can stay in the small cottage on the four-acre grounds. Relax in the parlor with a book, dream by the fire in the family room, or lock yourself away in the private, two-person whirlpool

There's Snow Place like Nebraska

*T*his is a story about never doubting the veracity of others' experiences until you experience them yourself.

I grew up hearing horrific stories of the Blizzard of 1888, the tragedy of nearly one hundred lives lost and the miraculous tales of those who survived. The Great Blizzard struck on January 12, 1888. The day started out warm, and most people anticipated the not-uncommon Great Plains phenomenon of a January thaw—the kind of day where people go ice-fishing in shirtsleeves. By late afternoon, however, the entire state was engulfed by gale-force winds whipping the snow into complete whiteout. The storm broke without warning; people became aware of it only when, as one survivor recounted, "the sheer front of the blizzard crashed against the schoolhouse like a tidal wave, shaking the wooden frame building and almost lifting it from its foundation." Those caught outside sought shelter in chicken coops, barns, haystacks, and even overturned wagons. One lucky girl found her way home by clutching a cow's tail. She was blinded by swirling snow, but the cow, sharing her intense desire to go home, led them to safety.

Rural children were trapped in country schools while desperate parents, unable to rescue them, prayed for them to not attempt a treacherous journey. Nebraska history books abound with stories of young women teachers saving their charges. Lois May Royce, a teacher in a small school near Plainview, was not so successful in her attempts. Three of the younger students were still at school with her when the storm roared in the afternoon. There wasn't enough fuel for the night, so they set out for her boardinghouse only 200 feet away. They lost their way in the whiteout and sought

room. The former owner made the best sugar cookies in the world. Not to be outdone, new owners Deb and Kyle Warren make a groan-inducing breakfast that includes delectables such as French toast, chocolate pancakes, potato and cheese frittatas, omelettes, meats, muffins, and fresh fruit. Children are welcome. No credit cards. The B&B is at 401 Plantation Street. To make a reservation, call (402) 843–2287 or (888) 446–2287. The Web site is www.plantation-house.com.

The community of **Neligh,** north of Elgin on Highways 14 and 275, gives you an example of an old-fashioned "daily grind" at the **Neligh Mills State Historical Site.** This flour mill on the Elkhorn River, at the corner of N and Wylie Streets, is one of the oldest examples of a water-powered mill in the United States. Built in 1873, it is now a branch museum of the State Historical Society. This is the only nineteenth-century flour mill in the state, and it still has all the original equipment. It's a fun tour and a peaceful place to watch the river flow by. The

There's Snow Place like Nebraska (cont.)

refuge in a haystack. The children died, and Royce lost both her legs.

Now here's the part about the wisdom of paying attention to the experience of others. The cynical part of me just could not believe that people could get lost only a few yards from where they wanted to go. Trust me, you can. And quickly. One winter night I was staying in a motel not far from Plainview. I woke up to a screaming, howling blizzard. I could barely see across the parking lot, but I was to meet some people for breakfast, so I dutifully bundled up. My car, parked right outside the door, was hopelessly buried, and I decided to walk. I should have gotten a clue when I didn't see a single soul about or any cars moving. My eyes were nearly pasted shut with snow and the wind was sucking my breath away within less than a minute of struggling through drifts.

This was not good. I decided to pass on the breakfast. As I turned around to go back, the intensity of the storm suddenly increased. I could not see anything. My mind flashed to the Blizzard of '88 victims. I had a piercing empathy for them and an equally piercing regret that I had ever doubted anyone could get irretrievably lost in two or three heartbeats. My brain was frozen with fear. I lost my sense of direction. I admit to a tendency for the dramatic; I imagined my lifeless body being discovered in a parking lot. I honestly cannot tell you how I got back the few yards to my room. Instinct? Luck? Divine intervention when my pitifully mewling prayers were heard? But I can tell you this: You should learn a lesson from history and from my stupidly cavalier attitude about Nebraska blizzards. Don't go out in one.

mill is open from May 1 through Labor Day. Hours are Monday through Saturday from 8:00 A.M. to 5:00 P.M. and Sunday from 1:30 to 5:00 P.M. From Labor Day weekend through September 30, it is open on weekends. From October 1 through April 30, it is open early by appointment. There is $3.00 admission fee. The telephone number is (402) 887–4999 or (402) 887–4975.

Neligh has one of the last remaining drive-in theaters in the state. If you have fond memories of smooching in a car on humid summer nights or if you'd like to create some similar fond memories, grab your sweetie and buy some tickets to the *Starlite Drive-in.* Or bring your kids and try to convince them you never did any such smooching and they shouldn't either when the puberty whammy hits them. It doesn't really matter what's playing (it's always family fare); just be there between April and September on a Thursday, Friday, or Saturday evening. The phone number is (402) 887–5021.

In Neligh you can go from moving pictures to still life with animals. The *Pierson Wildlife Museum Learning Center,* housed in a former church at 205 East Fifth Street, is a collection of one hundred full-body mounts and fifty shoulder mounts of creatures from four continents. According to Safari Club International, this museum has "one of the largest and most impressive private collections in the country." The collection was donated by retired Neligh physician and hunter Dr. Kenneth Pierson and his wife, Margaret. Hours are Sunday through Friday, 1:00 to 5:00 P.M.; and Saturday 10:00 A.M. to 5:00 P.M. Admission is $5.00 for adults, $4.00 for senior citizens, and $3.00 for children five years old and up. The number is (888) 266–4195.

Head north from Neligh on Highway 14, turn west on Highway 20, and go to the *Zoo Nebraska* at *Royal.* This is a wonderful, unpretentious little zoo, and you should stop here. The zoo is home to Reuben, a chimpanzee who knows American sign language, and to other animals such as bobcats, lemurs, snow monkeys, a miniature horse and donkey, llamas, pygmy goats, reptiles, and mountain lions. The birds-of-prey exhibit includes an eagle, barn owls, kestrels, and a Swainson's hawk. The pride of the zoo is the Przewalski's horse, one of only 1,000 of these animals in a handful of zoos around the world. This well-muscled animal is the ancestor of the modern horse, which was thought to be extinct until a Polish explorer in the Russian army found a small herd in the Mongolian desert. Sadly, it is now extinct in the wild. Another cool thing about the zoo is the excellent gift shop, with really neat toys

The Ponca Trail of Tears

*W*hen the Ponca Tribe was forcibly removed from land along the Niobrara River to Indian Territory (now Oklahoma) in 1877, the route became known as the Ponca Trail of Tears. The Ponca were forced to move because an error in the 1868 Treaty of Fort Laramie gave land already belonging to the Ponca to the Dakota Sioux. The arduous journey was marked with hunger, illness, and many deaths. White Buffalo Girl, the daughter of Black Elk and Moon Hawk, died near the community of Neligh. The community gave her a Christian burial, cared for her grave, and in 1913 erected a stone monument for her. A historical marker in the Neligh Cemetery in Antelope County, high on a hill with a dramatic view, tells the story of the Ponca Trail of Tears. (Thanks go to Pat Henkins, the sister of a friend who suggested that this site be included in future editions. Pat died unexpectedly in October 1998. I hope she gets a chance to talk to White Buffalo Girl herself.)

and games and stuff. Summer hours are Memorial Day through Labor Day, daily from 10:00 A.M. to 5:00 P.M. The rest of the year the hours are weekends from 10:00 A.M. to 5:00 P.M. They're closed during December except for a holiday light extravaganza held in the evening from December 10 through December 23. Adult admission is $4.50, and for kids it's $3.00. The telephone number is (402) 893–2002. The Web site is www.zoonebraska.org.

You won't have to drive far to get back to prehistory. *Antelope County* has one of world's finest archaeological sites. *Ashfall Fossil Beds State Historical Park* is 2 miles west and 6 miles north off Highway 20 on a well-marked turnoff between Royal and Orchard. About ten million years ago, a massive volcanic eruption in what is now Idaho sent a deadly cloud spewing ash down on a watering hole in the savanna-like region of what would become Nebraska. The ash suffocated and then buried creatures great and small, from birds to rhinoceros. Today there remains an astonishingly detailed tableau of death, which is being unearthed by paleontologists. You can watch as they sift and sort in the covered Rhino Barn. They will explain the intact and fossilized skeletal remains and make the tragedy real again after all these years. Visitors are endlessly fascinated, as they should be, by the fossilized skeleton of a tiny rhino fetus, still protected by its mother's rib cage, as they died together so long ago. Two of the rhino fossils are named after Sandy, a staffer, and Justin, her son. The visitors center and interpretive facility have equally fascinating exhibits on what the birds and mammals looked like, what they ate (grain seeds in stomachs became fossilized, too), and how they lived. As an added bonus to the enjoyable learning experience, the park is located high on a hill, and you can see for many scenic miles across the rolling plains. Nature trails interpret the area's current plant and animal life. This one-of-a-kind attraction is truly off the beaten path, and you'd be remiss to pass it up. A small admission fee is charged in addition to the park entry permit. Pay it; it's worth it, and it'll help keep the place open and build more trails. Besides, how often do you get to see something that *National Geographic* has called the "Pompeii of the Plains"? The park opens May 1 and has hours Tuesday through Saturday, 10:00 A.M. to 4:00 P.M. Expanded hours run from Memorial Day weekend through Labor Day weekend, Monday through Saturday, 9:00 A.M. to 5:00 P.M.; and Sunday, 11:00 A.M. to 5:00 P.M. After Labor Day through mid-October it's open Tuesday through Saturday, 10:00 A.M. to 4:00 P.M.; and Sunday, 1:00 to 4:00 P.M. The telephone number is (402) 893–2000; the Web site is www.museum.unl.edu/ashfall.

Madison County

N *orfolk* is where the former late-night host Johnny Carson spent most of his growing-up years. He has recently donated one whole bunch of his memorabilia, including several of his Emmys, to the **Elkhorn Valley Museum and Research Center** at 515 Queen City Boulevard. The museum has taken advantage of Mr. Carson's generosity by creating an impressive gallery that includes a set of the *Tonight Show* and other interactive displays. The museum also offers a look at an old movie theater, and it has a large collection of Elkhorn Valley historical items and genealogy materials. Most everyone who goes to the museum is in awe of the enormous (I swear it's bigger than an old bull elephant) Square Turn Tractor; it's the only surviving and operating tractor of its kind in the world. This is a sweet museum; you should go. Hours are Tuesday through Saturday, 10:00 A.M. to 4:00 P.M., Thursday nights until 8:00 P.M.; and Sunday, 1:00 to 4:00 P.M. Donations are accepted. The phone number is (402) 371–3886.

Go the Distance

You may have noticed towns getting farther apart. Many towns in rural areas are between 7 and 10 miles apart, and the reason for that is because when farm families traveled to town on horses or in wagons, it took one day to travel the distance to town, pick up or unload goods, and then get back to the farm before dark. Think of that when you cover these distances in just a few minutes.

The **Willetta Lueshen Bird Library** is in the same building but with a separate entry. This hands-on learning center has more than 1,200 books about birds and nature. A large glass wall looks out onto a very pretty little garden with a whole bunch of birdfeeders. It is only open on Wednesday from 1:00 to 4:00 P.M., but you can call (402) 371–2346 for information on special events. Donations are welcome.

No stop in Norfolk would be complete without visiting the **Norfolk Arts Center** at 305 North Fifth Street. It's a beautifully designed new structure with lots of light and great open spaces. There's a small permanent collection with monthly new exhibits from around the state. The sculpture garden is pretty wonderful, too. Hours are Monday through Friday, 9:00 A.M. to 5:00 P.M.; and Saturday and Sunday, 1:00 to 4:00 P.M. The phone number is (402) 371–7199.

If you want to stretch your legs or take a bike ride, head on over to **TaHaZouka Park** on the south side of town on Highway 81. Here you'll find the trailhead of the **Cowboy Trail,** which will be the longest rail-to-trail conversion in the United States when it's fully completed. This completed stretch runs 34 miles to Neligh. A $2.00 day pass is required. Call (402) 370–3374 for more information.

Continue south on Highway 81 for 13 miles to *Madison* and the *Madison County Historical Society Museum* at 210 West Third Street. This is a great little museum with a touching display about native-son Baseball Hall of Fame member Richie Ashburn. And check out the pencil collection; there's a zillion of them. It's open Monday through Friday from 2:00 to 5:00 P.M. The phone number is (402) 454–3373.

Southeast of Norfolk on Highway 121 is *Battle Creek,* with its spectacular park system. Fourteen parks are encircled by paved People Trails. You'll enjoy the Enchanted Forest minipark, the Heritage Park, with a life-size statue of the Ponca Tribe's Chief Petalsharo, and a carved wooden bear in Sandbox Park created by cowboy and chain-saw artist Joe Serres (read more about him in the section under Winnetoon in Knox County), to name just a few. Historic buildings from the community have been moved onto the Heritage Park grounds. Battle Creek, with a population of a little less than 1,000, is the winner of five Tree City USA awards, and a visit here will demonstrate why the community has been so honored.

Platte County

In *Columbus,* located on Highways 30 and 81 in Platte County, you'll find two good eating places: the beautiful *Gottberg Brew Pub* and adjoining *Dusters* restaurant, 2804 Thirteenth Street (402–564–8338), and *Glur's Tavern,* 2301 Eleventh Street (402–564–8615), said to be the oldest continuously operating saloon west of the Missouri. All are definitely worth a stop.

A man born in Columbus invented something that saved the lives of untold soldiers during World War II, the Korean War, and the Vietnam War. Andrew Jackson Higgins invented the LCVP (Landing-Craft, Vehicle, Personnel) boat that carried American soldiers ashore, most notably on D-Day. A full-size steel replica of the boat can be seen at *Andrew Jackson Higgins National Memorial* in West Pawnee Park at U.S. Highway 81 and Thirty-third Avenue. Three bronze statues of soldiers representing the aforementioned wars have recently been installed. Pawnee Park is very pretty—what better place to have a picnic than here in Columbus, the Picnic Capital of Nebraska? Call (402) 564–2769 for more details.

Platte County offers an abundance of water recreation at *Lake North* (a 200-acre lake 4 miles north of Columbus on Eighteenth Avenue) and

Chickens and Cattle and Pigs, Oh My!

This is one of the greatest agricultural states in the country, and we have the numbers to prove it! Nebraska has far more farm animals than people. For every human being there are four cows, two pigs, and eight chickens residing in the state at any given moment.

Lake Babcock (a 600-acre lake 4 miles north on Eighteenth Avenue and 1¼ miles west).

Platte County is perhaps the only site in the continental United States that was bombed during World War II by the U.S. Army Air Corps. On August 16, 1943, the tiny community of *Tarnov* was peppered with several one hundred-pound test bombs filled with sand and small charges. Some fell through a roof and passed inches from two sleeping young sisters. The *Omaha World Herald* reported it thusly: "The good people of this little Polish village (population 70), who were bombed accidently by an army plane early Monday, went to bed early Monday night. It has been a tremendous day—the biggest day for continuous excitement they had ever known." No one was hurt, not even the man who was deep in "an alcohol-induced slumber" inside his car after a harvest festival the night before. A bomb landed a few feet from the car; he woke up only when the sheriff roused him into a hung-over incredulity. It is speculated, but no one knows for sure (the results of the military investigation remain a secret to this day), that the bombs were intended for a test-bombing range outside of the community of Stanton, 25 miles from Tarnov.

Colfax County

In *Howells,* the *Prairie Garden B&B* is a beautiful example of the prairie-style architecture popularized by Frank Lloyd Wright. Located at 216 South Third Street, the B&B has oak floors, beamed ceilings, beveled and leaded glass, and great details such as electric lights inside columns, which accent the house. The two guest rooms look nice and comfortable. One has a second-story screened-in porch that looks perfect for sipping coffee and reading a good book. In the stairwell there hangs a charming example of folk art: a handmade altarpiece, made from wooden cigar boxes by the great-grandfather of one of the owners. Rates are $45 for two and $40 for a single; a full breakfast is included. For more information call (402) 986–1251.

A couple blocks away is *Bill's Food Mart,* 112 South Third Street, which displays a great collection of 900 cookie jars. The collection ranges from the common to the rare, from the tacky to the sublime. The hours are Monday through Saturday, 7:30 A.M. to 6:00 P.M. The telephone number is (402) 986–1141.

If you love to garden and work in your yard, a stop in the neighboring community of **Clarkson** is most decidedly worth your time. The **Bluebird Nursery,** in southwest Clarkson at 515 Linden Street, must not be missed. The nursery is the largest perennial plant grower between Chicago and the Pacific Northwest. To give you an idea of the magnitude of its operation, it employs 110 people in a community of 700 people. The nursery specializes in, but is not limited to, hardy perennial plants native to the Plains that are able to withstand the wild vagaries of four complete seasons. Bluebird Nursery has more than 1,000 perennial and ground-cover plants, with a large selection of annual plants as well. Each year, the nursery ships millions of plants (up to 1,800 different varieties) to nurseries, garden centers, and botanical gardens in the United States and Canada, as well as in England and Australia, from its massive greenhouses. During the summer months make a stop at the Bohemian Gardens, on Main Street, and the All-American Display Gardens and Proving Ground, at 521 Cherry Street, to be amazed at the plants and to garner gardening ideas. Store hours vary seasonally: May 1 through June 30, Monday through Friday from 8:00 A.M. to 5:00 P.M., Saturday from 8:00 A.M. to 4:00 P.M., and Sunday from 1:00 to 5:00 P.M. From July 1 through April 30, the store is closed on Sunday except during the Christmas season, when it sells poinsettias and Christmas trees. Call (402) 892–3442.

The **Saint Benedict Center,** *north of Schuyler in Colfax County, will give you a chance to pray. If you're not the praying kind, you can still ponder, or at least shop. There's a great bookstore and gift shop with greeting cards, religious gifts and statues, icons, rosaries, CDs, cassettes, and videos. Or take home some of the nice pieces of art from Africa, Peru, and Korea. The store hours are Monday through Saturday from 10:00 A.M. to 4:00 P.M. and Sunday from 1:00 to 4:00 P.M. Sunday mass is held at the Mission House across the street at 8:30 A.M. The complex is ½ mile east from Highway 15 (4 miles north of Schuyler) on St. Benedict's Road. Call (402) 352–8819, extension 358, for more information.*

You can overnight at **Annie's B&B** at 310 Cherry Street in Clarkson. This huge 1890s plantation-style home has three rooms. The second floor has both front and back balconies, and one offers a 4-mile view. Rooms are between $35 and $45. The phone number is (402) 892–3660.

There's a great little museum, the **Clarkson Historical Museum,** at 233 Pine Street. It is said to have one of the best collections of Czech immigrant historical memorabilia in the country. It's open by appointment; call (402) 892–3854. When you're in town, do not miss the **Clarkson Bakery** downtown at 113 Pine Street. *Kolaches* (a traditional Czech pastry), rye bread, strudel, and whole lot more are available with coffee to go. It opens at 6:00 A.M. The phone number is (402) 892–3131. Then go over to *Toman's Meat Market* at 219 Pine Street to load up on traditional, and award-winning, homemade specialties like sausages, wieners, and bacon. The phone number is (402) 892–3452.

Schuyler, on Highways 15 and 30, is home to one of the finest WPA (Works Progress Administration) buildings in the state. Although senior citizens who watched the *Oak Ballroom* being built in 1937 from huge native oaks and stones jokingly refer to the WPA as "We're Probably Asleep," this beautiful structure stands as tribute to the spirit of the Great Depression. Listed on the National Register of Historic Places, the Oak Ballroom is at the entrance to Community Park, which is situated on another historic site, the Mormon Trail. At present the ballroom is used for local events, and, if you're lucky, you'll be there when there's a big polka dance going on. Located on Lost Creek in the south part of town on Highway 15, the ballroom is open to visitors for free from 8:00 A.M. to noon on weekdays. Call (402) 352–9972 for details.

PLACES TO STAY IN NORTHEAST NEBRASKA

(ALL AREA CODES ARE 402 EXCEPT WHERE NOTED OTHERWISE)

CROFTON
The Argo Hotel,
211 West Kansas Street,
388–4200 or
(800) 607–2746

ELGIN
Plantation House,
RR 2,
843–2287 or
(888) 446–2287

HOWELLS
Prairie Garden,
216 South Third Street,
986–1251,
www.innsite.com/inns/
A002602.html

OAKLAND
Benson B&B,
402 North Oakland Avenue,
685–6051,
www.flinthills. com/
~atway/ne/benson.html

PIERCE
Willow Rose B&B,
rural,
329–4114

PLAINVIEW
Rose Garden B&B,
305 North Third Street,
582–4708,
www.virtualcitiescom/ons/
ne/e/nee2701.html

WATERLOO
J. C. Robinson House B&B,
102 East Lincoln Avenue,
779–2704 or
(800) 779– 2705,
www.jcrobinsonbandb.com

WAYNE
Grandma Butch's B&B,
502 Logan Avenue,
375–2759,
www.innsite.com/inns/
A00259.html

PLACES TO EAT IN NORTHEAST NEBRASKA

(ALL AREA CODES ARE 402)

COLUMBUS
Dusters (American and continental),
2804 South Thirteenth Street,
562–6488 or 564–8338

DIXON
Euni's Place
(burgers, pizza),
Second and Conway,
584–9309

FREMONT
Carey's Cottage (American and continental),
732 Park Avenue,
721–7640

HOOPER
The Office Bar and Grill (American),
Main Street,
654–3373

MARTINSBURG
Bob's Bar (giant burgers),
no street address (honest!),
but you can't miss it,
945–2995

PONCA
Centennial Lanes (burgers),
102 Third Street,
755–2678

ROYAL
Green Gables (American, home cookin'),
go north on the road leading to Ashfall Fossil Beds between Royal and Orchard,
893–5800

SCRIBNER
436 Main Steakhouse (eclectic decor and great food),
436 Main Street,
664–3436

STANTON
Uptown Brewery (American and Continental),
801 Tenth Street,
439–5100

HELPFUL NORTHEAST NEBRASKA WEB SITES

NORTHEAST NEBRASKA TRAVEL COUNCIL
www.travelnenebraska.com

COLUMBUS
www.thecolumbuspage.com

FREMONT
www.visitdodgecountyne.org

NORFOLK
www.norfolk.ne.us

OMAHA
www.visitomaha.com

SOUTH SIOUX CITY
www.sscdc.net/ssctour

WAYNE
www.waynene.com

Where the West Begins

The Sandhills region comprises approximately 19,300 square miles of grass-covered, stabilized sand dunes, covering roughly one-third of the state. From the air it looks like ocean swells. It has such subtle beauty that persons hurrying through are inclined to miss the wildflowers, the birds, and the glorious expanse of sky, which is matched by the seemingly endless undulating hills. If you're driving through the Sandhills on Highway 2, you're on a road that Charles Kuralt considered among the ten most beautiful routes in the country. Folklorist Roger Welsch is like many Nebraskans who are smitten with the Sandhills. He maintains "that any days you spend in the Sandhills are not taken off your lifetime allotment. It's so restful that God just gives them to you for free." The many small lakes, coupled with the lush grass on the hills, makes this prime ranching country. The Sandhills has its share of western history, with military outposts, horse-stealing

Pretty Prairie River

I learned three things as I watched an expensive camera float down the Niobrara River toward who knows where, maybe New Orleans. One, when you tip over you tend to grab things that are most important at that moment, like oars. Two, I should have listened when my friend Foster explained the necessity of either securing, or wearing, things you don't want to end up in places like the Mississippi Delta. And three, there's a reason why Backpacker magazine lists the Niobrara as one of the ten most challenging rivers in the United States. Have no fear, though—most of the time the river is fast but gentle, depending on the amount of snowmelt and rainfall. Keep in mind, there's also a very good reason Canoe & Kayak magazine lists the Niobrara as the "prettiest prairie river," among the top twenty-five places to canoe and camp. Several outfitters in and around Valentine can provide you with everything you need, plus they'll shuttle you to the river and pick you up hours downstream. You just need to bring food and a cooler. (Caution: If you do bring beer, be advised it's illegal to have alcoholic beverages on the river, even though sometimes the river looks like an armada of minibars.)

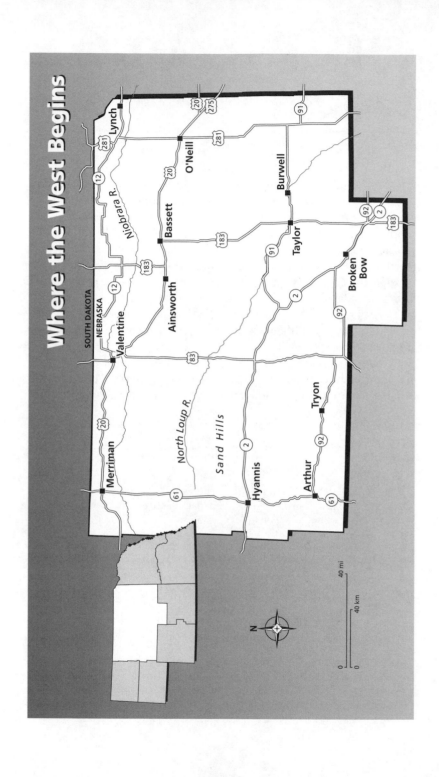

Where the West Begins

Lynch

SOUTH DAKOTA
NEBRASKA

Niobrara R.

Valentine

Merriman

Ainsworth

Bassett

O'Neill

Burwell

Taylor

Broken Bow

North Loup R.

Sand Hills

Hyannis

Arthur

Tryon

N

40 mi

40 km

0

0

outlaws, and frontier justice. The rivers of the Sandhills—the Niobrara, Cedar Dismal, Snake, and Loup—are popular with canoeists. Bicycling enthusiasts will enjoy the Cowboy Trail, which when completed will stretch more than 300 miles across the northern counties of Nebraska and will be the nation's longest rails-to-trails conversion. Sections of it are open now. An abundance of wildlife refuges, state parks, state historical parks, and reservoirs round out the outdoor offerings of the Sandhills.

Cherry County

You are now in one of the largest counties in the United States. Cherry County is larger than Rhode Island and Delaware combined. You might imagine there'd be a lot of things to see and do in such a large county, and you'd be right. Cherry County is most famous for the Niobrara River, a National Scenic River, and the biological crossroads it represents. The river valley is where several types of vegetation converge. You'll see everything from yuccas to alpine flowers, cacti, and birch trees. What you will see for sure are canoers, tubers, and kayakers on the enormously popular Niobrara River.

AUTHOR'S FAVORITE ATTRACTIONS IN THE SANDHILLS

Arthur Bowring Sandhills Ranch State Historical Park, northeast on Highway 61, Merriman, (308) 648–3428 or (800) 658–4024

Happy Jack Chalk Mine and Peak, 1 1/2 miles south on Highway 11, Scotia, (308) 245–3276

Heartland Elk Guest Ranch, south of Sparks on a gravel road, (402) 376–1124

Lovejoy Ranch B&B, 17 miles south on Highway 83, Valentine, (402) 376–2668 or (800) 672–5098

Nebraska National Forest, 2 miles west on Highway 2, Halsey, (308) 432–0300

Plains Trading Company Booksellers, 269 North Main Street, Valentine, (402) 376–1424 or (800) 439–8640

Everything Has a Price

One fine fall night I was in the Peppermill lounge in Valentine when in walks a woman of obvious wealth, a friendly and charming stranger. She had come to hunt, and she had fallen in love with the area in her few days there, as often happens. (This is an example of If You Don't Build It, They Will Come.) After a couple of drinks, she asked if anyone knew of land for sale along the river. No one did. When she left, one of the locals allowed that he'd rather set his face on fire than sell to an outsider. Another allowed that he'd sell anyone his grandmother's grave if the price was right. One thing's for sure: The land is hauntingly beautiful and will claim part of your soul if you let it, whether or not you can afford to own a piece of it.

On Highway 12 in **Sparks,** the Canoe Capital of Nebraska, Dryland Aquatics will provide canoes, tubes, camping, and shuttle service, as will several outfitters in Valentine.

Two miles south of Sparks is the **Heartland Elk Guest Ranch.** New log cabins are set in a secluded, heavily wooded area that opens onto an astonishingly beautiful view of the river valley. Owners Kerry and Lisa Krueger have done everything right. The two-bedroom cabins are great— the kitchens come complete with coffeemakers and microwaves, there's a radio but no TV, and an outdoor grill awaits your culinary creativity. And the best thing . . . there are no phones, so this really is a getaway. (I'm glad I had my cell phone, however, because I drove onto a muddy road I clearly shouldn't have, and Kerry had to come rescue this goofy city slicker.) They've built a horse barn, so you can ride down the bluffs to the valley. A gut-busting breakfast is served in a dining area that provides a perfect view of the elk pasture. Horseback riding through wooded trails and trout fishing at private ponds await. Call (402) 376–1124 for reservations. The Web site is www.valentine-ne. com/heartlandelk.

Ya Gotta Kiss a Lot of Toads

*Y*ou wouldn't think a grown woman would get excited about a toad. A fat little toad who wanted nothing more in the world than to make his way across the yard without being herded by a grinning woman on her hands and knees. I hadn't seen a toad since I was a little girl, more years ago than I care to admit. But I do admit to some of the responsibility for not seeing a toad since then. Because I, like most of my urban counterparts, routinely apply nasty chemicals to achieve a lush, barefoot lawn. Toads and chemicals don't mix. I do have a lovely lawn, but alas, a decided dearth of toads. So when I left the breakfast table at the Heartland Elk Guest Ranch near Sparks and walked down the sidewalk, what to my wondering eyes did appear but that fat little toad. I was enchanted; however,

my behavior was somewhat mystifying to Buffy, a three-legged bassett hound. I followed the toad; Buffy followed me. Lisa Krueger, the co-owner of the guest ranch, came to the front door and just looked at me. "IT'S A TOAD!" I exclaimed. "Oh," she said. I suppose her reaction to my toad sighting, something quite common to her, was not unlike my reaction to some Australians who were visiting Nebraska. There are no squirrels in Australia; we had to stop and marvel at every damn squirrel for about 100 square miles. Somewhere in Sydney there are several photo albums with about twelve rolls of squirrel pictures. And if I had had a camera at the guest ranch, there'd be pictures of the toad, of me and the toad, and of me, the toad, and Buffy hanging on my refrigerator door right now.

Valentine, Cherry County's largest community, with a population of just less than 3,000, is located at Highways 83, 12, and 20. Valentine serves the needs of the far-flung ranchers with grocery stores, gas stations, cafes, restaurants, and western supply stores. In addition, you'll find *King of Hearts Antiques and Things,* run by a Catholic priest who makes "blessedly" good fruit preserves, and a bookstore called the *Plains Trading Company,* which also has Nebraska products and a gift shop. Another wonderful store is *My Backporch Friends,* where you'll find intricate, handmade folk doll collectibles that are sold across the country in some pretty fancy stores. All the dolls spring from the mind of Cody Foster, who got his start by helping his grandmother make mop dolls. Even for people who think they won't like

African-American Settlement in the Sandhills

*N*inety years ago a community called **DeWitty** *was founded in the Sandhills of Cherry County. The adjacent area was settled by people who claimed portions of land under the terms of the 1904 Kinkaid Act, which opened the Sandhills to settlement and helped many who hoped for a new life in a new land. There's nothing unusual about this until you consider the fact that DeWitty was one of very few settlements in Nebraska founded by African Americans. At present DeWitty has disappeared from the landscape just west of the community of Brownlee in Cherry County, but the town does hold a place in Nebraska history. The town was named DeWitty after the first postmaster, and after he left the community it was called Audacious. Later on the town was known as Garden. In 1909 a group of black homesteaders led by William Walker and Charles Mehan took out homestead claims, and other black homesteaders joined them until the population reached a peak of about 175 people. They constructed sod*

houses, a post office, a grocery store, a church, and a school. There was a baseball team called the Sluggers. They lived just as the white settlers did, working the land, raising families, praying for good weather, and taking part in rodeos. DeWitty dwindled in population, and by 1940 there were no African Americans left in Brownlee.

Another small group of black settlers claimed land west of Westerville in Custer County. Three brothers, Moses Speece, Henry Webb, and Jerry Shores, all of whom had taken the last names of the slaveholders who once owned them, were the first to settle there. The Speece family, whose sixteen living children enjoyed music, was said to have worn out two pump organs and a piano in the twenty-five years they lived in their sod house. Both the Speece and Shore families were photographed by Solomon Butcher, whose work has been widely published. Their homes are gone and their families are scattered, but their images remain forever.

frog dolls, pumpkin-head dolls, Santa dolls, rabbit dolls, or kitten dolls, this place is a must-see.

Seventeen miles south of Valentine on Highway 83 is the unique *Lovejoy Ranch B&B.* The house, shaped like a geodesic dome, is filled with windows that offer great views of the Sandhills and skylights that offer great views of the stars. The two upstairs rooms are exceptionally beautiful and have private baths (the Meadow View Room has a whirlpool). Each afternoon guests receive complimentary hors d'oeuvres and beverages. Breakfasts can be hearty country or elegant gourmet. Horseback riding can be arranged. Room rates range from $75 to $95. Credit cards are accepted. Call (402) 376–2668 or (800) 672–5098.

Smith Falls State Park, 12 miles northeast of Valentine on Highway 12, has the state's highest waterfall. Spring-fed Smith Falls drops 70 feet from a birch-crowned canyon rim to the Niobrara River. You can rent a canoe to cross the river to the falls, and you should do this, as the falls are really quite lovely. Or take a stroll across the footbridge. Throw a penny in the river, but watch out for canoeists below. Picnic sites, rest rooms, concessions, tent camping, and showers are available on the north side of the river. The park is open from April 1 through November 30. A park permit is required. The telephone number is (402) 376–1506.

West of Valentine on Highway 20 is the *Arthur Bowring Sandhills Ranch State Historical Park,* which provides the opportunity to see a working cattle ranch in the Sandhills. The ranch is located 1½ miles

Lovejoy Ranch B&B

north of *Merriman* on Highway 61. The cattle industry in the Sandhills began in a serendipitous fashion in 1879, when a blizzard drove many cattle from the E. S. Newman ranch near Gordon, Nebraska, deep into unknown valleys, which had been prematurely judged to be inhospitable to cattle. Hoping to find a few surviving head, ranch hands ventured hopefully into the interior of the Sandhills to discover not only the Newman cattle but thousands more from other ranches that had wandered away and grown fat and content on the rich interior meadowlands. Voilà! A thriving industry was born. Arthur Bowring started ranching in 1894 and married Eve Kelly Forester in 1928. They were successful ranchers and also public servants. He was a member of the Nebraska legislature, and she was the first woman from Nebraska to serve in the U.S. Senate. Eve died in 1985 at the age of ninety-two and, having no living children, donated the 7,202-acre Bar 99 Ranch to the Nebraska Game and Parks Foundation, with the stipulation it remain as a living historical monument. At present the ranch house remains much as it was at the time of Eve's death. It includes a huge collection of glassware and silver, which she gathered on her extensive travels, and also photographs of many of the famous politicians she met, including Haile Selassie, the emperor of Ethiopia. (Eve's experience on the ranch was apparently a whole lot different than that of 1880s pioneer woman Ellen Moran, who wrote that the Sandhills were " . . . a great country for cattle and men, but hell on horses and women.") The barns, bunkhouses, corrals, and other ranch buildings are maintained as workplaces. The visitors center has interesting displays about the Bowrings, the history and geology of the Sandhills, and the ranching business in the state. The center is open from Memorial Day weekend through Labor Day, 9:00 A.M. to 5:00 P.M. daily. There is also a sod house, with periodic living-history demonstrations. A park permit, which costs $14.00 for a year and $2.50 a day, is required. The buildings are open from 8:00 A.M. to 5:00 P.M. daily from Memorial Day weekend through Labor Day. Call (308) 684–3428 or (800) 658–4024 for more information.

Keya Paha County

I f shopping malls make you shudder and you can't stomach the thought of another fast-food meal, then *Keya Paha County* will suit you just fine. In case you need to pronounce the name of the county you're in, the locals say *KIP-a-haw*, but other Nebraskans often pronounce it *Keya-pawhaw*. The name is from the Sioux language and means turtle hill. Keya Paha County used to be called Mob County because of the notorious Pony Boys, who had a propensity for horses other than their own.

Springview, at Highways 183 and 12, is the largest town in the county; it has 304 citizens. *Burton* has nine. And *Norden* is unincorporated. Springview has everything a traveler could want: a couple of cafes that offer home-cooked meals, a bar and grill, a liquor store, a grocery store, gas stations, and a hotel.

There are two B&Bs just outside of Springview: At *Larrington's Guest Cottage* you can rent the whole two-bedroom modern house and prepare your own meals, although continental breakfast "fixin's" are provided. There's a dang-wonderful view of the Niobrara River valley from this isolated cottage. Call (402) 497–2261 to make required reservations. The *Big Canyon Inn* also has a beautiful view of the prairie, and the modern home has four cozy rooms, a fireplace, and a deck. Guests can hike, ride horses, mountain bike, and hunt in season. Call (402) 497–3170 or (800) 437–6023 for reservations. The name Big Canyon is apt; it's adjacent to a seriously deep canyon. The owner of the B&B is developing a ski area, if that gives you an indication of how deep the canyon is. A 1939 guidebook about Nebraska, written by Federal Writers Project of the Works Progress Administration, described the terrain south of Springview as "almost mountainous, with cedar and pine trees, rolling hills, and the blue Niobrara winding far below." I'm here to tell you that when you're in that canyon, it's not *almost* mountainous, it *is* mountainous.

When you're about 1½ miles west of Springview on Highway 12, you'll see a couple of tall structures that look suspiciously unlike the more familiar windmills that commonly dot the Nebraska prairie. Windmills exist to draw up water for livestock and, less commonly these days, for human use. These two 296-foot-tall towers exist to harvest the wind sweepin' down the Plains. The turbines can furnish up to 40 percent of the electrical power needed in Keya Paha County. The Nebraska Tourism Office recently fielded a complaint from a tourist that the towers "spoil the view." Get a life, people! Two towers on one acre in a vast state do not a view spoil. And if you have ever, even for a nanosecond, shaken your head at the size of your electric bill or given a thought to the rapid depletion of natural resources, you'll just note their presence and how pretty they really are and drive on.

Before you leave Keya Paha County, you could check out a ghost town called *Meadville.* Keya Paha County had a wild and wooly western past. More than ten killings are documented, with grisly tales of many more. Meadville, had its share of colorful characters. Things slowed down considerably over the next several decades to the point in 1960 that the post office was closed; no mail for anyone, character or not. The community is now enjoying a little resurgence. There's a refurbished general store with food and drinks. The park is used by campers, hikers, anglers, hunters, bird-watchers, and outdoor enthusiasts. Also in the area are Bottomless Lake (I wonder if that's where some of the murder victims ended up), Oxbow Bayou, the largest and fastest moving fault line in Nebraska (there are occasional reports of small earthquakes in northeast Nebraska), and an old bridge over the Niobrara River. Brochures also tout the Meadville onions, "known far and wide for their flavor and extreme mildness." There's a great big Fourth of July blowout every year. On January 1 at least some people plunge into the icy river, making it the only Polar Bear Club I know of in the state. The year I went it was nearly 80°—so much for Polar weather. Call the General Store at (402) 497–2440, (402) 387–2440, or (402) 387–2212 for more information. Go north from Ainsworth on a little spur (watch for signs) to get there. Or go south a couple miles west on Highway 12 from Springview.

Brown County

South of Keya Paha County is *Brown County,* with the three communities of Long Pine, Ainsworth, and Johnstown strung along Highway 20 from east to west. *Long Pine* has great fishing on the Long Pine Creek and at the nearby Long Pine State Recreation Area. There are two great lodging opportunities at Long Pine: The *Pines* has ten housekeeping cabins that were built in the 1920s, and they are decidedly rustic and old-fashioned, with fishing right down the hill. You'll likely see wild turkeys on your walks around the place. Rates range from $37.80 to $59.40; call (402) 273–4483. *Pine Valley Resort* has seven housekeeping cabins (the honeymoon cabin has a Jacuzzi) on the other side of the highway. Rates range from $60 to $70 for two people. The telephone number is (402) 273–4351. Both these places are hilly, pine-covered, and secluded.

There's something about the water in the Sandhills. Perhaps it's so pure because it filters down through so much sand. In any case, the water around Long Pine is so naturally pure that Coca Cola was once made there. At present there's a home-grown company called *Seven Springs Water* that bottles up Mother Nature's elixir. Watch for it in stores. Or if you stop by the plant (go south on the main street past the old railroad tracks, turn west, and watch for the blue building with the red flagpole), you can buy some there. The number is (402) 273–4295.

I would love to tell you that one of the few remaining drive-in theaters is still in operation outside of Long Pine, but a big wind blew it over a couple of years ago. However, one of my favorite stories about Long Pine is driving by and seeing that local pranksters had altered a movie's title on the marquee. Have any of you ever seen *The Loin King*?

Another great fishing spot is **Keller Park State Recreation Area,** which is west and north of Long Pine on Highway 183. Keller Park has five ponds and is one of the few spots in Nebraska where anglers can catch both

Trout Fishing in the Sandhills

*M*y friend Bob agreed, with no small amount of trepidation, to take me fishing with him. Bob is someone for whom fishing is a highly spiritual experience. I am someone who once read a quote that some famous person's favorite season is "indoors" and who has subscribed to that ever since. Nevertheless, off we headed to Long Pine in Brown County and the Long Pine Creek, a legendary trout stream.

Bob supplied an astonishing amount of fishing paraphernalia. I supplied a good attitude—and gas money, as I recall. He had two stipulations: first, I had to bait my own hook, and second, I could not squeal like a girl at doing so. Fine. We crawled down a steep embankment, and tree branches did their best to ensnarl both my pole and my hair. Bob informed me that trout like to hang out in fallen brush, and that you had to cast beyond the brush, upstream even though you are downstream, so the trout would think the bait was a natural food source and not an implement of death. You couldn't let them see you, or even your shadow, because they were smart and wouldn't bite if you were

stupid enough to apprise them of your location.

We commenced what I called Stealth Fishing. I got to be very good at piercing worms and weaving their squirming bodies firmly on the hook. But I got much better at putting on new hooks themselves, because I lost hook after hook in the tangled undergrowth where the trout supposedly lived. I quickly grew to hate how and where trout lived. Then it occurred to me that there was a lesson to be learned: the Zen of Tying on New Hooks. I became a sort of Zen master after two days and dozens of new hooks. It didn't even matter if there were trout lurking about or not. My task to was to keep tying.

The last night of the trip, with not even one trout in either of our creels, was spent in the bar in Long Pine playing pool. No crafty fish, no wiggling worms, and no hooks. The final degradation, to the trout-free Bob, was when the bartender informed us that not only had we been using the wrong bait, but we had been fishing in the wrong part of the creek. No matter; my mission was accomplished. I had achieved Hookness.

AUTHOR'S FAVORITE ANNUAL EVENTS IN THE SANDHILLS

(Call ahead to verify dates)

St. Patrick's Day,
O'Neill, (402) 336–2355

High School Rodeo,
Thedford, early June,
(308) 872–6092

Middle of Nowhere Trail Ride, Ainsworth, mid-June,
(402) 387–2488

Middle of Nowhere Days,
Ainsworth, late June,
(402) 387–2740

Windmill Festival, Comstock, mid-July,
(308) 628–4369 or
(308) 728–3113

Nebraska Star Party
(a gathering of stargazers from around the world at Merritt Reservoir), Valentine,
mid-July, (402) 466–4170

South Loup River Rock and Blues Festival,
Arnold, mid-July,
(308) 845–2527

Nebraska's Big Rodeo,
Burwell, late July,
(888) 328–7935

Kite Flight *(stunt kite competition)*, Callaway, early
September, (308) 836–2620

Beaver Creek Knap-In & Primitive Skills Gathering,
12 miles north of Stuart, late
September, (402) 924–3180

Old West Days
(with cowboy poetry),
Valentine, early October,
(800) 658–4024

Evelyn Sharp Days,
Ord, mid-October,
(308) 728–5527

cold- and warm-water species. Pond #5 has rainbow trout. It's a really pretty area, with canyons and lots of trees, making it ideal for hiking and camping as well as fishing. A park permit is necessary.

Ainsworth, west of Long Pine at the junction of Highways 20 and 7, has a boardinghouse turned B&B called the **Ainsworth Inn.** Each of the five second-story rooms is decorated in a different floral theme, and there's an antiques shop, gift shop, and tea room on the first floor. You can stop here for tourism information, too. Room rates are $44 to $69. Call (402) 387–0454 or (888) 237–0954 for reservations. The other B&B in town is the **Upper Room,** a big old Victorian house with a twenty-three-acre yard and a fountain, a wishing well, and a footbridge. Be sure to notice the old bedstead with flowers planted in it, making it, of course, the flower bed. Sadly, the resident turkey named Fuzzy died, but there's a very nice dog named Mattie. Room rates are $45 to $75. For more information call (402) 387–0107.

Johnstown, west of Ainsworth on Highway 20, is forever immortalized on film. Many scenes from the Hallmark Hall of Fame made-for-TV movie *O Pioneers!* were shot here. The mc ￢e has a couple of Nebraska connections; it was b￢ ￢ed on a book by Nebraska author Willa Cather, and Hallmark Cards was founded by three brothers (William, Rollie, and Joyce Hall) from Nebraska. There's a little store there (it's the only store in town beside the gas station), the **House of Plants and Gifts,** which sells great craft items and antiques. My favorite is the candle holders made from tin cans. Call (402) 722–4296.

Boyd County

f you enter **Boyd County** from the east on Highway 12, you'll soon come to the tiny community of **Monowi.** Very tiny, indeed. With a population of three, it is the smallest incorporated town in Nebraska. Boost the population temporarily; stop in for a burger and a brew at the *Monowi Tavern,* open from 8:00 A.M. to 1:00 A.M. every day, the only business in town. Call (402) 569–3600.

As you continue your drive along Highway 12 in Boyd County, you'll notice Burma Shave–type signs concerning a political situation that involves the placement of a low-level radioactive waste-storage site. Nebraska once belonged to, and then withdrew from, a five-state Radioactive Waste Compact. The compact, after years of searching for what it considered the single most suitable location for a waste site, deemed Boyd County to be just that. Many citizens of Boyd County have taken exception to being selected for what they consider an environmental disaster waiting to happen, as you will see from the multitude of signs along the highway. So far, ground has not been broken for the waste facility, and the story continues to unfold.

The town of *Lynch* in Boyd County, 7 miles west of Monowi on Highway 12, is fast becoming at attraction for Lewis and Clark fans. Just north of town on a dirt road (keep going straight on the main street through town) is *Old Baldy.* Old Baldy, a tall hill naturally devoid of trees and grass on the Missouri River, is where the expedition members came upon their first prairie dogs. They didn't know what they were; they called them "barking squirrels" and were determined to capture a couple of them. Capturing a prairie dog is not easily accomplished. After digging down fruitlessly several feet into a mound they decided to form a bucket brigade to drown one the critters out into the open. They succeeded and, ultimately, that prairie dog was sent back alive to President Jefferson. There's a public viewing area in a field near Old Baldy. It's fun to imagine the expedition members struggling up that hill with water-laden buckets to capture a fat little hairy prairie dog. And there's a great vista of the Missouri River from the viewing area, too. The ladies of Lynch, in a promotional effort, get together weekly to sew little stuffed prairie dogs, called Lynch Dawgs, to sell and raise money for the new RV park in town. I do not normally like cute little stuffed toys of any sort, but these Lynch Dawgs are the best dang thing. I have one in my office. If you're in Lynch on a weekend, plan on going to the *Lynn Theater.* The theater, which is run totally by volunteers, is a great old structure that looks from the outside like it hasn't been touched in sixty years. For more information on Lynch, call (402) 569–2706 or see the Web site at www.lewisandclark trail.cjb.net. (You can order the Lynch Dawgs on line!)

Are you in the mood for a Gross Burger? Then you're in luck! In the Boyd County community of *Gross* you'll find the *Nebraska Inn.* Don't worry about finding the building; it's just about the only building in town, and it will be the one with pick-ups parked outside. Gross Burgers will fill you up for only $2.00. On Friday and Saturday evenings the inn also serves steak dinners ranging from $6.00 to $10.00. Coffee, if you can believe this, is only a nickel a cup. The inn is open every day at 8:30 A.M. until about 11:00 P.M., or later if the place is jumping. There are two more good things about the Nebraska Inn: The ceiling is plastered with dollar bills that are collected by the owner when people say dirty words, damn it all. And there's a friendly, happy dog named Windsor who hangs around outside. To get to Gross, turn north from Highway 12 from Bristow, go for a few miles, and then watch for signs to turn east. It's best to bring a map since it's a little hard to find, but it's well worth the drive. The number is (402) 583–9922.

In the beautiful Niobrara Valley, 5 miles south and 1³/₄ miles east of **Naper** from Highway 12, there once was a ranch that seemed to be from another world—a gentle world, where a devoted but childless couple, Cal and Ruth Thompson, started a riding school for disadvantaged youths and taught them how to ride and train the graceful white horses that were bred on the ranch. The **White Horse Ranch** closed in 1963 after owner Cal Thompson died. But during the 1940s and 1950s, the ranch was famous for the White Horse Troupe, which performed all over the United States and Canada. The ranch was featured in a photo-story in *Life* magazine in 1945. The horses, which were ridden bare-back, dazzled audiences with their many spectacular routines. Ruth Thompson was inducted into the Cowgirl Hall of Fame in 1990. After nearly thirty years the ranch is now being restored by Dean and Carley Daugherty. It is a labor of love for both of them, but particularly for Carley, who was one of the many children to whom the Thompsons opened their hearts and lives. Carley's love for the Thompsons is readily apparent as she leads visitors on a tour of the general store, which has been converted into a museum. Her love for the white horses, whom she chides softly after they muddy themselves in a springtime romp through a creek, is also apparent as she coaxes one of them into a grace-ful bow to the guests. The white horses, known as American Albino or American White, are the only horse breed to be developed in Nebraska. At present the White Horse Ranch is on the National Register of His-toric Places. The ranch is open to visitors from Memorial Day through Labor Day. It is closed on Tuesday and Wednesday. Hours are from 9:00 A.M. to 6:00 P.M.; Sunday hours are from noon to 6:00 P.M. There is no admission fee, but donations are a good thing. Camping, both primitive and with electrical hookups, is available, and there are fish ponds for you angler types. The telephone number is (402) 832–5560.

Holt County

'Neill, b'gosh and b'gorra, is the Irish capital of Nebraska. It was established in 1874 by Gen. John O'Neill, a native of Ireland, of course, and a Civil War veteran. General O'Neill founded three colonies in Nebraska for Irish Americans: one at O'Neill, one at Atkinson, and one in Greeley County. Before starting these colonies he was involved in the Fenian invasion into Canada. For this he was jailed, which apparently gave him time to think about his actions. In any case, he moved to Nebraska to start his colonies for Irish Americans. The town gained notoriety in 1892 when Barrett Scott, the county treasurer, disappeared about the same time some county funds disappeared. He was found in Mexico, brought back to face trial, and was kidnapped while out on bail. Frontier justice prevailed; Scott's body was found wrapped in a blanket, the rope from which he was hanged still around his neck and a nasty boot-heel mark on his forehead. By the 1930s, the town of O'Neill seemed safe enough to Mr. William Froelich of Chicago. He was the state's attorney who successfully prosecuted Al Capone and, fearing retribution against his family, moved them to O'Neill. At present O'Neill, at Highway 281 and Highways 20/275, is a thriving, pleasant community of just less than 4,000 people and is home to the Irish Dancers. There are plenty of places to find meals and lodging, and the world's largest shamrock has been painted on the street. If you're in town on St. Patrick's Day, enjoy a meal of corned beef and cabbage provided by the church ladies. And if you stick around into the wee hours, you might see one of the Irished-up locals ride his horse right into a bar. If you're ever in O'Neill at any time, do stop at a great Irish import store, **Saints and Shillelaghs,** at 1017 East Douglas. You can get high-quality Irish goods of all sorts, from clothes (the hand-knit sweaters are to die for) to china, crystal, jewelry, linen, and foods. You can even get Irish tin whistles and a handmade chess set with the "little people" as pieces. It has a whole lot of Irish music, too. Summer hours are 9:30 A.M. to 5:00 P.M. daily. Winter hours are 10:00 A.M. to 5:00 P.M. Monday through Saturday. The telephone number is (402) 336–2600.

From O'Neill continue on Highway 20 northwest for 18 miles to **Atkinson** in *Holt County*. I have many must-see places and must-do favorite things in Nebraska; however, your taste might differ from mine. But we all scream for ice cream! Go into the 1950s five-and-dime called **R. F. Goeke** at 110 South Main to buy a soda or sundae. That is, if you can tear yourself away from looking at the notions (lots of notions) and old-fashioned candy. Owners Randy Goeke and Mike Skulavik wanted to re-create a true five-and-dime, and they've succeeded admirably. A sundae will cost between $1.30 and $3.00 (for a humongous sundae providing a gut-busting experience). The recipes are all original from old, no-longer-existing soda fountains. A favorite sundae is the Klown, which was invented at a soda fountain in Fremont, Nebraska. They named the restaurant for Mr. Goeke instead of Mr. Skulavik because they thought "Skulavik's" might lead one to think it was a Jewish deli. But if you've got a hankering for a good egg cream, you could do a lot worse at a Jewish deli than at this store. Another plus, Mike Skulavik grew up in the South; he can't help calling all females past puberty "ma'am," and to a Midwesterner that is a refreshingly polite and oddly sweet gesture. It kind of made me feel like a dowager, but he can call me "ma'am" in his slow Southern drawl anytime he wants. The store is open Monday through Saturday from 8:30 A.M. to 6:00 P.M. The phone number is (402) 925–2263. If you decide you can't stop here, you'll be given another chance in Bassett at the R. F. Goeke Variety store.

Just west of Atkinson is *Atkinsons State Recreation Area,* and adjacent to it is the *Bluebird Trail.* Just as everyone loves ice cream, everyone loves bluebirds. Bluebirds, once common in Nebraska, have been making a comeback in the state, thanks to the efforts of people like those who created this trail. Stroll along the 1,500 feet of the trail and pick out a bench on which to sit quietly and observe. Twelve bluebird boxes are occupied by twelve bluebird families. It's pure magic to see them. You owe it to yourself to catch a glimpse of them.

Garfield, Loup, and Rock Counties

urwell, at Highways 11 and 91 in *Garfield County,* is most famous for *Nebraska's Big Rodeo,* held each July at the rodeo grounds/arena, which is a National Historic Site. The rodeo grounds are active all summer long, with colorful, action-packed ranch rodeos, open ropings held twice weekly, an old-timer's rodeo, and professional rodeos. If you've never been to a rodeo, or even if you have, check out the action at Burwell. Each April and October Burwell is host to two of the few fox hunts in the state.

West of Burwell off Highway 91 in Garfield County is a sign for *Dream Weavers Cabin.* Turn north here, following a curve. A very nice young woman has a shop in a log cabin there. You can watch her weave while you browse the store for herbs, woven items, handcrafts, vitamins, teas, and all sorts of cool stuff. She grows a lot of her own herbs in the gardens surrounding the cabin. The cabin is open from March through December,

Nebraska's Big Rodeo

Wednesday through Saturday from 10:00 A.M. to 6:00 P.M. and Sunday from 1:00 to 6:00 P.M. The phone number is (308) 346–4383.

Six miles northwest of Burwell is the *Calamus Reservoir State Recreation Area,* encompassing nearly 12,000 acres in both Garfield and Loup County. There is a huge lake, with 196 million gallons of fresh spring water entering it daily. The lake is great for fishing, sailing, boating, skiing, sailboarding—well, all those water-related things you'd expect to do at such a lake—plus there are sandy beaches. There's a modern campground with rest rooms and showers. A park permit is required. If you get tired of cooking out, the *Calamus River Lodge* (the only log-cabin restaurant in out-state Nebraska) is near the lake, as are a motel and a golf course. The telephone number at the Calamus Reservoir is (308) 346–5666.

The *Calamus State Fish Hatchery,* Nebraska's largest hatchery, produces an estimated forty million fish each year. It is located at the Virginia Smith Dam, 7 miles northwest of Burwell. Visitors are welcome daily from 10:00 A.M. to 4:00 P.M. with the exception of legal holidays. Hatchery activities can be seen from the visitors center, and you can feed fish in some of the outdoor raceways. Call (308) 346–4226 for more information. Tours can be scheduled forty-eight hours in advance.

From Calamus Reservoir take Highway 96 to Highway 183; go north from there for 59 miles and then go without fail to the five-and-dime/soda fountain in *Bassett* called *R. F. Goeke Variety.* This *Rock County* store transports you back to the 1950s with notions, candy, and soda fountain concoctions. There's a store in Atkinson in Holt County with the same notions and treats; it's called R. F. Goeke. The Bassett location is at 119 Clark. The store is open Monday through Saturday from 8:30 A.M. to 6:00 P.M. The telephone number is (402) 684–2263.

For an abundance of uninterrupted Sandhills scenery, many Nebraskans would recommend the drive from *Taylor,* in south-central *Loup County,* north on Highway 183 to Bassett, in north-central Rock County. This highway is a good place to practice your finger wave on the driver of the in-all-likelihood rare car you'll meet. In the days of the Wild West, the cattle-rustlin', hard-drinkin', and gamblin' Pony Boys, led by David C. "Doc" Middleton and Albert "Kid" Wade, frequented the Martin Hotel in Bassett. Wade was hanged east of town in 1884 by masked vigilantes who dragged him from jail, thinking this swift justice would put an end to horse stealing in the area. Middleton died an old man in the county jail of Douglas, Wyoming, in 1913, while serving a sentence for bootlegging.

Greeley and Valley Counties

Spalding, in **Greeley County,** will welcome you to the town where "a river runs through it." The spring-fed Cedar Creek flows into this valley town, and its 1910 Light Plant still provides up to 10 percent of the electrical needs of the community. A hand-dug millrace and waterwheels were originally constructed to power a flour mill. Tours of the original waterwheels can be arranged. A river might run through your golf game, too. A diversion of Cedar Creek cuts through part of the nine-hole course. If you'd rather be on the water than playing golf near it, the *T&T Canoe Service* will provide canoes, safety gear, and transportation back to your car from downstream. The telephone number is (308) 497–2120. As you drive into town on Highway 91, you'll see the Gothic spires of *St. Michael's Church,* an enormous church that is listed on the National Register of Historic Places. You're welcome to visit the church. The doors are open all the time, but the lights won't be on at night. Call (308) 497–2103 or (308) 497–2662 for more information.

In the opposite corner of Greeley County, southwest of Spalding, you'll find the *Happy Jack Chalk Mine and Peak* just 1½miles south of *Scotia* on Highway 11. Take a tour of the place where chalk was mined from 1887 until 1932. The chalk, used for paint, cement, whitewash, polishes, and chicken feed, is comprised of the fossilized remains of tiny sea creatures from the time when much of Nebraska was an inland sea. The mine is named after "Happy Jack" Swearingen, a fur trader who built a dugout dwelling for himself near the peak. (I haven't been able to find anyone to tell me why he was so happy; I guess he just was.) The mine fell into dangerous disrepair when it closed, the kind of place that draws teenagers who want to scare themselves silly with ghost stories in the dark of the night. A group of Scotia citizens acquired it, fixed it up, made it safe, and turned it into a sweet little tourist attraction. The guided summer tours, the hike to the peak, and the picnic area are well worth your time. Around Halloween there's a haunted house (or I guess it would be a haunted cave) that even grown men say is truly scary. Call (308) 245–3276.

Aviation fans are encouraged to head north on Highway 11 into *Valley County* and the *Evelyn Sharp Airfield,* on the north edge of *Ord,* to view the touching mementos of Nebraska's most famous aviator. Evelyn Genevieve Sharp was born in 1919, earned her commercial pilot's license when she was sixteen, and three years later became one of the nation's first female airmail pilots. At the age of twenty, she became a flying instructor and taught more than 350 men to fly. At the onset of World War II, Sharp joined the Women Airforce Service Pilots (WASPs), which was organized by Gen. H. H. (Hap) Arnold to deliver airplanes from the factories to shipping points. Sharp died in 1944 at the age of twenty-four in a crash of a P-38 in Pennsylvania. At the time of her death, she was a squadron commander just three flights shy of her fifth rating, the highest certificate available to women pilots at the time. The display about her career contains newspaper articles, photographs, and the propeller of the Curtis Robin airplane that was purchased for her by the businessmen of Ord in 1937.

Before you leave Ord, consider the joys of tanking down the river. Grab some drinks and some grub from an Ord grocery store and make plans to crawl into a stock tank. Stock tanks are large, oval, metal tanks that hold water from which cattle and horses drink. The stock tanks at the *North Loup River Trails* outfit will hold *you* ... and off you go down the river. A one-and-a-half-hour trip costs $10; an all-day trip costs $15. These guys also do trail rides as well as hunting and fishing stuff. To get there, leave Ord going east on Highway 70, cross a river bridge after $1\frac{8}{10}$ miles, and take the second right after the bridge onto Springdale Road, which you follow for 6 miles to the ranch house. The telephone number is (308) 728–5950; the Web site is www.trailrideusa.com.

WHERE THE WEST BEGINS

Six miles north of Ord on Highway 11 you'll come to the town of *Elyria* and the exit to *Fort Hartsuff State Historical Park.* Fort Hartsuff was built in 1874 as a buffer between homesteaders along the North Loup River valley and the Native Americans who had lived there for a lot longer. The troops also assisted local authorities in catching horse thieves and train robbers until the fort closed in 1881. Its nine main buildings were built of concrete, which has made the task of restoration somewhat easier than at other abandoned prairie outposts. Although it seems a strange adjective for a military post, Fort Hartsuff can easily be described as lovely. All the buildings around the parade ground are picture perfect, and when you walk into the enlisted men's quarters, you can almost hear them chatting around the stoves before crawling into their lined-up cots. The jail looks exceedingly uncomfortable and, one suspects, served as a silent admonition for good behavior. Staff and volunteers are often outfitted in period uniforms, and the baker turns out crusty golden loaves of bread for guests to sample. There's a picnic area shaded by big old trees. A park permit is required—$14.00 for a year, $2.50 for a day. The grounds are open daily from Memorial Day weekend to Labor Day from 8:00 A.M. to 8:00 P.M. and from 9:00 A.M. to sunset the rest of the year. Buildings are open daily from Memorial Day weekend to Labor Day from 9:00 A.M. to 5:00 P.M. Call (308) 346–4715 for more information.

Wheeler County

The *Hungry Horse Saloon* in *Ericson,* 7 miles off Highway 281 on Highway 70, is a great place to stop for a burger or a brew. You can't miss it; there's only one bar in town, and the Hungry Horse looks just the way you'd expect a western bar to look—wonderfully weathered, just a little worse for wear, and on an unpaved street. It's dimly lit, as a good bar should be, and it offers great burgers. On weekend nights they rustle up a great steak, just like the kind you'd expect from a saloon in ranch country. The interior of the bar is rough wood paneling, and the restaurant is separated from the bar by a partition of authentic barn siding. You can tell this ain't one of them snooty wine-drinker bars. For one thing, there's a decided dearth of hanging ferns, and the wine glasses hanging above the bar look slightly dusty and little used. For more than twenty-five years, the Hungry Horse has sponsored the hilarious Sandhills Turtle Races on the first weekend in August. You don't happen to have a turtle in the car? No problem—you can rent one. But remember, the use of steroids is strictly prohibited! In September the bar sponsors greyhound dog races. You probably can't rent one, but you are certainly encouraged to cheer for your favorite. The Hungry Horse is open daily from noon to 1:00 A.M. The telephone number is (308) 653–3100.

Hooker and Grant Counties

I f you fancy yourself a good golfer, you will find the next few sentences frustrating. That's because you'll be reading about the *Sandhills Golf Club,* south of *Mullen* off Highway 97, a private membership club where you can play only if you're a sponsored guest or you make written arrangements well in advance of your arrival. Now is the time to plan ahead and consider how to make those arrangements. This golf course, one of the finest natural courses in the country, was designed by Ben Crenshaw and Bill Coore to take advantage of the contours of the Sandhills on a plateau above the Dismal River. Magazine and newspaper articles have referred to the eighteen-hole, 7,000-yard, par-71 championship course as a "masterpiece" and a "work of art" and in other terms generally reminiscent of a mother talking about her favorite child. The owners and managers are intent on maintaining the high-quality atmosphere of the club. If you are a golfer, you'll understand why the club prefers not to have casual tourists. If you are not a golfer, think of something you are passionate about and how much better it is in the company of persons who share your passion. To make golfing arrangements, call (308) 546–2237.

Hooker County has plenty of other outdoor activities for non-golfers, however. The Middle Loup and Dismal River offer canoeing and tubing. If you want to rent canoes, stop at the Sandhills Motel in Mullen on West Highway 2. The number is (308) 546–2206 or (888) 278–6167. Be forewarned that the Dismal River is not for a beginning canoer. It is tricky, and it can be hazardous for the inexperienced. Fishing and hunting in the county are excellent, but again, heed a word of advice: Always get a permit, and always get permission from landowners before crossing onto private land.

The drive along Highway 2 in *Grant County* provides still more spectacularly serene Sandhills scenery. And Grant is another county where the cattle easily outnumber humans. *Hyannis* has 210 people; *Whitman* and *Ashby* are both unincorporated. On the west edge of Whitman, you'll come to the *Whitman General Store,* which is a perfect example of a modern general store that sells a little of everything. It looks like a tiny place, but room after room reveals food and snacks, soda, beer, health and beauty products, jewelry, cologne and perfume (this is ranch country, so Stetson for men and Annie Oakley for women are good choices), cleaning products, boots, hats, caps, belts, belt buckles, blankets, rodeo eos, leather bags, socks, and western clothing for both genders of all ages. It's a great store! Hours are Monday through Saturday, 8:00 A.M. to 6:00 P.M.; and Sunday, noon to 5:00 P.M. The telephone number is (308) 544–6489. Just a little way west of Whitman there are lakes on the north side of Highway 20, and, yes, those birds you see are pelicans, right here in landlocked Nebraska.

Blaine and Thomas Counties

*H*ave you ever heard of a Sandhills monkey? It's closely related to the jackalope and just as rare. You can see one in Blaine County, albeit stuffed, at **Uncle Buck's Lodge** in **Brewster.** Uncle Buck's is a big log-cabin lodge, restaurant, and lounge in this community of twenty-two people, at Highways 7 and 91. The three-story, 15,000-square-foot, cedar-sided building is surrounded by a deck, and the rooms are comfortable. The dining room has huge windows that open onto a view of the North Loup River. Plus it's got light fixtures made of horns and animal heads on the wall. The food is fine, and the pastries are great (guests have been known to make midnight raids on the pies). It's a popular place for hunters in season and a pleasurable getaway for anyone at any time. The number is (308) 547–2210. Oh, about that Sandhills monkey—it's the rear end of a deer, disguised to look like a scary toothsome creature you'd never ever want to meet. And about those jackalopes—well, ask anyone where you can see one. If they tell you that your leg has been pulled mightily,

TREEmendous!

*N*ow, please consider the gentle irony of Nebraska, a state that has the bad (and incorrect) reputation for being flat and treeless, producing trees for reforestation in other states. The Bessey Nursery, in the Nebraska National Forest, produces millions of seedlings to be planted in forests all across the United States. During the first fifty years of the nursery's existence nearly 200 million of its seedlings were planted. Seedlings are still distributed across the

country to provide shade and shelter for farms, schools, parks, and other forests, which have suffered from overlogging or fires. So let's not hear another word about Nebraska being treeless. Well, even if some parts of it are fairly treeless, somebody is probably busy planting a tree or two right now as you read this. Also, keep in mind that those fairly treeless places are good for growing the food you eat—without clearing forests or digging up a bazillion rocks.

Trivia:

South of Arthur, on Highway 61, you'll notice well-worn cowboy boots upside down on fence posts. No one can say with absolute certainty how this custom originated, but some people contend it's because cowboys like their "soles" facing heaven.

just tell them you know they exist because you saw one on a postcard. While you're at it, ask someone of the opposite sex for the best place to snipe hunt.

You could opt to stay at the **Sandhills Guest Ranch B&B** in rustic cabins set on a lush Sandhills meadow. The five rooms cost $75; some have private baths. A huge country breakfast (they even make their own syrup) is served at the nearby working ranch of owners Lee and Beverly DeGroff. Call (308) 547–2460 for reservations.

You might wonder why you're seeing more trees in **Thomas County** than you have in other Sandhills areas. It's because they've been planted, by hand, to create the 93,000-acre **Nebraska National Forest,** the largest hand-planted forest in the country. The forest was established in 1902 by Teddy Roosevelt, and by 1921 more than thirteen million seedlings had been planted. You see the forest better when you drive in and look around. The entrance is 2 miles west of **Halsey** off Highway 2. It's quite pretty, and you can climb to the top of the lookout tower in the summer between 2:00 and 4:00 P.M. to see off into forever. If you climb to the top, you'll realize how big the forest is, and, seeing the contrast between the forest and the Sandhills, you'll be able to judge for yourself how much work it must have been to plant all those trees. Remember, this is not an old-growth forest, but it's pretty darn impressive just the same. There's a swimming pool, picnic areas, some great hiking, and you can camp year-round. For more information call (308) 432–0300.

Arthur County

The tiny community of **Arthur** is located at the junction of Highways 92 and 61. Even though it's quite small, with a population of 128, Arthur has two attractions you should see. The first is a church made of bales of hay, which was built in the late 1920s. It is said to be the only baled-hay church in the world. If you find another, do let the people at *Ripley's Believe It or Not* know. The bales of the Pilgrim Holiness Church have been plastered inside and out, so you'd never know by looking that it's made from hay; however, you might think it's just a little lumpy here and there. In case you tend toward the more critical approach to life, ask yourself if you could do a more ingenious job of devising a structure in a country where hay is more common than trees. If the door isn't open, there's generally a note on the door giving you a number to call to get inside. You should also see the no-longer-in-use, one-room courthouse, which remains the smallest courthouse in the United States. Again, if it's not open, there should be a note on the door. Or ask anyone you see how to get in. For more information call the Arthur Enterprise at (308) 764–2426.

May's Place, in a restored older home in Arthur, has some fine items made by craftspeople in the Sandhills. Of particular note are silver jewelry and silver belt buckles made by Hanna Silversmiths. Actor Danny Glover has a Hanna buckle, as do several people who've crewed on his movies. You'll also find hand-woven items; a tour of the weaving shop can be arranged. Other items included in the inventory are goat milk soaps, quilts, collectible dolls, Sandhills Pottery, quilts, crafts, and lots of old stuff in an Antique Room. Someone is generally around on Monday mornings. At other times you are encouraged to call the numbers listed on the door: (308) 764–2376 and (308) 764–2362.

Logan and McPherson Counties

The best attraction in these two counties is what makes them so eminently qualified to be in a book about off-the-beaten-path places. The whole of both counties *is* off the beaten path and comprises

One Really Horny Guy

*O*nce upon a time, not all that long ago, a national tabloid newspaper printed a story about a man named Horace Easterwood, who was supposed to have lived north of Broken Bow. Now there's nothing unusual about that. But he had a 40-inch, unicorn-like horn on the top of his head, and that is highly unusual. This fanciful story came as news to the residents, none of whom had ever heard of the afflicted Mr. Easterwood. Because this is a part of the country where everybody knows everybody else, it is safe to assume that someone—a pastor, a doctor, the mail carrier, the mother's best friend— would have known of the wee horned one. Now I suppose it might be that little Horace's mother was so horrified by his appearance that she hid him away forever; it just took some enterprising tabloid reporter to ferret him out. (All the truth that's fit to print, doncha know.) Anyway, the whole suspicious Easterwood affair was taken in highly amused stride by the locals, who now promote him as one of their own. The mayor proclaimed February 16 to be Horace Easterwood Day, and the annual festival on that date continues to be enjoyed by all.

only three communities, with a grand total of fewer than 350 people. (It's a pretty safe bet there are metropolitan areas where more people than that live in just one building.) Of the twenty-five least-populated counties in the country, eight of them are in the Sandhills. Take the time to slow down, see the scenery, hear birds sing, and breathe clean air. Stop for a meal, stop for a soda, or just stop and enjoy a slower pace of life than usual. Take a stroll around **Gandy, Stapleton,** or **Tryon** and let the kids play in the park. It's also a pretty safe bet you won't get mugged and the kids won't get abducted; you won't even have to lock your car. If you want to see small-town America, you're looking at it. Oh, one more thing—when you're driving in the Sandhills, make sure to watch your gas supply. Not every one of these widely-spaced-apart towns has a gas station, and even if they do, it might not be open when you need it.

Custer County

It seems like all roads lead to **Broken Bow,** which is located at the junction of Highways 2, 21, 91, and 70, in Custer County. A good place to stay is the **Arrow Hotel,** across from the town square. It's a great old hotel that has been modernized without compromising any historic integrity. It has twenty-two suites with full kitchens. The restaurant is appealing, and the food is excellent. Lunches are served Monday through Friday, 11:00 A.M. to 2:00 P.M.; dinners are served Monday through Saturday, 4:00 P.M. to 10:00 P.M.; and weekend brunches are served 7:00 A.M. to 2:00 P.M. The telephone number is (308) 872–6662.

Northwest of Broken Bow is the town of **Anselmo** on Highway 2, which is becoming famous for the sheepish behavior of the nearby ranch family of Larry, Kim, and Luke Curtis. Out here in cattle country you'll find a herd of fuzzy white sheep. There is one black sheep, which seems only appropriate. **Shepherd's Dairy** is the first and only certified sheep dairy in Nebraska and the second in the United States. That's right, they milk sheep! The milk is shipped, frozen, to a processing plant in New York where it ultimately becomes cheese or yogurt. A sideline of this sheepishness is a beautiful line of hand-crafted soaps made from sheep milk that will leave your skin soft and supple. They are advertised as "ewenique" soaps—ya gotta love that! There are nearly a dozen different kinds of soap, from Creamy Oatmeal to Lime Zest to Prairie Rain. Individual soaps or pretty handmade gift boxes can be ordered from the Web site at www.simplerway.com/shepherds-dairy/. At the ranch there are also several gargantuan hairy white dogs whose job is to protect the sheep. The dogs are a Turkish breed called Akbash. The puppies, which seem about as big as your typical ATV, like to greet visitors and stick their face in your car window while you decide if they're more likely to eat you or kiss you. They're more likely to kiss you. The adults are more reserved but will, with great dignity, accept your petting and will ultimately herd you around gently when they get the signal from the Curtises that you're okay. Be forewarned; dogs that weigh up to 140 pounds tend to drool. The dogs' friendly demeanor is for humans, and sheep, only. The Curtises say the dogs like hanging out with the sheep, and each dog tends to pick out a favorite sheep buddy. When it comes to predators, sheepkill from coyotes is now nil. The local coyote population has learned to keep a healthy distance from the Akbash and their sheep charges. To get to Shepherd's Dairy, turn off of Highway 2 at Anselmo, go east through town on Spur 21A toward Victoria Springs, watch for the 3-mile marker, and then turn east again and watch for signs. Call ahead if you want a tour; the number is (308) 749–2349 or (888) 966–5496.

Power to the People

*W*orking together to achieve a common goal is a time-honored tradition. But how do you organize far-flung farmers across the country to obtain a fair price for farm products and a good value for money spent? If the year is 1867, you start a movement called the National Grange of the Patrons of Husbandry. The Nebraska State Grange was organized in 1872. (In case you're wondering was a grange is, the dictionary defines it as a farm with outlying buildings and as a national fraternal organization of farmers.) During the 1870s the Grange played a huge role in farmers' lives and offered political, social, educational, and fraternal activities. "Granger Laws" put in place by state governments set the pattern for modern America's regulated free-enterprise economy.

Within a decade the Farmers' Alliance, and the Farmer's Equity Union after that, replaced the Grange as the farmers' organization of choice. By the time of the Depression the Farm Holiday Association became the political arm of the farmers' movement. Other movements supporting farm owners have come and gone as the economic pendulum has swung. However, the Grange Movement was reestablished in 1911 in Custer County and is the oldest Grange organization in the state. The State Grange, likewise, was reorganized in the same year. At present, local Granges are important to community life and sound farm policy.

A Nebraska State Historical Marker about the Nebraska Grange is located northwest of Broken Bow on Highway 2 in Custer County.

Northeast of Broken Bow, near *Comstock,* is the *Dowse Sod House,* one of the few original intact sod houses in the county, at one time known as the Sod House Capital of the World. In this area wood was scarce, and settlers were forced to build shelter from the very ground on which they stood. Sod, known as Nebraska Marble, housed many pioneers until they could afford to build wooden homes. The Dowse Sod House was built by William Dowse for his bride-to-be in 1900. The original house had three rooms and a sleeping loft. For fifty-nine years the Dowse family lived there and overcame drought, blizzards, grasshoppers, prairie fires, rustlers, and isolation. Many of the furnishings in the house are period pieces and similar to those used by the family. You can stop by on your own, but guided tours are available with a little advance notice by calling (308) 527–3462. There is no charge, but do leave a donation if you go on your own. To get there, take Highway 183 and go east at the Comstock sign; continue on 21C to the Dowse Sod House sign; then turn south and east for 3½ miles to the home place.

After leaving the Dowse Sod House, go back to the highway, drive into Comstock, and see two very pretty parks. One park is in the downtown area; it is now a great garden that was created by volunteers after two businesses burned down a few years back. The fire left Comstock with three remaining businesses, those being—as the locals say with tongue in cheek—the bar, a pay phone, and a pop machine. If you turn north just before the baseball field on the edge of town, go north 3 miles and

The Tunes They Are a-Changin'

This I hold to be true: Nebraskans are friendly and tolerant. So when I hear of rare instances that contradict this belief, it hurts my heart. During the 1960s the community of Arnold was reputed to be quite unfriendly. Cautionary remarks such as "pray your car doesn't break down in Arnold" were abundant. In 1968, two members of a group of cross-country bicyclists were beaten to a pulp while camped at a park. Two weeks later, another bicyclist was saved from the same fate by a local whose testosterone level was not poisonous. Luckily, the shallow gene pool

those troglodytes were spawned from decades ago seems to have evaporated. Today, Arnold's bad reputation has gone the way of all flesh. Nearly 2,500 non-locals (about four times larger than the town's population) are welcomed at the annual South Loup River Rock and Blues Festival. Major blues luminaries such as Koko Montoya and Tab Benoit have graced the stage on the baseball field west of South Broadway Street and south of the fire department. Close your eyes and you might feel like you're in a Chicago blues bar—and don't fear to close your eyes at night.

east 1 mile and you'll come to one of Nebraska's newest attractions. The *2nd Wind Ranch* is comprised of a beautifully restored farmstead home that is now the Dempster House B&B (with a restaurant open Thursday through Saturday nights), the Crosswind Mercantile store with arts and crafts housed in an old barn, and dozens of windmills. The number of windmills on the ranch increases with every year. The owners hope to have 200 windmills within the next few years, which will make it the world's largest collection of standing windmills. The house has a great big wraparound porch that invites a good settin' spell. If you're lucky, there'll be a stupendous lightning storm in the west of an evening, and you can gasp with delight as the windmills are silhouetted by dramatic lightning flashes. The phone number is (308) 628–4369 or (308) 728–3113. The Web site is www.windmillenterprises.net.

Northwest of Broken Bow is *Victoria Springs State Recreation Area.* This secluded sixty-acre park, called an oasis in the Sandhills, is located 6 miles east of Anselmo or 9 miles north of Merna. It is named after the mineral springs in the park, the water from which was said to have restorative powers and which was bottled and sold by homesteader and judge Charles Mathews. Log cabins he built are still on the site. The recreation area has two modern housekeeping cabins, camping, picnicking in wooded areas, fishing, and boating. A park permit is required and costs $14.00 for a year and $2.50 for a day. Reservations for the cabins are a real good idea. For more information call (308) 749–2235.

**PLACES TO STAY
IN THE SANDHILLS**

AINSWORTH
Ainsworth Inn B&B,
400 North Main,
(402) 387–0454 or
(800) 237–0954,
www.innsite.com/inns/
A002611.html

The Upper Room B&B,
409 North Wilson,
(402) 387–0107

BROKEN BOW
The Arrow Hotel,
509 South Ninth,
(308) 872–6662

O'NEILL
The Golden Hotel
(restored),
Fourth and Douglas,
(402) 336–4436 or
(800) 658–3148

SENECA
McCawley House B&B,
(308) 639–3300 or
(308) 639–3229

SPARKS
Heartland Elk Guest
Ranch,
rural,
(402) 376–1124

SPRINGVIEW
Larrington's Guest Cottage,
rural,
(402) 497–2261

Big Canyon Inn,
rural,
(402) 497–3170 or
(800) 437–6023,
www.innsite.com/inns/
A002595.html

STUART
The Sisters' House B&B,
412 Garfield,
(402) 924–3678

VALENTINE
Lovejoy Ranch B&B,
rural,
(402) 376–2668 or
(800) 672–5098,
www.lovejoyranch.com

**PLACES TO EAT
IN THE SANDHILLS**

BREWSTER
Uncle Buck's Lodge
(American),
Highways 7 and 91,
(308) 547–2210

BROKEN BOW
The Lobby Restaurant
(American) in the
Arrow Hotel,
509 South Ninth,
(308) 872–3363

ERICSON
Hungry Horse Saloon
(American),
(308) 653–3100

ELYRIA
The Country Neighbor
(American),
¹/₂ mile south of
Fort Hartsuff,
(308) 346–5049

GROSS
Nebraska Inn (steaks,
burgers), about the only
building in town—you
can't miss it,
(402) 583–9922

LONG PINE
Hidden Paradise (American), in gorgeous canyon
on Long Pine Creek,
(402) 273–4576

SPENCER
Angel's Strawbale Saloon
(American), 2 miles south
of the junction of Highways
281 and 12 on the south
side of the Niobrara River,
(402) 589–1017

VALENTINE
Jordan's (American),
Highway 20,
(402) 376–1255

Peppermill (American),
112 North Main,
(402) 376–1440

**HELPFUL SANDHILLS
WEB SITES AND
E-MAIL ADDRESSES**

**NORTH CENTRAL NEBRASKA
TRAVEL AND TOURISM
COUNCIL**
www.nebraskaoutback.com

AINSWORTH
www.co.brown.ne.us/
ainsworth.htm

BROKEN BOW
bbchamber@navix.net
(e-mail)

BURWELL
haskell@micrord.com
(e-mail)

O'NEILL
www.cl.oneill.ne.us

VALENTINE
www.valentine-ne.com

Land of Cowboys and Indians

The Pine Ridge area of northwest Nebraska is a land where the drama of the landscape is more than matched by the drama of events in western history. This canyoned, pine-covered territory was home to the Sioux, who occupied it permanently beginning in 1810. This is where the Oglala Sioux warrior Crazy Horse was killed in 1877 and where fur traders set up early trading posts. This is the land of novelist Mari Sandoz, who wrote about history and the incontrovertible effect the land had on shaping the destiny of the people who lived here. Although there is a Cowboy Museum in the Pine Ridge, you'll find cowboys around every corner, still making a living from cattle and the land. And, if you're lucky, you'll catch a glimpse of the lake "monster," which rivals the Loch Ness Monster in its elusiveness. Prehistoric wonders and paleontology digs round out experiences for travelers in the Pine Ridge.

Sheridan County

Sheridan County is where the Sandhills meet the Pine Ridge. The northern part of the county has the topography of the Pine Ridge, with Beaver Wall, a nearly vertical rock cliff that extends for several miles north of Hay Springs. The central and southern areas of the county are prairie country. In *Gordon,* at Highways 20 and 27, is the *Tri-State Old-time Cowboy Museum.* It's located in a city park 1 block west of Main Street between Third and Fourth Streets. This log cabin contains a collection of cowboy artifacts from the late 1800s to the present day. The collection includes tools and gear such as saddles, hats, and boots, plus a chuck wagon, with more than 200 cattle brands. If you think branding cattle is barbaric, bear in mind the words of South Dakota rancher/writer Linda Hasselstrom, who wrote in her book *Land Circles* that she'll "consider another method of marking my cattle when we stop licensing cars to identify them and prevent their theft." The museum is open from Memorial Day through September 15 daily from 1:00 to 5:00 P.M. Admission is free. The phone number is (308) 282–0887.

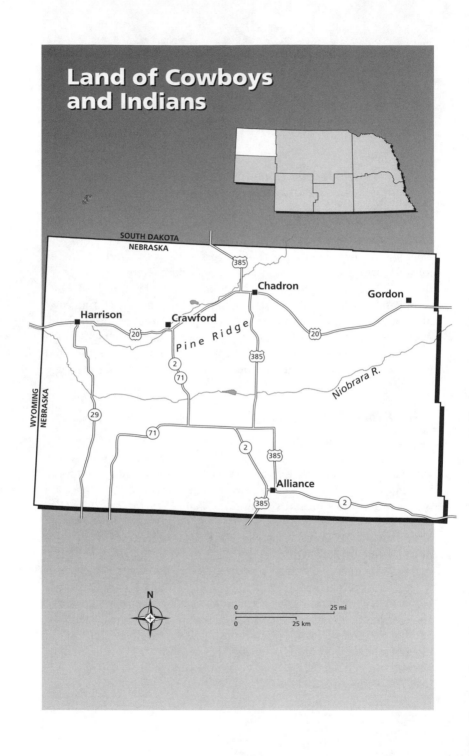

Land of Cowboys and Indians

SOUTH DAKOTA
NEBRASKA

385

Chadron

Gordon

Harrison   Crawford

20   385   20

Pine Ridge

2

71   385

Niobrara R.

WYOMING
NEBRASKA

29

71

2   385

Alliance

385   2

N

0   25 mi

0   25 km

LAND OF COWBOYS AND INDIANS

AUTHOR'S FAVORITE ATTRACTIONS IN THE PINE RIDGE

(All area codes are 308)

Agate Fossil Beds National Monument,
24 miles south of Harrison or 34 miles north of Mitchell, 668–2211

Carhenge,
2½ miles north on Highway 87, Alliance, 762–1520 or 762–4954

Olde Main Street Inn,
115 Main Street, Chadron, 432–3380

Sioux Sundries,
downtown Harrison, 668–2577

Sowbelly Canyon,
northeast off Highway 20, Harrison, 668–2466

Toadstool Geologic Park,
northwest from Highway 2, Crawford, 432–4475

Sheridan County is also known as Sandoz Country for novelist/historian/biographer Mari Sandoz. The **Mari Sandoz Room** is located at 117 North Main in Gordon in a little printing shop. All her books are available here, and you can see manuscripts and interesting memorabilia about her life. Sandoz, who grew up on a ranch south of Gordon, has been credited with creating a Great Plains legacy with sensitive portrayals of pioneer men and women and Native American history and culture. Not bad for a woman whose taciturn (and some say downright tyrannical) father kept her out of school until she was nine years old. Some of her most famous novels are *Old Jules* (pioneer stories; some describe life with her father), *Cheyenne Autumn* (it's been made into a movie), and *Crazy Horse*. Four of her books have been included in the 100 Best Books about the West, which are selected by the Chicago Corral (the parent group of the Westerners). Sandoz died in 1966 and is buried on her beloved land south of Gordon, at the privately owned ranch where she grew up. Several miles south of Gordon on Highway 27, near the ranch, a historical marker commemorates her life and work. The Mari Sandoz Room is free and open year-round, Monday through Friday, 9:00 A.M. to 5:00 P.M.; and Saturday, 9:00 A.M. to noon. The telephone number is (308) 282–1687. Circle Tour maps of sites around Sheridan County are available here.

Beaver Road, north out of **Hay Springs,** is located in Beaver Valley and extends the length of **Beaver Wall.** Beaver Wall is an escarpment with breathtaking views. You can see for nearly 150 miles from the Black Hills to the buttes at Crawford. According to Sioux legend, if someone made a wish and spent the night in the cavelike depressions in Beaver Wall, the wish would be granted the next morning. The drive is pretty spectacular. If you must get out to hike, always find a landowner to ask his or her permission. Or if you want to climb Beaver Wall, seek out the owner and ask permission. Beaver Wall is 10 miles north of Highway 20 on a county road at the west end of Hay Springs.

South of Gordon on Highways 27 and 2 is the tiny town of **Ellsworth,** with a ranch store called **Morgan's** that is also the post office. Morgan's sells all kinds of horse gear as well as riding hats and boots. The store is old-fashioned with a tin ceiling, but the supplies are not. A lot of the equipment is made on-site from a wear-like-iron modern fabric known as cordura. In the store you can buy luggage, from garment bags to backpacks, boot bags, saddlebags, sports bags, ditty bags, hat bags, bridle bags, pistol cases, outfitter packs, panniers—well, the list goes on and on. Ask to see a mail-order catalog if you don't want to schlepp stuff around on your trip. The store is open Monday through Saturday from 8:30 A.M. to 5:00 P.M. The telephone number is (308) 762–2666. The bathroom has this no-nonsense poem on the wall: "With these two rules to live by, / You've got it put' near skinned: / Never whittle towards you, / And don't spit against the wind."

Just west of **Antioch,** north of Highway 2 across the railroad tracks, you'll see some ruins that look as though a very small, bizarre cathedral once stood there. These are the ruins of a potash plant. Potash was a component of a fertilizer used in the Cotton Belt of the United States. When World War I broke out and cut off the supply of European potash, a plant was built near Antioch to extract potash from the alkaline lakes in the area. Five plants were built by 1918, and the potash was used for fertilizer, epsom salts, soda, and other products. When peace was achieved, the

Believe It or Not: The Mouth That Roared

*T*ry to catch of glimpse of the fabled, elusive **Walgren Lake Monster** at the **Walgren Lake State Recreation Area** near Hay Springs. This benign, Loch Ness–like creature has been the subject of spirited local legend and debate for decades. Verified sightings have yet to be confirmed. Some locals insist on the authenticity of sightings; folklorist Roger Welsch says the creature has been seen only by fishermen who've been out too long in the sun without a hat, while others say it's seen by teenagers on a toot. Here are some of the things that have been written about the monster: It eats a dozen calves when it comes ashore; it flattens the cornfields; its flashing green eyes spit fire; the gnashing of its teeth sounds like a clap of thunder. Newspaper accounts from the mid-1930s claim that a skeptic from Omaha bravely spent the night alone at the lake. He returned home haggard, white-haired, and voiceless with fear. Three days later, upon regaining speech, he said the monster was 300 feet long and its mouth was big enough to hold Omaha's Woodmen of the World building. It's a great legend (although a great big hoax), and you'll enjoy the peaceful surroundings of this beautiful lake, where you can camp, hike, and fish. A park entry permit is required and can be obtained from stores in town. To try your luck at seeing the creature, go 3 miles south of Hay Springs on Highway 87 and then 2 miles east.

European potash was again imported, and at a cheaper cost than that needed to keep the plants open. The last of the plants closed in 1921.

Dawes County

hree miles east of **Chadron** on Highway 20 is the **Museum of the Fur Trade.** This fascinating, one-of-a-kind museum features an extensive collection of items associated with the fur trade and the daily lives of traders, trappers, and Native Americans. The museum does not limit itself to the American fur trade; there are also displays of international fur trading. Plan on spending a long time here viewing trade goods like knives, beads, cloth, traps, blankets, and other items used either for trade or treaty payments. The collection of guns made for the Native American trade from 1750 to 1900 is the largest and most complete in the world. You'll see all types of fur, from buffalo robes to beaver, mink, wolf, badger, and sea otter. (Shoppers take note: The gift shop is where I always leave some of my money.) On the grounds is the site of the re-created Bordeaux Trading Post. Built in 1837, the original trading post was part of the American Fur Company until 1849, when it became an independent post operated by James Bordeaux for trade with the Sioux until 1872. Four years later, with the Indian Wars in full cry, the U.S. Cavalry confiscated illegal ammunition being sold to the by-then-hostile Sioux, and the post was abandoned by the subsequent owner, James Boucher. The trading post is built on the original foundations. Inside you'll see evidence of the far-from-fancy life of the frontier trader. Imagine sleeping on the willow bed, cooking in the kettles hung over the fire hearth, and selecting from the store shelves stocked with trade goods. This museum is a must-see for anyone interested in western history. Admission price for those eighteen and older is $2.50; children seventeen and younger are admitted free when accompanied by parents. The museum is open from Memorial Day through September 30 from 8:00 A.M. to 5:00 P.M. The museum is not heated, so winter visits are not recommended; off-season tours can be arranged by calling (308) 432–3843 in advance. The Web address is www.furtrade.org.

A great place to stay in Chadron is the **Olde Main Street Inn,** at 115 Main Street. Chances are you'll find owner Jeanne Goetzinger at her spinning wheel in the evening. This eclectic B&B, now listed on the National Register of Historic Places, has ten rooms on the second and third floors. Some are charmingly restored to reflect the original days of the 1890 hotel; others are awaiting renovation. There's a restaurant for lunch and dinner, with a variety of foods that include buffalo, mesquite chicken, steak, and some of the best green-chili stew found in these parts. On the first floor is the Longbranch Saloon, where locals and guests gather to swap stories. There's a pool table, too. If you don't like bars, you can enter by a private outside door, to which you'll get a key when you register. If you decide to forgo the bar, however, you'll miss the chance to meet other guests, who have ranged from rodeo stars to barnstorming pilots, foreigners who come for the nearby Sioux Sun Dances, and people who are riding a mule-driven wagon across the country. If you ask, Jeanne will turn back the guest book pages to show you Dick Cavett's name. The history of the hotel is the history of the area as well. In December 1890 and shortly into the following year, the hotel was the military headquarters for Gen. Nelson Miles, who commanded the Wounded Knee operations in the Native American campaigns. Jeanne will make breakfast pretty much to your order, and, if she has the time and you have the inclination, might join you for stories of the area and to share insights on life. Reservations aren't necessary but are encouraged. Credit cards are accepted. Rates range from $35 for one person to

I Dream of Jeanne

I groggily stumbled down the steps for breakfast one morning at the Olde Main Street Inn in Chadron. I was greeted by a smiling and serene Jeanne Goetzinger, who said, "Whatever you want, I'll make whatever you want." She was referring to breakfast, but in my grumpy morning mood I thought, "I want to be 4 inches taller and twenty pounds lighter." I don't remember what she made to eat, but I do remember her making me feel better about pretty much everything. It wasn't a busy morning, so she sat down with me. For an hour we talked about life, family, books, spirituality, and local Native American history. She

glowed with pride about her mother, with whom she operates the inn, and her daughter, an accomplished artist who fills in as a cook. Jeanne has since become a bust-yer-buttons grandma; my congratulations to all, particularly her son-in-law, who has a great big laugh and the sense to align himself with a family of hard-working, smart, and strong women. If you have the time, and Jeanne has the inclination, sit down with her and learn a little. Say hello, and indulge in some ear-scratchin' with the dogs Ginger and Trapper. Ginger's always in the mood. Trapper's a bit shy, and you may have to coax him.

$50 for two people and up to $72 for the three-room General Miles suite. The telephone number is (308) 432–3380.

Before you leave Chadron, spend some time at the *Mari Sandoz High Plains Heritage Center* on the Chadron State College campus. The center is devoted to the culture and history of the High Plains as well as the personal and professional life of Mari Sandoz. The hours are Monday through Friday, 9:00 A.M. to 4:30 P.M. The phone number is (308) 432–6066.

Just 8 miles south of Chadron on Highway 385 is *Chadron State Park*. This heavily wooded retreat can come as a surprise to persons unfamiliar with the rugged terrain of the Pine Ridge's Nebraska National Forest. A few years ago, when then-governor Ben Nelson visited there with his wife, Diane, she is reported to have exclaimed delightedly, "This looks just like Colorado!" To which her diplomatic husband replied with a smile, "No, Colorado looks just like this." There are several housekeeping cabins tucked among the ponderosa pines of this 972-acre park. Or you can pitch a tent or park your RV. Established in 1921, this is Nebraska's oldest state park, but the campgrounds are modern, as are the showers and rest rooms in the camping areas. Trail rides and jeep rides can be arranged. There are tennis and sand volleyball courts, paddle boats, a swimming pool, a craft center, horseshoe games, and picnic shelters. Cabin reservations must be for a minimum stay of two nights, but cabins can be rented for one night on a first-come, first-served basis. Even if you can't stay, stop for a hike or unload your bikes. The park is at an elevation of nearly 5,000 feet; mountain bikers sing the praises of the park and surrounding trails. The required park permit is available at the park office for $14.00 per year and $2.50 per day. To make reservations for a cabin (from $50 to $60 per day) or to get more information, call (308) 432–6167. The Web address is www.ngpc.state.ne.us/parks.

Tunnel Vision of a Ghost Town

*I*f you want to see a **ghost town,** go to what was once **Belmont.** It's near **Crawford,** 1 mile east of Highways 71 and 2. This former town once had fifty buildings, most of which are gone except for the brick school building and a few others. The town was established in 1886 by a dairy farmer who used a pooch-powered treadmill to separate the cream. (Do you suppose townspeople back then thought the business was going to the dogs?) A short walk north from Belmont takes you to the only railroad tunnel in the whole state. Built in 1888, it was used for nearly a century until 1983.

Since we're on the topic of mountain biking, the Pine Ridge is an excellent place to do so. There are approximately 70 miles of marked bike routes that will challenge even the scoffers who say that mountain biking isn't possible in Nebraska. The Nebraska Game and Parks Commission and the U.S. Forest Service have produced a wonderful weatherproof topographic map for bikers. It is available for $6.95 from the Chadron Chamber of Commerce (call 308–432–4401) or from local bike shops. *Soldier Creek Wilderness Area* (to find it, follow Soldier Creek Road at the entrance to Fort Robinson State Park) is a particularly wonderful place to bike. It's off-limits to motorized vehicles. No matter where you bike in the Pine Ridge, whether in state parks or U.S. Forest Service land, follow these rules: Stay on the marked and visible trails, don't scare the slower-moving hikers and horse riders, don't trespass, always leave any gate as you found it, take water, and wear your helmet. And remember, prickly pear cactus is common in the area. If you get off the trails, your tires are in peril. If you go too fast and take a spill, your body is in peril. Call (308) 432–4475 for more information.

Southwest of Chadron, on Highway 20, is *Crawford.* Here you can sample the wares of Nebraska's third winery. Stop in at *Lovers Leap Vineyards* at 432 Second Street. Nearly ten varieties of wine await your judgment and ensuing pleasure. One of the vintages is Turkey Run Red, named after the greedy wild birds that consumed much of one year's harvest. The winery itself is named for a well-known rock formation just west of Crawford that looms over the landscape around the winery. The winery is open Sunday through Wednesday, 1:00 to 6:00 P.M.; and Thursday through Saturday, 10:00 A.M. to 8:00 P.M. The telephone number is (308) 665–2712. The Web site is www.loversleapvineyards.com.

Fort Robinson State Park is just about five minutes west of town. It's hard to say enough good things about this park. Not only is it Nebraska's largest state park (with 22,000 acres of incredibly beautiful scenery), but it's simply dense with history and great things to see and do. It was an active military post from 1874 to 1948. Chief Crazy Horse was killed here in 1877, at a site now marked by a simple stone monument outside the guardhouse. He had freely agreed to come into Fort Robinson for negotiations with the military; when he realized he had been betrayed and was about to be imprisoned, his struggle ended when he was bayoneted and lay bleeding to death on the floor of the Adjutant's Office. Fort Robinson was a post for the Ninth Cavalry's famous black "Buffalo Soldiers" and, in later years, was a training ground for the Army's Olympic equestrian team, a World War II K-9 Corps, and a prisoner-of-war camp for German prisoners.

At present guests can stay in any number of original and reconstructed historic buildings: the ranch house, the lodge, cabins, and officers' or enlisted men's quarters. Primitive and modern camping facilities are available. There is a long list of things to do: ride horses in the buttes, hike, bike (you can rent bikes there), fish, see the buffalo herd, swim in the indoor swimming pool, see a free rodeo, take a hayrack or stagecoach ride, or go to the evening buffalo-stew cookout and campfire sing-along. As for biking, don't miss nearby Smiley's Canyon. If you're a theater buff, each season the Post Playhouse Summer Repertory Theater offers three really good productions that include musicals, comedies, and melodramas. One melodrama title of recent years was *Run to the Roundhouse, Nellie, He Can't Corner You There*. The Lodge has a nice restaurant for all three meals. Fort Robinson is immensely popular with Nebraskans and residents of nearby states, so rooms are often booked in advance for the summer. But you might get lucky if there's been a cancellation. Cabins are available only from early April through mid-November. Even if you can't stay at the park, you can stay in motels at Crawford and take advantage of Fort Robinson's activities. Call (308) 665–2900 for reservations or for more information. A park permit is required. You can buy one for the year for $14.00 or just a day for $2.50. The Web address is www.ngpc.state.ne.us/parks.

Also on the grounds of Fort Robinson is the *University of Nebraska State Museum at Trailside.* The Trailside Museum has paleontology

The Mysterious Burial of Crazy Horse

*W*hen Crazy Horse was killed at Fort Robinson in 1877, his family came to get his body, taking it away on a horse-drawn travois. Apparently they placed the body in a tree on a scaffold in Beaver Valley. After a period of mourning, the body was removed. But to where? The site of his final resting place remains a sacred, and decidedly secret, place. Historians, professional and amateur alike, have tried for more than a century to find that place. Some say Crazy Horse's remains are in a crevice near Scout Point in Beaver Creek Valley. A book called To Kill an Eagle: Indian Views on the Last Days of Crazy Horse by Edward and Mabell Kadlecek supports this view. Other theories support likely burial places in South Dakota, such as Wounded Knee, Eagle Nest Butte, Pepper Creek, or Porcupine. Many believe his remains were divided and placed in several locations so as to avoid discovery by unscrupulous profit-seekers. Charles Trimble, himself an Oglala Sioux and a former board member of the Nebraska Historical Society, has been quoted as saying, "To us, he's all over. That's where his spirit is. Your spirit is what is important. Your body is not."

exhibits that include a giant mammoth, a fossil rhino, and a giant tortoise, plus geology exhibits of rocks and minerals. Special demonstrations include flint knapping, and there are temporary exhibits and traveling art shows. The museum's gift shop has a good selection of educational (and fun) games, toys, and books for children of all ages, as well as Native American crafts from nearby reservations. Hours are daily June through August, 9:00 A.M. to 5:00 P.M.; September, October, April, and May, Monday through Friday, 10:30 A.M. to 3:30 P.M. Admission is (with a valid park permit) $2.00 for adults; children with adults, free. Children without adults, 50 cents. Call (308) 665–2929 for more information or to arrange field programs.

The *Fort Robinson Museum,* on the grounds of Fort Robinson, is operated by the Nebraska State Historical Society. The interpretive exhibits are housed in the 1905 Post Headquarters building. The museum's wonderful collection, which spans the entire history of the fort, is nicely designed and curated. Of special interest is a Sioux Ghost Dance shirt (the shirts, believed by some Sioux to make the wearers invisible and impervious to soldiers' bullets, were worn during the Ghost Dance in a spiritual effort to make the white man go away and the buffalo, as well as all Sioux ancestors, come back). Also of interest to visitors is a collection of McClellan saddles, which were designed for use by the military. The McClellan saddles are very lightweight, with a slot down the middle. If you're hoping to see a photograph of Crazy Horse at the museum, prepare for your hopes to be dashed, for Crazy Horse never allowed his photograph to be taken by anyone. Hours: Memorial Day through Labor Day, Monday through Saturday, 8:00 A.M. to 5:00 P.M., Sunday, 1:00 to 5:00 P.M.; September through May, Monday through Friday, 8:00 A.M. to 5:00 P.M. Hours may vary a bit during the off-season; call ahead at (308) 665–2919. The admission is $1.00 for adults; children accompanied by adults are admitted at no charge.

It might take you a while to follow these directions (and I assure you—you'll think you're way lost en route) to the *Hudson-Meng Bison Bone Bed Enclosure,* but you'll be glad you did. Go 4²/₁₀ miles north of Crawford on Highway 2 to Forest Development Road 904, turn left on 904, and go for 7⁴/₁₀ miles to Sand Creek Road; then turn left on Sand Creek Road and go 6³/₁₀ miles to the Hudson-Meng turnoff—you'll be truly off the beaten path. Be forewarned that after a rain, the roads turn into what the locals call "gumbo." Also, don't drive fast unless you're adept on gravel roads. At the end of the road is the final resting place of more than 600 bison who died en masse about 10,000 years ago. What, you might ask yourself, caused so many bison to die in one place at one time? The answer is literally being unearthed. Archaeologists and paleontologists at first thought the place might have been a buffalo jump where Native Americans stampeded the beasts over a cliff. But if it had been a buffalo jump, there would have been more arrowheads and tools unearthed; there have only been a couple, and those might have been dropped at a later time. There are other theories: A prairie fire may have trapped the bison around a watering hole, or a fierce winter storm could have covered the grass with snow too deep to paw through, causing the bison to starve to death. The prairie-fire theory is the most probable. (A graduate student I knew who worked the dig one summer postulated it was an alien attack, but she hastily pointed out it was a *joke*.) A new enclosure, with staff to explain what you're seeing, has been built over the dig area. There's a pretty little pond with cattails there, too, complete with a critter I couldn't identify. Beaver? Muskrat? Call for more information at (308) 432–4475, (308) 432–0300, or (308) 665–3900. Hours from mid-May through September 30 are 10:00 A.M. to 6:00 P.M. daily. Admission is $4.00.

When you leave Hudson-Meng, stop by for a meal or a piece of killer-good pie at the ***Drifter's Cookshack.*** Or if looking at all those old bones made you tired, then just stay the night at the adjacent ***High Plains Homestead Bunkhouse.*** I swear this is one of the coolest places in the whole state. Not only is the food good (I have dreams about the sour cream raisin pie), but the whole dang place looks like a movie set that has been perfectly placed on a windswept plain surrounded by buttes. The Cookshack is full of antiques and neat stuff to look at while you wait for the food. Do not fail to look up at the really creepy enormous dried and intact hornets' nest hanging from a rafter. The rooms at the Bunkhouse are cozy, with private baths and no phones or televisions. If you're coming from Hudson-Meng, you'll drive right past it. In addition to the room, overnight accommodations include RV hookups and primitive camping. You can even bring your horse for a restful overnight stay. If you're coming from Crawford, take Highway 2 north and follow the signs. The phone number is (308) 665–2592, and the Web site is www.bbc.net/highplainshomestead/.

North of Crawford is ***Toadstool Geologic Park.*** This awesome landscape is absolutely lunarlike. Take a walk through these badlands and watch for fossilized tracks of ancient creatures. The "toadstool" formations were created when erosion affected the different strata of sediment deposited by ancient volcanoes. Toadstool Park is 4 miles north of Crawford on Highway 2 and then 15 miles northwest on Toadstool Road (an all-weather road). Toadstool Park is on federal land, is open year-round, and is free. You can even camp here. The phone number is (308) 432–4475.

Toadstool Geologic Park

Now we're headed 10 miles south of Crawford to the *JX Cattle Ranch and Guest Ranch.* This working cattle ranch offers visitors a variety of experiences. From May until October you can do ranch work such as rounding up cattle or riding fence (riding along the fenceline to make sure it is in good repair). If you're feeling a little crafty, they can teach you how to make your own chaps. Rent a cabin year-round; they have full kitchens, plus a woodstove for that rustic ambience. In the winter there's cross-country skiing through some pretty spectacular scenery. The cabins rent for a two-day minimum at $130, with additional days costing $60 per day per cabin. If you want to polish up on your foreign languages, they speak French, German, and Swedish. To get there, go south of Crawford on Highway 2/71, turn east at Saw Log Road (you'll see a sign for the Ponderosa Wildlife Area), go 2 miles, and cross a railroad track. Turn south and go 3 miles to where the road divides; here there's a sign for the JX Ranch, so go 2 more miles to the headquarters. The phone number is (308) 665–1585, and the Web site is www.jxranch.com.

Sioux County

I t is only appropriate that this huge county, which has but one incorporated community, *Harrison,* does have "America's largest hamburger." The people of this tiny town, population 290, seem to have a good sense of humor: The signs on the edge of town read HARRISON, NEXT FOUR EXITS. Harrison is located at the junction of Highways 20 and 29. Stop in at *Sioux Sundries* for a twenty-eight-ounce hamburger, which is 6 inches in diameter and sports a bun that is dwarfed by the burger's sheer enormity. It is called the Coffee Burger after a local rancher, Mr. Coffee, who reputedly wanted giant burgers for himself and his crew. The burgers got bigger and bigger until the Coffee Burger was born and the rancher pronounced it good. Once upon a time it was decreed that if you could eat two Coffee Burgers, you'd get a third for free. It is doubtful, however, that anyone could survive the attempt. One burger can feed a whole family for just $8.00. People from all over the world have stopped for a burger, and you should, too. Another great thing about Sioux Sundries is that it is a true general store. Merchandise includes everything from canned goods to greeting cards, personal-hygiene products, toys, jewelry, dishes and cutlery, baking pans, towels, and cleaning products. Items made by local ladies, such as crocheted dolls and hand-embroidered pillowcases, are also sold here. Hours are Monday through Friday, 7:00 A.M. to 5:30 P.M.; and Saturday, 7:00 A.M. to 7:00 P.M. The telephone number is (308) 668–2577.

When you look at Sioux County on a state map, you'll see lots of boxes filled with what look like little green dots in the northern tier of the county. This is the 95,000-acre *Oglala National Grasslands,* a veritable ocean of prairie administered by the U.S. Forest Service. The area is great

A Bellyful of Scenic Wonder

You ou must, without fail, take a drive through **Sowbelly Canyon.** If you could visit only one place in Nebraska, this is the place to go. All the adjectives in the world cannot describe the sheer, jaw-dropping beauty of this canyon, so I won't even try. You decide for yourself which words best describe it. Take your time, relax, enjoy the view. Pull off the road when you can, because you will want to firmly fix the view in your memory.

The canyon was dubbed Sowbelly when some soldiers were trapped there by unhappy Native Americans. The soldiers ran out of food, and when they were rescued they were fed dry salt bacon, or sowbelly, which probably seemed downright tasty.

You won't find Sowbelly Canyon on a state map, so pay attention. If you're coming from the east on Highway 20, turn north at Hillside Service in **Harrison** and watch for signs. If you see signs for Coffee Park, that means you're on the right road. When traveling from the south on Highway 29, go straight through town (the highway ends at Harrison), then watch for Hillside Service and the SOWBELLY CANYON sign. Or you can go 3 miles east of Harrison on Highway 20 and turn north on Pants Butte Road. If all else fails, ask someone in Harrison how to get there. For more information call (308) 668–2466.

for hiking, wildlife viewing, photography—and great for the soul. The grasslands begin approximately 15 miles north of Harrison on an unpaved road. It is open year-round, and admission is free. A request: If you find a fossil bit, leave it there, and please don't pick any wildflowers. Leave the place as you found it for future generations. The phone number is (308) 432–4475, and the Web address is www.fs.fed.us/r2/nebraska.

A lovely 24-mile drive on the high plains of Sioux County, south of Harrison on Highway 29 (or 34 miles north of Mitchell), will bring you to **Agate Fossil Beds National Monument.** Start your visit at the visitors center. It has exhibits on the now-extinct animal life of nineteen million years ago, whose fossilized remains are part of a permanent diorama. Other exhibits feature the current plant and animal life of the region. Fossils were first discovered by Capt. James Cook on the land in 1878. Cook was a colorful character who counted many people as friends; among them was his close friend Chief Red Cloud, who gave him many beautiful handmade items. Many of these items are on display in the Cook Collection. This display, beautifully curated, is honestly one of the nicest Native American collections I've ever seen. There's a piece of pipestone that Crazy Horse had on his person when he was killed. A 2-mile trail leads to the Fossil Hills, which was the site of the early 1900s excavations. Another trail, the 1-mile Daimonelix Trail, will take you past some "devil's corkscrews," or preserved burrows of an ancient beaver called the paleocaster. If you take a hike, watch for rattlesnakes (yes, it's true, but they often want to avoid you just as much as you want to avoid them) and take water with you. There are sheltered picnic areas near the visitors center, where you can gaze for miles at the scenery. The monument is open daily, year-round except Christmas, New Year's Day, and Thanksgiving. Hours from Memorial Day to Labor Day are 8:00 A.M. to 6:00 P.M. The trails are

Buffalo Bill and the Cheyenne

*W*arbonnet Battlefield, *in northern Sioux County, was the site of an 1876 skirmish between the Fifth Calvary, with Buffalo Bill Cody serving as chief scout, and a group of 800 Cheyennes, mostly women and children, who were fleeing the Red Cloud Agency. This battle took place not long after the Battle of* Little Big Horn, where Custer got what he so justly deserved. At Warbonnet, Buffalo Bill fought a duel with Yellow Hair, sometimes referred to as Yellow Hand. Buffalo Bill killed and scalped Yellow Hair, whereupon he is said to have held the scalp aloft triumphantly and declared, "The first scalp for Custer."

open from dawn to dusk. Fees are $2.00 per person, $5.00 per car, or a $15.00 annual pass. The telephone number is (308) 668–2211. The Web site is www.nps.gov/agfo/.

Box Butte County

Alliance, with a population of nearly 10,000, is the largest community in Box Butte County. In fact, it's one of only two communities in the county. A must-see attraction near Alliance is **Carhenge,** a wonderfully whimsical re-creation of Stonehenge—but instead of giant stones, it's made out of old cars. One imagines that the builders of Stonehenge would be pleased by this modern-day version. It's been featured in several magazine stories and on *Good Morning America* and the *Today* show; it was the answer to a *Jeopardy* question, and it graces the cover of Steely Dan's *Greatest Hits.* There's a summer solstice gathering each year when a new sculpture, made, of course, of car parts, is installed on the grounds. (My favorite one is of a giant fish.) It's open year-round and admission is free, but do leave a donation. Carhenge is 2½ miles north of Alliance on Highway 87. Call (308) 762–1520 or (308) 762–4954 for more information. The Web address is www.carhenge.com.

What do a bordello, a Chinese laundry, a mortuary, and a bootlegger's cabin have in common? They are just a few of the buildings at *Dobby*

A Cemetery with a View

I found myself softly weeping at the remote **Montrose** church cemetery, and I'll never know if it's because of the stories I extrapolated from the headstones or the achingly beautiful view. From the hilltop I could see across a broad expanse of valley to a row of buttes, soft in the spring sunshine. Maybe my tears were triggered by the clusters of tiny, deep-purple irises, or maybe because I had been watching my sister die for several months. The cemetery served as a reminder of what I was about to lose, which was unbearably overwhelming.

I do not remember the names and dates on the headstones, and maybe that's just as well. However, I do remember a headstone with a relief of a man, Beloved Father and Son, seated on his horse with that same glorious view etched in the background. I remember headstones for babies and a headstone for a young woman, unmarried and childless; I wondered about her life. Moist-eyed, I drove away, sad and happy at the same time. Sad for all the lives, now extinguished, represented on that windswept hilltop. Happy for all the love in those lives.

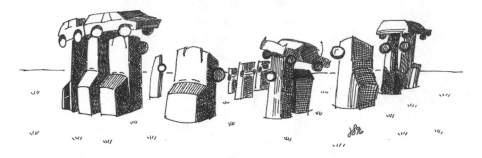

Carhenge

Lee's Frontier Town in Alliance, at 320 East Twenty-fifth Street, just east of Box Butte Avenue. A local resident named Dobby Lee has been preserving buildings and gathering artifacts for years in an effort to create his frontier village. And he has done a nice job. (Although, to be honest, it has been suggested I should take it out of this book. To that I say, *you* try to create and maintain an entire village by yourself, with your own time and money, and see what it looks like. Me, I have a hard time maintaining my one little house.) Other buildings include a general store and meat market, a post office, a saloon, a blacksmith shop, an original home of a black homesteader, and more. All the structures have antique furnishings, tools, and appliances. Weather permitting, summer hours are from 10:00 A.M. to 6:00 P.M., and winter hours are from 10:00 A.M. to dusk. The village is closed Monday, most major holidays, and in December. Admission is free, but donations are accepted. To verify the hours, call ahead at (308) 762–4321.

The *Sallows Arboretum and Conservatory* is a good place to learn about western Nebraska's indigenous plants and also those not indigenous. The greenhouse measures 1,800 square feet, and a conservatory houses forty different types of tropical and subtropical plants that are not typical to western Nebraska. An arboretum has sixty-four types of woody plants that will thrive in the local climate. Besides seeing lots of colorful plants, you can learn ways to landscape your yard to conserve energy, supply shade, and reduce wind velocity. In this part of the country, the matter of reducing wind velocity is important. There's an old story that a turn-of-the-twentieth-century traveler, remarking on the wind, asked if it always blew that way. He was told, "No, sometimes it blows real hard." The arboretum and conservatory are in Central Park, at Eleventh and Niobrara Streets. Visiting hours are Monday through Friday, 7:00 A.M. to 4:30 P.M. Admission is free. If you want more information, call the Alliance Chamber of Commerce at (308) 762–7422.

PLACES TO STAY IN THE PINE RIDGE

(ALL AREA CODES ARE 308)

CHADRON
Olde Main Street Inn,
115 Main Street,
432–3380,
www.chadron.com/
oldemain

GORDON
B&B Bunkhouse (one
cottage on a working
cattle ranch,
open March through
October),
282–0679

Horse Thief Cave Ranch
(private building on
2,000 acres),
282–1017,
www.nabb1.com/
gor1017.htm

HARRISON
Sowbelly Canyon B&B
Hideaway (partially earth-
sheltered home 5 miles
north of Harrison,
open year-round "if the
roads are passable"),
668–2537

HEMINGFORD
Hansen's Homestead
B&B,
rural,
487–3805

MERRIMAN
Twisted Pine Ranch B&B
(log cabin and
one-room addition,
open March through
October),
684–3482

PLACES TO EAT IN THE PINE RIDGE

(ALL AREA CODES ARE 308)

ALLIANCE
Bistro on the Butte
(California cuisine),
508 Box Butte Avenue,
762–2101

Martin's Family Restaurant
(Mexican),
1307 West Third Street,
762–8548

CHADRON
Angela's Eatery (Mexican),
251 Main Street,
432–5500

China House (Chinese),
1240 West Highway 20,
432–4080

Giovanni's
(Greek and Italian),
239 Main Street,
432–8397

Olde Main Street Inn
(American),
115 Main Street,
432–3380

GORDON
Italian Inn (Italian),
220 North Main Street,
282–0247

HARRISON
Sioux Sundries
(giant burgers),
downtown,
668–2577

HEMINGFORD
Carol's Cafe (country
cookin'; try the stuffed
potatoes),
downtown,
487–4322

HELPFUL PINE RIDGE WEB SITES

PANHANDLE AREA DEVELOPMENT DISTRICT
www.westnebraska.com

ALLIANCE
chamber.prema
online.com

CHADRON
www.chadron.com

GORDON
www.gordonchamber.com

Highways to History

hen you're in the Panhandle of Nebraska, you'll be reminded again and again of the many historic trails that crossed the region. The Oregon Trail, the Mormon Trail, the Sidney-Deadwood Trail, the Pony Express, and stagecoach routes all had major roles in the development of the area and of the Old West. Several excellent museums will show you how the West was won, and numerous historical markers dot the Panhandle like porcupine quills. The Panhandle is also dotted with recreation areas and wildlife refuges, where you can enjoy the great outdoors in uncrowded settings.

Scotts Bluff County

our miles west of Morrill on Highway 26, you'll come to a historical marker. This marker will tell you about the 1851 *Horse Creek Treaty* and the largest gathering of Native Americans in history. More than 10,000 people, representing the tribes of the Sioux, Blackfeet, Crow, Assiniboin, Mandan, Gros Ventre, Arikara, Cheyenne, and Arapahoe, assembled near the North Platte River and Horse Creek to sign the first Treaty of Fort Laramie. The treaty's purpose was to ensure the safe passage of westward-bound pioneers and to end intertribal warfare; however, the treaty was broken by the United States almost immediately after it was signed. While imagining the land covered for miles in all directions with Native Americans camped in unprecedented numbers, one wonders how history might be different if the thousands of Indians there had decided to fight instead of sign that treaty.

If you continue southwest from *Mitchell* on Highway 26, you'll come to the communities of *Scottsbluff* and *Gering.* The most outstanding attraction in the area is *Scotts Bluff National Monument,* which is 3 miles west of Gering on Highway 92. Scotts Bluff was a famous landmark along the Oregon Trail. The Sioux name for this geologic formation meant "the hill that is hard to go around." You'll soon see why this is an appropriate name. Scotts Bluff got its current name from Hiram

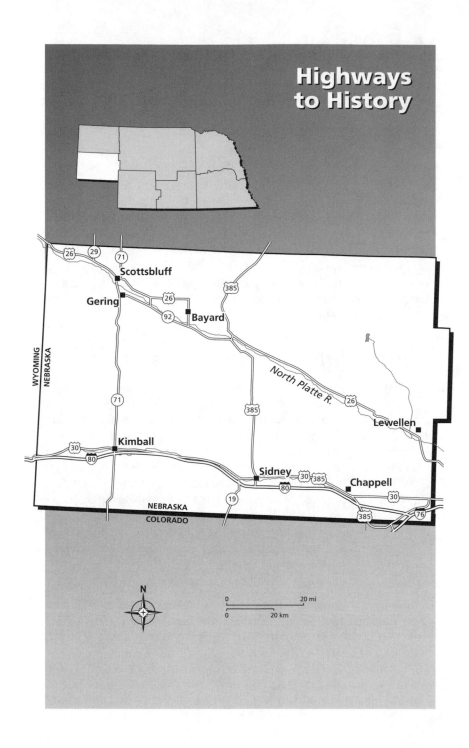

Highways
to History

Scottsbluff

Gering

Bayard

WYOMING
NEBRASKA

North Platte R.

Lewellen

Kimball

Sidney

Chappell

NEBRASKA
COLORADO

N

0   20 mi
0   20 km

HIGHWAYS TO HISTORY

Scott, a fur trader who was abandoned by his expedition and whose remains were found in the area the following spring. Several theories exist about where he died (near the river or at the base of the bluff), why he died (Indian attack, broken leg, or illness), and when he died (1828 or 1829). Although there are mysteries about the demise of the unfortunate Hiram Scott, there is no mystery why you should see the place named after him.

The visitors center has fascinating displays about the Oregon Trail, and wagon ruts are still visible. You can drive to the top of the bluff on Summit Road for a spectacular 100-mile view, or you can hike to the top on trails. There's also a bike trail, but it doesn't go all the way to the top. Summer hours are 8:00 A.M. to 7:00 P.M. daily. From Labor Day weekend through Memorial Day, the hours are 8:00 A.M. to 5:00 P.M. daily. Admission is free, but donations are accepted. For more information call (308) 436–4340 or visit the Web site at www.nps. gov/scbl.

Author's Favorite Attractions in the Panhandle
(All area codes are 308)

Barn Anew B&B,
170549 County Road L,
Scottsbluff, 632–8647

Cabela's, north of Interstate 80 at the junction of 385, exit 59, Sidney, 254–7889

Chimney Rock National Historic Site, 1 mile south of the junction of Highways 92 and 26, Bayard, 586–2581

Oregon Trail Wagon Train, 2 miles south, 1 mile west of Bayard, 586–1850

Scotts Bluff National Monument, 3 miles west on Highway 92, Gering, 436–4340

Wildcat Hills Nature Center, 10 miles south on Highway 71, Gering, 436–3777 or 436–3394

Not far from the monument is the *Farm and Ranch Museum,* at 2930 M Street in Gering. This little museum has a lot of old equipment that was used for planting and harvesting crops in the region. They have an 1831 reaper that, I was told, is probably the oldest reaper in existence. There's also an 1863 hay baler that could, with lightning speed, crank out seventy-two bales of hay a day. (Modern balers can produce up to 2,500 bales in the same amount of time.) You can see plows, corn pickers, drills, grinding equipment, tractors, corn shellers, threshing machines, and a giant steam engine used to power the equipment. All the equipment is donated, and all the enthusiastic staff are volunteers. This sweet little museum is free and open May through September, Monday through Saturday, 10:00 A.M. to 5:00 P.M.; and Sunday, 1:00 to 5:00 P.M. Open October through April by appointment. Call (308) 436–1989. The Web site is www.farmandranchmuseum.com/.

From the Farm and Ranch Museum, go take a hike at the *Wildcat Hills State Recreation Area,* 7 miles south on Highway 71. This picturesque, 935-acre setting with rugged buttes and pine-covered canyons has walking trails, stone shelters with fireplaces, picnic tables, and water and toilets for your convenience. Camping is also available. The

Nature Center, dedicated in 1995, has great displays on the flora and fauna of the region, plus raptor displays and murals. It also has a bee colony that you can view from inside the Nature Center. (Don't worry—you can see them, but they can't get near you.) There also is a large aquarium with some fat fish; visiting children often catch grasshoppers outside and come in to feed the fish. It's pretty fun to watch the fish leap up out of the tank for this tasty treat. A park permit is required. The trails are open year-round, and the Nature Center is open daily in the summer and Monday through Friday in the winter, from 8:00 A.M. to 4:30 P.M. The telephone number is (308) 436–3777 or (308) 436–3394. The Web address is www.ngpc.state.ne.us/parks.

The *Wildlife World at the Wyo-Braska Museum* in Gering, housed in a charming old railroad depot at 950 U Street, has more than 300 mounted animals. More than 200 species from six continents are displayed in a creative and interesting fashion. Two of the most popular displays are a lion bringing down a Cape buffalo and a lioness chasing a zebra. (These displays make you appreciate your superior position in the food chain.) You'll see a replica of the largest land animal that ever roamed the earth, the Baluchithere, which is 19 feet tall and 30 feet long. The museum is open May 1 through October 1, Monday through Saturday from 9:00 A.M. to 5:00 P.M.; from October 2 through April 30, it's open Tuesday through Saturday from 10:00 A.M. to 4:00 P.M. Admission is $3.50 for adults, $3.00 for seniors, and $1.00 for students; children age five or younger visit free. For more information call (308) 436–7104.

Another nice little museum in Gering is the *North Platte Valley Museum* at Eleventh and J Streets. It's different from a lot of country museums in that it's not jammed to the rafters with so much stuff that you don't quite know where to look first. (Not that there's anything wrong with that, of course; it's just that this museum feels good.) It's spacious and airy and very nicely curated. They have areas decorated like old rooms of several kinds, and there is a log cabin site. You can spend quite a lot of time looking at items from the country's past. A recent renovation has allowed for room to display one of the nation's finest collections of Oregon Trail memorabilia. It's open from May through September, Monday through Saturday, 8:30 A.M. to 5:00 P.M.; and Sunday, 1:00 to 5:00 P.M. Admission is $3.00 for anyone age thirteen or older and 50 cents for children age twelve or younger. The phone number is (308) 436–5411. The Web address is www.npvm.org/.

The *Riverside Zoo* in Scottsbluff, the largest zoo in western Nebraska, is well worth a stop. There's a wonderful prairie-dog town with a viewing

AUTHOR'S FAVORITE ANNUAL EVENTS IN THE PANHANDLE
(Call ahead to verify dates; all area codes are 308)

Banner County Museum Annual Open Event,
Harrisburg, early June, 436–5074

Sugar Valley (Car) Rally,
Scottsbluff/Gering, early June, 632–2133

Wheat King Festival,
Chappell, early June, 874–2800

Ash Hollow Pageant,
Lewellen, mid-June, 778–5548

Cabela's Sidewalk Sale,
Sidney, late July, 254–7889

Farmers Day Off Golf Tournament,
Kimball, mid-August, 235–3782

Greek Festival,
Bridgeport, mid-August, 262–1825

Chimney Rock Pioneer Days,
Bayard, mid-September, 586–2830

Octoberfest, Sidney, early October, 254–2932

Old West Weekend, Scottsbluff/Gering, mid-October, 635–8479

bubble so that you can see the animals close up without disturbing them. The beautifully maintained zoo has more than 300 exotic and regional animals in natural-looking habitats. There's an unusual sculpture, carved from a single cottonwood tree, with likenesses of about fifteen animals, including a giraffe, an alligator, an elephant, a chimpanzee, a fish, and a bird. Kids like it and will also enjoy lots of hands-on activities. A recent $2.5 million renovation granted accreditation as well as facilities to house such endangered species as vultures, chimpanzees, red pandas, spider monkeys, Bengal tigers, and Persian leopards. The zoo is 1 mile west of Broadway Street on the South Beltline Highway. From May 1 through September 30, the hours are 9:30 A.M. to 4:30 P.M. daily. Winter hours are 10:30 A.M. to 3:30 P.M. daily. There's an admission fee. Call (308) 630–6236 for details. The Web address is www.riversidezoo.org/.

Two miles east of Scottsbluff on Highway 26 you'll see a historical marker for **Rebecca Winters' Grave.** Rebecca was with a group of Mormon families traveling to New Zion to flee religious persecution. She died near here on August 15, 1852, one of thousands who died on the Mormon Trail. For years her grave was tended to by the Norman DeMott family, who farmsteaded there beginning in 1887. Her grave was relocated when the land was sold to the railroad. Stop and appreciate the price too many people have paid for intolerance.

A great place to stay in the area is the **Barn Anew B&B.** At a time when most people would be looking forward to retirement, Dick and Jane Snell bought a huge, crumbling old barn, without a roof but with about forty years' worth of debris. They spent the next two years turning it into a beautiful B&B, which opened for guests in 1998. Ask Jane to see the before-and-after pictures; the difference is astonishing. The four rooms are comfy and have private baths, and there's a sitting room upstairs with a balcony view of the back of Scotts Bluff National Monument. The landscaped grounds are courtesy of Dick, and there's a little antiques store behind the house—do you need a hog oiler? There is one other permanent resident besides Dick and Jane, and it isn't Spot or Puff. Baby, a cat, found his way to the Snells after being abandoned out in the country. He now has the run of the house and amuses guests by carrying around his stuffed mouse toy. Prices range from $75 to $90 per night. The phone number is (308) 632–8647, and the Web address is www.prairieweb.com/barnanew. Directions are complicated, so call and ask.

South of Gering, in Carter Canyon, is the **Robidoux Trading Post,** a beautifully reconstructed trading post made from one-hundred-year-old, hand-hewn logs. The post is 1 mile south of Gering on Highway 71 and then 8 miles west on Robidoux Road. Tours can be arranged by calling (308) 436–6886. Or follow the marked 23-mile Robidoux Loop, which begins here. Admission to the post is free, and it's open year-round. Nearby are **Robidoux Pass, Blacksmith Shop,** and **Pioneer Grave Sites** in the Wildcat Hills. The graves of Oregon Trail travelers can be found here, including the grave of twenty-six-year-old F. Dunn, who died of cholera on June 13, 1849. Robidoux Pass is 1 mile south of Gering on Highway 71 and 8 miles west on Robidoux Road. For more information about Robidoux Trading Post and other sites, call (308) 436–6886.

A lighthouse in a landlocked state? Yes, and you'll find it just 5 miles east and 4 miles north of Scottsbluff at **Lake Minitare State Recreation Area.** The recreation area is accessible on a paved road from either Highway 26 or Nebraska 71. The 55-foot-tall lighthouse was built in 1937–39 entirely of native stone by the Veterans Conservation Corps. It's the only structure of its kind in the state and one of only seven inland lighthouses in the country. It is open to the public, and you can climb to the top. If it's locked, you can get the key from the Game and Parks office, just down the road, and besides, you'll need to stop there to get a park permit. As the brochure says, "Those with the stamina to climb its winding staircase to the top will have a spectacular view of the lake and the river valley." But you really don't need all that much stamina; it's an easy climb. If you've ever climbed a winding staircase in one of those massive cathedral towers in Europe or to the top of the Statue of Liberty, this is a piece of cake in comparison. The lighthouse is open from April through mid-September, Friday through Sunday, 9:00 A.M. to 8:00 P.M. Call (308) 783–2911 for more information. The Web address is www.ngpc.state.ne.us/parks.

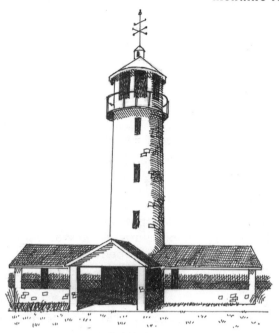

Lake Minitare State Recreation Area Lighthouse

Morrill County

*J*ust inside Morrill County you'll discover the ***Oregon Trail Wagon Train,*** south and west of ***Bayard*** on Oregon Trail Road off Highway 92. Make arrangements beforehand to enjoy a covered-wagon train right on the Oregon Trail. The drivers can tell you a lot about Oregon Trail history. You can choose either a three-hour ride or a one- to four-day trek. The owners make the experience as authentic as it can possibly get, with chickens in crates tied to the wagons (for fresh eggs) and cooking over a fire. The owner will ask you if you want an authentic ride or a fun ride. If you want an authentic ride, you're jokingly advised to get out and walk because that is how most people traveled on the Oregon Trail; the precious space in wagons was taken up by items that would be used to start a new life in the West. Reservations can be made for a chuck-wagon cookout that will leave you full to bursting, followed by a rousing campfire sing-along. Camping and canoeing are available. For reservations call (308) 586–1850.

You are now within sight of the ***Chimney Rock National Historic Site and Visitors Center.*** Chimney Rock, a compelling spire jutting up into the landscape, was visible for days to Oregon Trail travelers and was mentioned in journals and diaries more often than any other natural formation along the entire stretch of the trail. It still amazes and delights travelers. The visitors center has wonderful displays about the geology and history of Chimney Rock (including the fact that the Native American name for it was Elk Penis). There's a great interactive exhibit for children, with a miniature wagon and miniature supplies with the number of pounds marked on them. Children can learn the realities of pulling up stakes and traveling west by deciding what to take on the trek. If they pack too much, the oxen or horses can't pull the weight. Do they pack tools at the cost of leaving behind treasured heirlooms? Do they pack supplies to start a new crop, or do they pack a lot of extra food in case wild game is not in abundance? This is a great museum, and you should stop. Admission is only $3.00 for adults age eighteen or older; young people age seventeen or younger visit free. The visitors center is open from 9:00 A.M. to 6:00 P.M. daily in the summer; closing time is an hour earlier in the winter. It is closed on Veteran's Day, Thanksgiving, Christmas, and New Year's Day. The telephone number is (308) 586–2581. The Web address is www.nebraskahistory.org/sites/rock.

Two more impressive natural formations along the Oregon and Mormon Trails are **Courthouse** and **Jail Rocks.** The site, open year-round and free, is just a few miles south of Bridgeport on Highway 88.

Banner and Kimball Counties

The **Banner County Historical Museum and Village** in **Harrisburg,** at 200 North Pennsylvania, has a fascinating collection of historic structures, particularly when you consider that Harrisburg is the only town in the county and that the population of the entire county, according to the latest census, is 819. Consider further that Harrisburg isn't even located on any highway; it's 4 miles west of Highway 71 on S4A. Seventy-five people live in Harrisburg, and they are justifiably proud of their museum. It has a sod house, a church, a log schoolhouse, and a log house. The buildings are full of well-designed displays, and the museum building has a spectacular collection that ranges from Native American to pioneer artifacts. The official hours at the museum are Memorial Day through Labor Day, Sunday afternoons from 2:00 to 5:00 P.M., but if you call (308) 436–4514, there's a recording with a list of volunteers who will let you in. Please leave a donation. Harrisburg, and the museum, are well worth a stop. There's no restaurant in town, but the

Prairie Inn, south on Highway 71, has a reputation for great hamburgers. According to one resident, the food is "good and there's plenty of it!"

The highest point in Nebraska is in the extreme southwestern corner of **Kimball County. Panorama Point** is 5,424 feet above sea level. On clear days you see almost forever—to the Rocky Mountains to the southwest, anyway. You can drive to Panorama Point from Interstate 80 by getting off at the Bushnell exit, and then going 10 miles south, 4 west, 1 south, 2 west, and 2 more miles south to the entrance road. There's a guest book to sign, and if you "rappel" the marker, the Chamber of Commerce in Kimball will happily send you a certificate. Better yet, stop in at the chamber office, at 119 East Second Street in Kimball, to get the certificate. And make a stop at **Gotte Park** to see a 100-foot Titan missile on display. The park is on Highway 30, 9 blocks east of Highway 71.

Kimball is in the middle of the largest complex of intercontinental ballistic missiles (ICBMs) in the world (more than 200 are deep in the earth in the immediate tristate area), and the town has declared itself to be Missile Center, USA. Also deep in the earth is oil; more than 1,400 oil wells have been discovered since 1951 in Kimball County. The brochure for Kimball says it's "a place where strangers are greeted on the streets, and senior citizens are respected." Don't you just love that? There's also a brochure with "101 Ways to Satisfy Your Curiosity About the Kimball Area." Some suggestions: Pet a goat; go bowling; tee off on the highest tee box in Nebraska; play cards or dominoes at a corner bar; pull weeds at the arboretum; watch the wheat grow; hug a tree; plant a tree; or climb a tree. Ya just gotta love it.

Cheyenne County

Prepare yourself for a wonderful experience at **Cabela's,** near Sidney. Self-proclaimed to be the world's foremost outfitter for fishing, hunting, and outdoor gear, Cabela's is located just outside Sidney at the junction of Interstate 80 and Highway 385. You can't miss it; it rises out of the hill next to the interstate like something out of a fairy tale. There's also a fairy tale–like story about the early days of this business. It all began more than thirty years ago, when Jim and Dick Cabela of Sidney placed a classified newspaper ad that offered twelve hand-tied flies for only $1.00. Their business is now one of the country's largest mail-order outfits. At present this massive building, measuring 62,000 square feet, contains more than 60,000 products. There's not nearly enough space on this page to tell you everything you can buy, but trust me, if it concerns the outdoors, you'll find it here. You'll also find more

GERING

*North Platte
Valley Museum,*
Tenth and J Streets;
436–5411

MORRILL

*Fillingham & Sons Exotic
Animal Farm,* east of
Morrill on Highway 26,
Ostriches, emus, rheas,
llamas, Z-donks, camels,
fallow deer, reindeer, yak,
muntjack deer, zebus,
miniature horses and
donkeys, and oryx. Seasonal
weekend tours, Saturday 9:00
A.M. and 10:30 P.M.; Sunday
1:00 and 3:00 P.M. Picnic area
and pond. Call 623–1164 for
reservations.

OSH KOSH

*Crescent Lake National
Wildlife Refuge,*
28 miles north of Osh Kosh
between Highways 26 and 2;
772–4566. Forty thousand
acres serves as a nesting site
and stopover for migratory
birds.

SCOTTSBLUFF

*Mexican American
Historical Museum,*
in Pioneer Park at the corner
of Broadway and Twenty-
seventh; 635–1044. Call
ahead; sometimes the building is not open during posted
hours.

than 500 wildlife mounts from around the world, an 8,000-gallon aquarium with Nebraska game fish, an art gallery, a gun library, a bargain center with first-quality merchandise no longer listed in the catalog, a great gift selection, and even a snack area with smoked meats—including buffalo, ham, and turkey—and roast-beef sandwiches. Outside you'll see the amazing *Royal Challenge,* a larger-than-life bronze sculpture of two battling elks (it's so big it had to be shipped in on two separate trucks). You should stop here even if you think you already have every outdoor item you'll ever need. Cabela's is open Monday through Saturday from 8:00 A.M. to 8:00 P.M. and Sunday from 10:00 A.M. to 6:00 P.M. The telephone number is (308) 254–7889; the Web address is www.cabelas.com.

You'd never know by looking that the pleasant town of **Sidney,** just north of Interstate 80 at Highways 385, 30, and 19, used to have the reputation as the roughest town in the West. When gold was discovered in the Black Hills of South Dakota, the town became a jumping-off place for miscreants and reprobates of all sorts. (Historical note: Gold was discovered when a group led by Gen. George Custer violated an agreement with the Sioux that kept whites from even setting foot in the sacred Black Hills. Some scientists in the group discovered gold, and whoops—there goes another promise.) At one time there were twenty-five bars in just a 1-block area. Citizens became inured to the frequent murders, and railway passengers were advised not to disembark in Sidney because thieves had grown bold enough to smack them on the head and throw them, robbed and dazed, back onto the train. Historians recount an episode when a dance was interrupted briefly by one murder, the unfortunate victim of which was dumped in a corner. The dancing went on, briefly interrupted by another murder and another corpse in the corner. It wasn't until a trio of corpses graced the corner that the dance came to an end.

Visitors today can quite safely venture into Sidney to see the interesting *Fort Sidney Complex,* on Sixth Avenue and Jackson Street. The original mission of the fort was to protect the people who were building the Union Pacific railroad from Indian attack and later to protect travelers against "depredations" inflicted by these same "hostiles." Soldiers at the fort also played a role at Wounded Knee. The complex has a powder house, officers' quarters, and the restored post commander's home. The museum is open daily May 1 to Labor Day from 9:00 to 11:00 A.M. and 1:00 to 3:00 P.M. The post commander's house is open daily Memorial Day to Labor Day the same hours as the museum. There is no admission fee. The telephone number is (308) 254–2150.

A final note about Sidney: Calamity Jane is said to have given birth to an illegitimate child in Sidney. Others say this was impossible; she was really a man, or at least a hermaphrodite. Who knows?

Garden County

In the southeast corner of Garden County, you'll find *Ash Hollow State Historical Park* 3 miles southeast of *Lewellen* on Highway 26. This park is chock-full of history: fossils, the cave where prehistoric native peoples lived, Oregon and Mormon Trail lore, and Plains Indians conflicts. The Bidwell-Bartelson group was the first emigrant train to pass through Ash Hollow in 1841. Early emigrants commented on the sweet spring water and abundant ash trees that made the hollow so attractive to them. Before too many years passed the water became less sweet, due to the sheer number of people and animals who used the stream, and the ash trees all but disappeared as they were used for fuel. The grave of the newlywed, eighteen-year-old Rachael Patterson, a victim of cholera, is in the cemetery, just ½ mile west of the park entrance on Highway 26. It's sure to strike an emotional chord as well as make you ponder how easy life is for modern travelers. The visitors/interpretive center is located on a bluff that offers a marvelous view, and it has displays that describe the history of the area and a video you can watch, too. The gift shop has great books about western and plains history. Take the time to have a picnic in the wooded grassy area at the entrance to the park, or walk down to see the cave where native people lived. Do make a stop at Windlass Hill, just 2½ miles south of the park entrance on Highway 26, which can be easily hiked. Try to imagine the difficulty of coming down this steep hill with a team of animals and a fully loaded wagon. For the emigrant trains, this tricky descent was the first frightening inkling of the increasingly arduous journey ahead into mountains, after the relatively flat crossing of the plains along the Platte River valley. The visitors center is open 9:00 A.M. to 5:00 P.M. daily from Memorial Day to Labor Day. A park permit is required. The telephone number is (308) 778–5651. The Web address is www.ngpc.state.ne.us/parks/hollow.html.

If something seems fishy to you about now, it's because you're getting close to the **Coldwater Fish Farm** by **Lisco** on Highway 26. The Fish Farm annually hatches and grows approximately 750,000 pounds of freshwater trout and salmon. That comes out to about 1.5 million fish and a taste treat for you. Stop by and buy packages of the fresh, frozen, or smoked delicacies ranging in price from $4.00 to $9.50 per pound. Or pick up a catalog and order from home. Check out the Web site at www.cohofish.com or call (308) 772–3474. To get there, go south through Lisco over a one-lane bridge, go left at the Y in the road, and it is about a mile farther, on the south side.

The Meat of the Matter

A few years ago in Acapulco I made the mistake of seeing my first, and last, bullfight. To my everlasting surprise I became an immediate, and involuntary, vegetarian. My choices at restaurants and delis have become quite limited, because for some reason it's not only red meat I can't eat, but pork, chicken, and fish, as well. Perhaps someday I will be able to sink these once-carnivorous teeth back into a juicy Nebraska steak or pan-fried chicken breast, but for now I'm into salads, soups, and pastas. I cannot begin to tell you how bothersome this is nor describe people's incredulous reaction to vegetarians. When I asked a very pleasant young man standing behind the counter of the deli/meat department of the grocery store in Lewellen to make me a big cheese and veggie sandwich (hey, I was hungry), he said, "You don't eat meat?" I shook my head meekly and steeled myself for the inevitable "Why not?" or at least the equally inevitable

look combining curiosity and surprise—and caution. Caution because nobody wants to get lectured by some knee-jerk, fuzzy-thinking, pea-brained, whining, liberal malcontent. So there we were, for one brief moment, him behind the meat counter not wanting to be lectured to, me in front of the meat counter not wanting to explain a deeply personal, painful reaction to that bullfight. Then he smiled and said, "I don't eat much meat either after looking at it and working with it all day." I smiled back. We smiled at each other for a few seconds and I left, happy, with my cheese and veggie sandwich.

Now, you may be asking yourself, what does any of this have to do with Nebraska? It has everything to do with Nebraska. Everything from tolerance, hospitality to strangers, to the very reasonably priced sandwich, which would have cost about four times as much in Los Angeles or New York.

Deuel County

Amystery exists in the public library in a small town called **Chappell** on the high plains of western Nebraska, just north of Interstate 80 at exit 85. The **Chappell Memorial Art Gallery,** in the Chappell Public Library at 289 Babcock Street, has three pieces of art that might be original works by Rembrandt. Or they might not. The staff is quick to point out that the works have never been verified as authentic and they don't really know the genesis of this story, but everyone can agree that the work is important. The pieces are called *Self Portrait, Rembrandt and Saskai,* and *Dr. Faustus and the Magic Disk.* If you're an art historian, or in a position to shed some light on the mystery, stop in for a look at the works. The works of art, and the money to build the library itself, were donated by Mrs. John Chappell, a wealthy resident of Chicago's Lake Shore Drive. Mrs. Chappell seems to have adopted the town of Chappell after seeing it from the train and appreciating the fact that they shared a name. The library also has a collection of pieces by a local artist named Aaron Pyle, who studied with Thomas Hart Benton. While you're in the library, you should also see the **Bergstrom Rock and Gem Collection,** which features fossil finds from the area such as mastodon teeth and bones, plus a collection of polished gems and stones. The library is open

America's Main Street

*I*f you've traveled on Highway 30 across Nebraska at all, you should be aware that you were on the historic **Lincoln Highway.** *The Lincoln Highway, which stretches all the way across the state from Omaha on the eastern border to Bushnell through to the Wyoming border, was the first transcontinental highway across the United States. It all started in 1903, when a Vermont physician accepted a fifty-dollar bet to prove he could drive a car from San Francisco to New York.*

Sixty-five days later the physician, his mechanic, and a stray bulldog named Bud arrived in New York. In 1913 the Lincoln Highway, named after President Lincoln, came into being. For many years the route across the country seemed to be comprised either of mud or choking dust. One early traveler called the Lincoln Highway "a red line connecting all the worst mudholes in the country," but now the paved route provides a delightful alternative to Interstate 80. If you're interested in learning more, there's a great book entitled *The Lincoln Highway,* Main Street Across America *by Drake Hokanson. There's also a book by Gregory Franzwa,* Nebraska's Lincoln Highway, *that includes incredibly detailed maps and the history of the Lincoln Highway in Nebraska.*

Death from the Sky

During World War II, Nebraska was home to eleven air bases that filled the sky with air crews in training. On June 7, 1944, fifteen B-24 bombers departed from the Lincoln Army air base en route to the West Coast. One of the planes caught fire during a thunderstorm and began circling **Chappell** *in* **Deuel County.** *It exploded 2 miles southeast, resulting in the tragic loss of life for all ten men on board. A historical marker in Chappell commemorates their supreme sacrifice.*

Tuesday through Thursday from 1:00 to 7:00 P.M. and Saturday from 2:00 to 5:00 P.M. There's no admission fee. The telephone number is (308) 874–2626.

Big Springs, just north of Interstate 80 on Highway 138 in Deuel County, was the site of the first and greatest robbery of a Union Pacific train. In 1877, Sam Bass and five other men stopped the UP express train, stole $60,000 in gold and currency, and relieved passengers of their cash and watches. They split up the booty and went their separate ways. Legend has it that some of the twenty-dollar gold pieces are still buried in the area. After the robbery, Bass returned home to Texas and resumed his larcenous ways. He formed a new gang and robbed four trains within a few months. Bass was generous with his ill-gotten gains and earned the nickname of the "Robin Hood of Texas." He was mortally wounded and died on his twenty-seventh birthday, ten months after the Big Springs

Not What You'd Call a Fair Fight

A historical marker near **Lewellen** tells the story of the **Battle of Blue Water.** In 1855, a 600-man expedition commanded by Col. William Harney attacked and destroyed a small Lakota village 3 miles north of Blue Creek. The fight, if you want to call it a fight, is also known as the Battle of Ash Hollow, or more appropriately, the Harney Massacre. Eighty-six Native Americans were killed, seventy women and children were captured, and all the tepees were looted and burned. The battle was fought to avenge the death of Lt. John Gratton, which took place near Fort Laramie the year before. Lieutenant Gratton went into a large Indian encampment where a lot of hungry Native Americans had taken, and eaten, a cow belonging to passing Mormons. Retribution was called for. Lieutenant Gratton, an interpreter, and three others tried to arrest High Forehead, the man responsible for the theft. Chief Conquering Bear offered a mule to take the place of the cow. No dice. More talking led nowhere, and Lieutenant Gratton decided a show of force was in order. In fact, it was his last order. He ordered the infantry to fire a volley, and this resulted in a skirmish in which he and all of his party were killed. The marker is located in a turn-off area $1/2$ mile west of Blue Creek, west of Lewellen, and 3 miles from the battle site.

robbery. His headstone in Round Rock, Texas, was erected by his grieving sister and reads: A BRAVE MAN REPOSES IN DEATH HERE. WHY WAS HE NOT TRUE? Indeed, why was he not? In the park at the south edge of downtown, near the railroad tracks, you'll find a charming, chain-sawed wooden folk-art memorial to this historic Big Springs event. When I first saw this tableau it consisted of several small train cars that were dwarfed by the oversize figure of Sam Bass, wearing a painted red bandana over his face. The sense of scale of Mr. Bass in comparison to the train made the scene seem a little like Godzilla attacking a Japanese village. A couple of years later the Sam Bass figure had been moved just far enough away that the Godzilla-like effect was diminished.

Drive up the main street through Big Springs and look for the *Phelps Hotel B&B,* on the east side on a downtown street. In the area next to it you'll see Buffalo Joe's five buffalo, all made of barbed wire.

PLACES TO STAY IN
THE PANHANDLE

(ALL AREA CODES ARE 308)

BAYARD
Flying Bee
Beefmaster Ranch (4,000-acre working cattle ranch. Cabin, RV or tent camping. Bring your hiking boots and even your horse.),
Route 2,
783–2885 or
(888) 534–2341,
www.flyingbee-ranch.com

BIG SPRINGS
Phelps Hotel B&B,
401 Pine,
889–3246

SCOTTSBLUFF
Barn Anew B&B,
rural Scottsbluff,
632–8647,
www.prairieweb.com/
barnanew

PLACES TO EAT IN
THE PANHANDLE

(ALL AREA CODES ARE 308)

BAYARD
Corner Cafe (American; giant cinnamon rolls), downtown,
586–1666

GERING
Bush's Gaslight Lounge,
Scottsbluff/Gering
Highway,
632–7315

LEWELLEN
Vic's Steakhouse and
Lounge,
junction of
Highways 26 and 92,
778–5801

MELBETA
Maggie's Main Street Grill & Bar (steaks, fish, seafood), Highway 92 southeast of Gering,
783–1727

MORRILL
La Pazadita (Mexican),
113 Webster Street,
247–2473

SCOTTSBLUFF
Cheers Smokehouse Grill,
1605 Avenue A,
635–6969

El Charrito (Mexican),
802 Twenty-first Avenue,
632–3534

Rosita's (Mexican),
1205 East Overland,
632–2429

Taco Town (Mexican),
1007 West Twenty-
seventh Street,
635–3776

SIDNEY
Dude's Steakhouse,
2126 Illinois,
254–9080

**HELPFUL PANHANDLE
WEB SITES**

**PANHANDLE AREA
DEVELOPMENT DISTRICT**
www.westnebraska.com

GERING
www.geringtourism.org

KIMBALL
www.ci.kimball.ne.us

SCOTTSBLUFF
www.visitscottsbluff.com

SIDNEY
www.sidney-nebraska.com

Prairie Lakes Country

J ust as the name implies, the Prairie Lakes Country in southwest Nebraska has several large lakes, recreation areas, reservoirs, and rivers, which makes it ideal for outdoor activities. The Texas-Ogallala Cattle Trail passed through the area, and history books are full of accounts of cowboy fights and stampedes. Native Americans favored the area for its hunting, and it is still renowned for that same purpose. This is the land that marks the transition from the tallgrass prairie in the eastern part of the state to the short-grass prairie of the high plains. The land is surprisingly hilly, with tree-covered canyons hidden along river banks deep in the hills. If you're traveling on Highway 30, remember that the old Lincoln Highway—the first transcontinental road, which led from New York to San Francisco—followed the same approximate path, beginning in 1913. Only then the road was mostly dirt trails and a bit more challenging. Present-day travelers will find museums, restaurants, guest ranches, and golf courses that early travelers could not have even imagined.

Keith County

O *gallala,* just north of Interstate 80, on the terminus of the Texas-Ogallala Trail, was at one time a wild town that earned a well-deserved reputation as the Gomorrah of the Plains. It all began when cowboys finished the cattle drive after weeks on the trail and went looking for diversions. They got paid, got a bath, got a drink (or several), and often got taken by gamblers and businesswomen of easy virtue who were eager to separate the freshly bathed and freshly paid cowboys from their money. The ten-year span between 1875 and 1885 saw Ogallala change from a quiet small town to one where gunshots were not uncommon. One odd fight erupted when a drunken cowboy from somewhere in the South took curious and great umbrage at two cowboys from the North when they ordered baked beans as part of their meal. He kicked over his chair and howled, "Just what I thought! A couple of Yankee bean-eaters." The

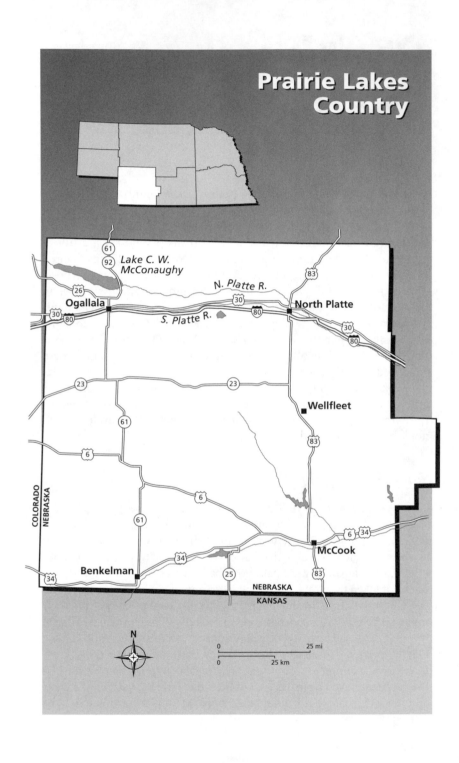

Prairie Lakes Country

61
92 Lake C. W.
McConaughy

83

N. Platte R.

26

Ogallala

30

North Platte

30
80

30
80

S. Platte R.

23
23

Wellfleet

61

83

6

COLORADO
NEBRASKA

6

61

6 34

McCook

34

Benkelman

25

83

NEBRASKA

34

KANSAS

N

0   25 mi

0   25 km

unarmed Yankees ran for their guns, followed more slowly by the alcohol-impaired but decidedly armed Southerner. As happened in the Civil War, the North won. The Yankees were never arrested because it was clearly a case of self-defense, as anyone who heard the soon-to-be-dead man bellowing about what he was going to do to them when he caught up with them could testify. Ogallala is considerably safer now, and you can order whatever you want at a restaurant without risking the ire of fellow diners.

The frontier history of Ogallala is encapsulated at **Front Street,** at 519 East First Street. It looks from the outside like an Old West street from the 1800s. Inside is the Livery Barn Cafe, with a western-style menu, a saloon, a free cowboy museum, and a gift shop. In the summer months you should see the family-oriented **Crystal Palace Revue,** with dancers, singers, and musicians, and which can only be described as western burlesque. It is Nebraska's oldest summer theater production, and you might be tempted to think that some of the jokes are equally as old. But it's great fun, and you'll enjoy it. There's a nightly shoot-out at 7:15 P.M.; the revue starts at 7:30 P.M. The stage show is $4.35 for adults and $2.75 for children five through twelve years of age. The telephone number is (308) 284–6000.

Also connected to the Front Street attractions is the **Kenfield Petrified Wood Gallery** at 525 East First Street. Here you'll find art and music boxes and wall hangings made from teensy-weensy pieces of petrified wood about the size of a baby's fingernail. They're truly amazing. Do take the time to look at the wonderful collection of rocks and stones. Admission fees are: families, $7.00; adults, $2.50; students, $1.00; seniors and tour groups, $2.00. It is open in the summer from Monday through Saturday from 9:00 A.M. to 7:00 P.M. and Sunday 1:00 to 5:00 P.M. Winter hours are Monday through Saturday from noon to 6:00 P.M. The phone number is (308) 284–9996 or (800) 658–4390.

Boot Hill is where both residents and visiting rowdies were buried. A man named Rattlesnake Worley was killed over a $9.00 poker bet. The

---

AUTHOR'S FAVORITE ATTRACTIONS IN SOUTHWEST NEBRASKA

(All area codes are 308)

Dancing Leaf Earth Lodge and Cultural Learning Center,
6100 East Opal Springs Road, Wellfleet, 963–4233

Fort Cody Trading Post,
intersection of Interstate 80 and Highway 83, northeast corner, North Platte, 532–8081

Junie Mae's Roadhouse Barbeque,
1815 Highway 61, Keystone, 726–2626

Kenfield Petrified Wood Gallery,
525 East First Street, at the Front Street attraction, 284–9996 or (800) 658–4390

La Casita Mexican Restaurant,
1911 East Fourth Street, North Platte, 534–8077

Ole's Big Game Steakhouse and Lounge,
east side on the main block of downtown Paxton, 239–4500

Pool Hall,
downtown Eustis, 486–3801

most famous and tragic resident of Boot Hill, however, was Mrs. Lillie Miller, who died along with her baby during childbirth in 1861. She and the baby were exhumed twenty-five years later in order to be moved to a new cemetery. Mrs. Miller, by all accounts, was perfectly preserved and perfectly petrified. Her remains were so heavy that a crane was required to move her. (The baby was neither preserved nor petrified.) Boot Hill is on West Tenth Street, 4 blocks west of Highway 61. It's always open, and it's free.

The new *Bayside Golf Course* outside of Ogallala is located on Lake McConaughy, a huge reservoir with 100 miles of beaches. Its eighteen holes are tough, but five tee boxes allow those of all skill levels to enjoy the

Pork Out

*Y*ou know you've hit restaurant pay dirt when the sign has a winged pig on it. **Junie Mae's Roadhouse Barbeque,** *on* **Lake McConaughy** *at 1815 Highway 61 near Ogallala, lived up to my every expectation foodwise. And a bonus: It's owned and managed by two of the nicest and most talented people on the planet. But more about them later. The food is all exquisitely fresh. They make their own sausage (Cajun and Italian), and they bake their own buns. They smoke or grill all the meat (chicken, ribs, brisket) in a steamy-hot back room. They have fresh salads, the kind you can't find in a lot of little towns in western Nebraska, and they have a potato salad that's to die for. (On the menu it doesn't list the ingredients, but it does say that if they told you what was in it they'd have to kill you.) A good selection of sandwiches and simple but yummy desserts are also offered. Postmeal selections include espresso, cappuccino, latte, and mocha; again, items not routinely found in a small-town restaurant. Last, but far from least, there's a beer garden.*

The people responsible for all of this are Paula Crofuett and her husband, Tom Barkes. Paula is a local girl who met Tom in Texas in the 1970s, and they commenced a lifelong adventure. They most recently lived in Seattle, where they made their living designing and making seats and seat cushions for boats. Paula wanted to be closer to her family, and Tom wanted to be close to a big body of water. It just so happened that her family and Lake McConaughy, the largest body of water between the Great Lakes and Salt Lake, were all in the same place. They opened Junie Mae's (it's named after Paula's mother) in May 1997, and the rest is history. When they aren't cooking they manage to find time to develop their other skills. Paula is a talented potter; her work is in the restaurant. Tom is a wizard welder; his workshop is full of gates, curtain rods, candle holders, and table legs. Oh, they also find time to ride around on their great big motorcycles. Go to Junie Mae's; the food is good, and so are the people.

course with its great view of the lake. When you've had your fill of golf, you can go boating or fishing, or play tennis or volleyball. It's a public course, but do make reservations. To get to Bayside from Ogallala, take Highway 61 north to Highway 26 west. Go west approximately 7 miles to Lakeview Road (watch for a billboard), then turn right and go north 3 miles to Lakeview Road West. Turn left here and go another 2 miles to the entrance. The phone numer is (308) 284–2800.

If you didn't know much about Nebraska and found yourself inexplicably transported to the white-sand beach of **Lake McConaughy,** you'd likely not guess correctly as to your location. This enormous lake, or Big Mac, as it is referred to locally, is 22 miles long and nearly 4 miles wide, and it has 100 miles of shoreline. It is very popular for fishing, and several fish caught here hold state records. In some parts the lake is 142 feet deep, so who knows what lunkers are lurking in the depths? Boating, Jet-Skiing, scuba diving, camping, and sailboarding are also popular. One of the nation's largest sailboarding competitions, the Toucan Open, is held here each September. Resorts, marinas, and restaurants are sprinkled around the lake, mostly on the north side. The July 2000 issue of *Trailer Boat* magazine included Lake McConaughy as a boating and camping "hotspot." Lake Ogallala is a smaller lake, just below Kingsley Dam to the east; it has camping and fishing, too. The dam is 3.1 miles long, 162 feet tall, and is the second-largest hydraulic-filled dam in the world. The dam complex supplies hydroelectric power and irrigation water for nearly half a million acres. Free tours of the plant are offered daily from Memorial Day to Labor Day, with the exception of Monday and Tuesday. Big Mac is 7 miles north of Ogallala on Highway 61. Call (308) 284–8800 for additional information. A new visitors center/water interpretive center opened at the lake in 2002. Learn about the lake, where its waters come from, and where its waters go.

If you're in a hurry for a bed, you might check out the **Super 8** in Ogallala. A housekeeper there named Ida Doggett won the 1999 national bed-making championship. She can make a bed to specifications in two minutes, thirty-one seconds. (Her husband makes his own side of the bed at home.) She entered the contest because she wanted to win the car that was being offered as first prize. Before winning this competition Mrs. Doggett had never been on an airplane, but she's been on some since to be interviewed on national talk shows such as David Letterman's *Late Show.*

East of Ogallala is **Paxton,** located 1 mile north of Interstate 80, where you'll find **Ole's Big Game Steakhouse and Lounge** on the main street through town. Before stepping into Ole's you might imagine you'd be stepping into the old west. Instead, you'll be back in the era of Hemingway, when men traveled around the world shooting things. In these politically correct times, this is not considered such a cool thing to do, but you'll still be fascinated by more than 200 mounted trophies from every continent, which were personally bagged by former owner Ole Herstedt. When you walk in, there's a behemoth polar bear in a glass case. Everywhere you look there are animals and birds and animal parts. It might be disconcerting at first, but just chill; the animals have been dead for a long time, and they were bagged in a different time, when the world had a vastly different mind-set. Ole's has one of the world's largest privately owned trophy collections. The bar has a colorful history; it opened its doors in 1933, one minute after Prohibition ended. The steak house serves Nebraska grain-fed beef, plus chicken and fish. The food isn't fancy, but it is very good, and there's a lot of it. If you're wondering what Rocky Mountain oysters are, here's a clue: The menu says that you'll go nuts over these. The hours are Monday through Saturday, 8:00 A.M. to 1:00 A.M.; and Sunday, 7:00 A.M. to 10:00 P.M. Food is served from 8:00 A.M. to 10:00 P.M. daily. Call (308) 239–4500.

You should change your watch now. Mountain time changes to central time (and vice versa depending on which way you're headed) between Paxton and Sutherland.

Lincoln County

North Platte, just north of Interstate 80, was home to one of the most famous characters from the Old West. In 1886, William "Buffalo Bill" Cody built an eighteen-room French Second Empire mansion and started his Scouts Rest Ranch northwest of town after he retired from a series of quintessentially "Western" jobs. He was a trail hand at the age of nine, a trapper, a Pony Express rider (he was fourteen years old when he responded to ads seeking riders who were young, wiry, and preferably orphaned), a buffalo hunter (he supplied meat for crews who were building the Kansas Pacific Railroad, and he shot 4,280 buffalo in eight months), and chief of scouts for the Fifth Cavalry during the Plains Indian wars. In 1882, the town fathers of North Platte asked him to plan something special for the Fourth of July. What he came up with ultimately brought him out of retirement and into international fame. He devised what is now thought to be the first organized rodeo in the nation, and it led to the inception of the wildly popular Buffalo Bill's Wild West Show and Congress of Rough Riders of the World, which performed to capacity crowds internationally. His home and ranch are now part of the ***Buffalo Bill Scouts Rest Ranch State Historical Park and***

State Recreation Area. The house is full of mementos and articles from his life (check out the beaded buckskins), and the huge barn has films from the Wild West Show and even some footage shot by Thomas Edison. Horseback rides on the adjacent 233-acre recreation area are available. The grounds, house, and barn are open daily from Memorial Day weekend through Labor Day weekend from 10:00 A.M. to 8:00 P.M. In April, May, September, and October the house and barn are open Monday through Friday from 9:00 A.M. to 5:00 P.M. A park permit is required. To find the ranch, take Highway 83 north to Highway 30; then go west 2 miles and follow the signs. Basically, follow Front Street for 6 miles through North Platte. The telephone number is (308) 535–8035.

You must stop at *Fort Cody Trading Post,* at the intersection of Interstate 80 and Highway 83, if you have any intention of buying souvenirs for yourself or for anyone. This place has the most eclectic collection of gifts, from astonishingly tacky trinkets to exquisite jewelry, pottery, western clothing, antiques, and leather goods. There are a zillion too many things to mention, but at one end of the taste spectrum is an ink pen that has Buffalo Bill dropping his trousers to reveal red-and-white polka-dot drawers, and at the other end is an incredibly beautiful Navajo silver story bracelet. The store has a very good selection of western literature, both fact and fiction. Do not fail to see the miniature, hand-carved, mechanized Buffalo Bill Wild West Show, with all its 20,000 pieces. Watch for the teensy woman with the cigarette being flicked out of her mouth by a whip. Words fail me as to how wonderful this place is—just see it. Don't miss the two-headed stuffed calf. Did you notice the raging battle up top on the outside of the building between the cavalry and the Indians? The front facade of the building looks like a stockaded fort with mannequins dressed and posed as cavalry soldiers and Indians. This place has something for everyone. The trading post is open from 8:00 A.M. to 9:00 P.M. most of the year; winter hours

---

AUTHOR'S FAVORITE ANNUAL EVENTS IN SOUTHWEST NEBRASKA
(Call ahead to verify dates; all area codes are 308)

Buffalo Commons Storytelling Festival,
McCook, late May, 345–3200

Nebraskaland Days
(PRCA rodeo and nationally known country music performers),
North Platte, mid-June, 532–7939

Nebraskaland Days Mexican Fiesta,
North Platte, mid-June, 532–4156

Wurst Tag Days,
Eustis, mid-June, 486–3611

Kites and Castles,
Ogallala, late July, 284–3584

Chase County Fair
(nationally known performers), Imperial, mid-August, 882–2118

Indian Summer Rendezvous,
Ogallala, mid-September, 284–4066

Toucan Open
(sailboarding), Ogallala, mid-September, 284–4066

Heritage Days,
McCook, late September, 345–3200

are 9:00 A.M. to 6:30 P.M. Closed for major holidays. The telephone number is (308) 532–8081.

Have you ever wondered how it's decided to put which train cars on which trains and how to route them to where they need to go? If so, you're in luck, because you can see it happening at the *Union Pacific Bailey Yard,* in North Platte. It's the largest rail-car classification complex in the world, and about 130 trains are put together on a daily basis. Visitors are welcome to enjoy the panoramic view, day or night, from the observation platform. A short audio description of what you're seeing is available. Admission is free, and the facility is open year-round. To get there, take exit 170 from the Interstate to Highway 83 (Dewey Street) through downtown and connect with Front Street behind the ALCO store, where you go west; then watch for directional signs to Bailey Yard. For more information contact the North Platte Chamber of Commerce at (308) 532–4966. Plans are in the works to build a giant Golden Spike observation tower. Come back and visit again during the year 2004.

What can you say about a Mexican restaurant with an Elvis/Kennedys/ Pope decorating theme? You can simply say it's one of the very best Mexican restaurants in the state. *La Casita,* also in North Platte, serves authentic homemade Mexican food that is not even remotely akin to fast-food fare. If you're very hungry, get the all-you-can-eat combo plate for $7.65. The chicken mole dinner, which out-of-town visitors have been known to load up in coolers and take home for those who are mole-deprived, is $5.75. The beef fajita dinner is only $7.75. Chile relleno dinners are $6.25. All dinners come with beans and rice. Six different kinds of enchiladas are $2.25 each. Bean burritos start at $1.75. An appetizer popular with Generation Xers, the Hippie Dip, is gravy made from cheese and chile verde. Yum. Well, you get the idea by now—the food is quite reasonably priced and more than reasonably good. La Casita has been keeping diners fat and happy for about forty years. The address is 1911 East Fourth Street, and the hours are Tuesday through Saturday, 11:00 A.M. to 10:00 P.M.; and Sunday, 11:00 A.M. to 9:00 P.M. The telephone number is (308) 534–8077.

Near North Platte on a high hill is *Sioux Lookout.* Except it's no longer topped by a large statue of a Native American, with his hand raised to his eyes, looking for settlers. The statue was damaged by vandals; it was removed, restored, and placed on the courthouse grounds in North Platte. Visitors used to be able to climb the hill to see the statue, but they can still see for themselves what a great view the Sioux had in scouting for interlopers. If you want to see the hill, take Highway 83 south of North Platte and turn east on State Farm Road. Follow the blacktop road, which curves twice to the right and once to the left. A marker on the south indicates the spot.

Glenn Miller of big band fame lived in North Platte as a toddler for one year. His family then moved 30 miles north to *Tryon,* where they lived for five years. Today the stretch of highway linking the towns is designated as the *Glenn Miller Memorial Highway.* Take a little "Moonlight Serenade" drive yourself on Highway 97; the Memorial Highway begins at the intersection of Highway 83 north of town.

To see the *Dancing Leaf Earth Lodge Cultural Learning Center,* take Highway 83 about a half hour south of North Platte to *Wellfleet.* Owners Les and Jan Hosick have built an authentic earth lodge in which guests can spend the night. You can also learn about the lives of early native people from the very knowledgeable couple. The site is on an old Boy Scout camp. The view is spectacular, as is the hiking. Tours are offered a couple times a day during the summer hours. There's a nice gift shop, too. This is well worth a stop. It's at 6100 East Opal Springs Road, 2 miles east of Wellfleet. Reservations are necessary; call (308) 963–4233.

Two miles south of Interstate 80's Maxwell exit 190 is the beautiful, twenty-acre *Fort McPherson National Cemetery,* Nebraska's only national cemetery. More than 6,700 veterans, and some spouses, who served in conflicts from the Civil War to Vietnam, are buried under row after row of white marble monuments. The utter silence and peaceful beauty combine to make a visit here a moving experience. Gates are open from dawn to dusk. Fort McPherson was established in 1863 to protect the Oregon Trail travelers. No buildings remain, but you can see a statue of a cavalryman about a mile east of the cemetery, which is situated on the former parade grounds. The cemetery was established in 1873. Call (308) 582–4433 for more information.

You can also take exit 190 to *Valley View Guest Ranch.* This is a working ranch where you can go on trail rides through some exceptionally pretty, cedar-studded canyons. The horses are gentle. The campground has a couple of housekeeping cabins, or you can camp. The cabins are $35 for two people. There are shower and laundry facilities, a grocery and a gift store, hayrack rides, and a playground. And you can stick your face into a cutout of a cowboy or cowgirl and get your picture taken. Valley View is open from April 15 through November 1; if the weather is fine, it stays open longer. To get there from Interstate 80, go south 2 miles to Fort McPherson National Cemetery, then ½ mile west and ½ mile south. The telephone number is (308) 582–4320.

Chase and Hayes Counties

Champion Mill State Historical Park, in *Chase County* near *Champion,* is a water-powered flour and grain mill now operated by the Nebraska Game and Parks Commission. It began operation in 1889 and remained open until 1968, when it was the last operating mill in the state. Visitors can see how grain was milled in this cavernous place and can even purchase small bags of pancake flour, whole-wheat flour, corn meal, and bran. The tranquil millpond is a state recreation area, with primitive camping and day-use facilities. It is open from Memorial Day weekend through Labor Day weekend from 9:00 A.M. to 5:00 P.M. The interpretative facility is open daily from Memorial Day weekend through Labor Day weekend from 9:00 A.M. to 5:00 P.M. and on Saturday from 9:00 A.M. to 5:00 P.M. and Sunday from 1:00 to 5:00 P.M. in May and September. A park permit is required. Costs are $14.00 annually and $2.50 daily. The park is located on the edge of Champion, which is southwest of Imperial on S15A. For more information call (308) 882–5860.

The *Camp Duke Alexis Recreation Area,* near *Hayes Center* in *Hayes County,* was at one time an important hunting ground for Native Americans. It's hard to keep a good thing secret, and, lo and behold, the next thing you know you have royalty coming to pay a call. In 1872 Grand Duke Alexis, the twenty-two-year-old brother of the Russian czar, came to see the "wild life of America, including the Indians." The hunting party was led by Buffalo Bill Cody and was hosted by Gen. Philip Sheridan. Buffalo Bill persuaded a band of Indians, led by Sioux chief Spotted Tail, who were camped nearby, to give a presentation of Indian-style hunting, followed by a war dance. The whole event was declared a brilliant success, and the Duke was pleased to shoot several buffalo. The recreation area, located 8 miles east and north of Hayes Center, covers 140 acres and includes a well-stocked, one-hundred-acre lake.

Frontier County

Frontier County has some of the reasons that southwest Nebraska is known as the Prairie Lakes Country. Strung along the southern tier of the county are *Harry Strunk Lake* and the *Medicine Creek* and *Red Willow Reservoirs.* These lakes offer a variety of activities and amenities: Among them are both primitive and modern camping, boat ramps, fish-cleaning stations (there are abundant fish to catch), hunting in season, picnic tables, grills, shelters, modern rest rooms, and vault toilets. For information on these and other southwest reservoirs, call (308) 345–1472.

In the northeast corner of Frontier County is **Eustis,** on Highway 23. By all means make a stop at the **Pool Hall** for some excellent Mexican food (the smothered burrito with green chili attracts diners from miles around), imported and microbrewery beers, and the locally famous margarita. In addition to the burritos (which will set you back only about $5.00), the menu includes chicken fajitas, enchiladas, rellenos, tacos, and taco salad. If you don't feel like Mexican food, try the steak, smoked pork chops, shrimp, burgers, or Polish sausage. The sweet-corn-nuggets appetizer alone will make your trip to Nebraska worth-while. Not only is the Pool Hall a great place for food and drink, but the

Oh, Give Me a Home Where the Buffalo Roam

*B*ecause Grand Duke Alexis of Russia came all the way to southwest Nebraska in 1873 to shoot buffalo, this chapter is an appropriate place to talk more about them. Two hundred years ago, fifty million buffalo roamed the Great Plains. In 1804, Lewis and Clark reported "seeing buffalo in such magnitudes that we cannot exagger-ate in saying in a single glance we saw 3,000 of them." Early fur traders who crossed the Plains told stories about seeing so many buffalo they blackened a valley stretching 10 miles across. That's a lot of buffalo. Initially, buffalo were hunted by whites in the millions for their hides and their tongues; their bodies were left to rot where they fell. Later, buffalo were killed to feed crews building the transcontinental railroad. A skilled shooter could kill 300 buffalo in one day. Killing buffalo also became a political tool. If you want to get rid of pesky Indians on the Plains, get rid of their primary food source. In 1876, Rep. James Throckmorton of Texas said, "I believe it would be a great step forward in the civilization of the Indians and the preservation of peace on the border if there was not a buffalo in existence." Ultimately, the Army paid hide hunters to hasten the demise of the buffalo. By the early 1900s, fewer than 500 remained. Five hundred! About 250 wild buffalo remained at Yellowstone National Park, and the rest were mostly scat-tered in private collections. Today there are 250,000 buffalo flourishing in their native lands, many of them on ranches in Nebraska and surrounding states. Ted Turner owns a buffalo ranch in Cherry County. The buffalo there, and on Turner's other ranches, come to more than 12,000 in number and are part of the largest private herd in the world. He's been quoted as saying, "I guess I've gone buffalo batty." Good for him. Oh, for you scientific purists out there, yes, I know *there are no* buffalo *in North America. There are* bison *in North America, as you have snootily thought to yourself this whole time.*

OTHER ATTRACTIONS WORTH SEEING IN SOUTHWEST NEBRASKA

KEYSTONE

Keystone Church was built in 1908 to serve both Protestants and Catholics. Neither group could afford to build their own church, so they pooled their money to build one church with a Catholic altar at one end and a Protestant one at the other. Pews with reversible, hinged backs were installed so they could be switched to whatever group had the floor. The church was used until 1949. It's located on McGinely Street. For tours call (308) 726–2281 or (308) 726–2312.

NORTH PLATTE

In Cody Park there is an amazingly intricate, life-size bronze **statue of Buffalo Bill,** donated by a British sculptor in 1998. The park is on Buffalo Bill Avenue; (800) 955–4528.

Lincoln County Historical Museum and Western Heritage Village is a great little museum. Don't miss the display on the North Platte Canteen, commemorating the effort of the people of North Platte, who met every single World War II troop train and offered the men a treat of candy, cigarettes, cookies, or cake. The museum is at 2403 North Buffalo Avenue; (308) 534–5640.

OGALLALA

Mansion on the Hill is a huge brick house built by a local man in 1887 for his bride-to-be from the East Coast, who decided to forget the whole thing. She never showed up, and the heartbroken groom-to-be never lived in the house; in fact, nobody ever did. The house is on the corner of Tenth and North Spruce Streets, 4 blocks west of Boot Hill. For more information call the Ogallala Chamber of Commerce at (800) 658–4390 or (308) 284–4066.

decor is curiously wonderful and defies categorization. Like a lot of small-town eateries, the tin ceiling is original, and the exposed brick walls and wooden floor add a warm and homey touch. But the similarity ends there. The decor is a combination of *Mayberry RFD* and Planet Hollywood. The walls are covered with everything from jazz posters to photographs of gypsies who came to town at the turn of the twentieth century. Pink-flamingo figurines are colorful accents behind the large oak bar and are scattered throughout the room. The Pool Hall opens at 11:00 A.M. and serves food throughout the day and into the night. Even though the kitchen may be closed after 10:00 P.M. Monday through Thursday and 11:00 P.M. on Friday, Saturday, and Sunday (the kitchen closes a little earlier during winter), do hang out and have some brews. It's the only restaurant in town, and you'll find it downtown. The telephone number is (308) 486–3801.

Dundy and Hitchcock Counties

I n 1867 Lt. Col. George Custer camped in *Dundy County* on the Republican River, just south of the present-day community of *Benkelman,* at Highways 61 and 34. His camp was attacked one June dawn by a group of Cheyenne and Sioux, led by Pawnee Killer. Apparently the leader was better at killing Pawnee than cavalrymen; a sentry was wounded while an unscathed Custer, according to historical records, "rushed from his tent into the midst of the battle." He lived a while longer before meeting his death at the Battle of Little Big Horn. Benkelman's most famous citizen is Ward Bond, who is best known for his role as

For the Birds

*E*ach year some 200,000 cliff swallows fly 3,000 miles from wintering grounds in Argentina to nest in western Nebraska. They represent the largest concentration of cliff swallows in the world. The cliff swallow earned its name from the practice of building gourd-shaped mud nests on cliffs or canyon walls, but these birds also seem to like making their homes on the smooth concrete facing of bridges and culverts. Biologist Charles Brown, fondly referred to as Captain Swallow, and his wife, Mary, a research assistant, have studied the swallows for several years at the Cedar Point Biological Station near Ogallala. They've discovered some fascinating things about cliff swallows' behavior. Like humans, their behavior runs from generous cooperation to mean-spirited competition. They share information about where to find food, and they work together to drive off predators such as sparrow hawks and bull snakes. But, they steal from each other, they're aggressive, and, none of this mate-for-life stuff, they engage in frequent adultery. Females often lay their eggs in

another's nest, thereby getting the fun of messing around without the drudgery of raising the little buggers.

Both Keith and Garden Counties are known as hot birding spots. A viewing station at Lake Ogallala gives a great view of lots and lots of bald eagles. Paul Johnsgard, professor of life sciences at the University of Nebraska-Lincoln, has written that there are close to 310 bird species in the region. "It's the best place in the state and third-best in the country to go birding," Johnsgard is quoted as saying in the Keith County News. "It has the third-largest local list for any locality in the United States." The others are in Texas and Kansas, but you'll need to read about those in other books in the Off the Beaten Path® series.

A checklist of birds in the area is available at the Ogallala Chamber of Commerce; call (800) 658–4390. In addition, a sizable number of Sandhill Cranes gather at the west end of Lake McConaughy every late winter and early spring.

the wagon master in the TV series *Wagon Train*. The **Dundy County Museum,** at 522 Arapahoe Street, has twenty-six rooms jam-packed with historical items. The Doll Room alone contains close to 250 dolls. There's a soda fountain that serves malts, frosties, and sundaes. The museum is open Thursday in summer from 1:00 to 4:00 P.M. and on the first and third Sunday of each month. Call ahead for tours by appointment during the rest of the year. The phone number is (308) 423–2791.

Just east of **Trenton,** in **Hitchcock County,** is a monument and marker that commemorates the final battle between the Pawnee and Sioux tribes. In 1873 a band of 700 Pawnee (300 warriors and 400 women and children) on a buffalo hunt were surprised by a Sioux attack. The Pawnee were outnumbered, and as they fled along the Frenchman River toward the Republican River, they came to a narrow canyon, where the heaviest fighting occurred. Because the Pawnee were friendlier to the whites than the Sioux, soldiers from Fort McPherson were sent to help, but they arrived too late Twenty-first-century visitors are invited to the annual Massacre Canyon Pow-Wow, held on the first full weekend of August. Native Americans perform traditional dances. A rodeo, a wagon-train ride, and a barbecue provide additional fun. Pioneer burial grounds can be viewed. A visitors center is open from Memorial Day through Labor Day. Massacre Canyon is one hour south of Interstate 80, at the Sutherland exit off Highway 25, 5 miles north of Trenton.

West of Trenton on Highway 34 is **Stratton.** In 1859 newspaperman Horace Greeley, heeding his own advice to "Go west, young man," was westward-bound on a stagecoach to Denver. He stopped at a temporary station, housed in a tent at Stratton, and wrote, "I would match this station and its surroundings against any other scene on our continent for desolation." That just goes to show what kind of trained observer he was. This is some of the prettiest country in the state.

Red Willow County

*M*cCook, located at the junctions of Highways 83 and 6/34, has Nebraska's only structure designed by the famous architect Frank Lloyd Wright. This two-story frame and stucco Prairie-style house, at 602 Norris Street, was completed in 1908. Other structures similar to this one are in Chicago; LaGrange, Illinois; and South Bend, Indiana. The original appearance was altered a bit after a 1932 fire destroyed part of the veranda roof and it couldn't be determined how to rebuild it. New columns were added, which changed the proportion and location of the roof. World War II saw more changes, when the house was converted to apartments; additional changes came in 1960 when the house was used as a medical clinic. It is listed on the National Register of Historic Places, but it's a private home, so please respect the privacy of the owners.

It's Bean Wonderful

*B*esides a whole lot of cattle, hogs, corn, and wheat, Nebraska produces a bunch of beans. We're first in the nation in great northern bean production, third in pinto beans, sixth in dry edible beans, and seventh in soy beans. A lot of these beans are grown here in western Nebraska. In honor of that, and given the fact that I've become interested in veggie recipes, here's something from the Cookbook for Beans and Peas, *which is published in Nebraska:*

Black Bean Chili with Cilantro

4 c. cooked black beans

¼ c. dry sherry

1 T. olive oil

2 c. chopped onion

½ c. chopped celery

½ c. chopped carrot

½ c. chopped red bell pepper

1 can (14½ oz.) vegetable broth (or 2 c. water)

2 T. minced garlic (6 cloves)

1 c. chopped tomatoes

2 t. ground cumin

4 t. chili powder (or to taste)

½ t. dried oregano

¼ c. chopped fresh cilantro

2 T. honey

2 T. tomato paste

In a large, heavy pot, heat sherry and oil over medium heat and cook onions until soft but not browned. Add celery, carrot, and bell pepper; cook five minutes, stirring frequently. Add beans, broth, garlic, tomatoes, cumin, chili powder, oregano, cilantro, honey, and tomato paste; bring to a boil. Lower heat and simmer forty-five minutes to one hour, covered. Chili should be thick with most liquid absorbed. Serve garnished with onion, grated cheese, and a dollop of yogurt.

The Nebraska Bean Cookbook, *published by the Nebraska Dry Bean Growers Association, is another great little cookbook. There are even recipes for bean desserts like Pinto Bean Fudge and Pinto Pecan Pie. I swear this cookbook is like a love poem to beans. Page four lists fourteen things about beans that, if they were set to music, would make a helluva country song. Here's a sample, but I've rearranged them to suit my own purposes:*

Beans are beautiful.

Beans are exciting, versatile, and delicious.

Beans were once used for money.

Beans are tops in nutrition and low in cost.

We all know that Benjamin Franklin's curious nature led to his flying a kite in a lightning storm, which led, in turn, to him being credited with discovering electricity. What not many people know is that electricity was brought to many people in the country because of Nebraska senator George Norris. Most famous as the father of the Tennessee Valley Authority, Senator Norris was also instrumental in creating the Rural Electric Administration. He was a sponsor of a bill that abolished the lame-duck session of Congress and changed the date of the presidential inauguration. The creation of the unicameral (one-house) legislature, which is unique to Nebraska, is another of Senator Norris's achievements. So great were his accomplishments that the U.S. Senate named him among the five greatest senators in American history. The *Senator George Norris State Historic Site,* at 706 Norris Avenue in McCook, is now a branch museum of the Nebraska Historical Society. This unprepossessing home is filled with artifacts and items used by Senator and Mrs. Norris in their simple, daily lives. The home is open year-round: Tuesday to Saturday, 9:30 A.M. to noon and 1:00 to 5:00 P.M. It is closed Monday and on major holidays. The admission fee is $1.00 for adults; free for children accompanied by an adult. The telephone number is (308) 345–8484. McCook was also home to three Nebraska governors: Governor Ralph Brooks, who served for one year before dying in office in 1960; Governor Frank Morrison, who served from 1961 to 1967; and Governor Ben Nelson, who was elected in 1990 and reelected in 1994.

Heritage Hills Golf Course, at 6000 Clubhouse Drive on the west edge of McCook, has been rated as one of America's top one hundred public courses by *Golf Digest.* Its 270 acres offer Scottish-style golf on a course that incorporates the natural crests and canyons of the land rather than something bulldozed and tortured into something alien to the landscape. The brochure states that the unsuspecting golfer will find the "gaping jaws of fifty-three bunkers and sandtraps . . . prepared to snatch his ball if he chooses to attempt to cut the corner of our doglegs." Despite the challenges of snatched balls, the course is absolutely beautiful, with native prairie grasses and yucca plants. Also according to the brochure, a U.S.G.A. official said that Heritage Hills is among the fastest and best courses in an eight-state area. The eleventh hole is rated as one of the best eighteen holes in Nebraska. An eighteen-hole game is $27 and a nine-hole game is $16. Try to call a week in advance for a tee-off time. The telephone number is (308) 345–5032.

If you're sick of gas station coffee, stop in at the *Bieroc Cafe* at 312 Norris Avenue for a great cuppa joe and a gourmet sandwich. The telephone number is (308) 345–6500.

PLACES TO STAY IN SOUTHWEST NEBRASKA

(ALL AREA CODES ARE 308)

CAMBRIDGE
Cambridge B&B,
606 Parker Street,
697–3220

MADRID
Clown 'N Country,
rural,
326–4378

MCCOOK
Best Western Chief Motel,
612 West B Street,
345–3700

NORTH PLATTE
Knoll's Country Inn,
6132 West Range Road,
368–5634 or
(800) 337–4526

TRENTON
Blue Colonial B&B Inn,
rural,
276–2533 or
(888) 276–2533

Flying A Ranch B&B,
334–5574,
(800) 434–5574
(out of Nebraska)

PLACES TO EAT IN SOUTHWEST NEBRASKA

(ALL AREA CODES ARE 308)

BRULE
Mac's Trailside Inn
(American),
108 State Street,
287–2470

EUSTIS
Pool Hall (American,
Mexican),
112 East Railroad,
486–3801

KEYSTONE
Junie Mae's Roadhouse
Barbeque (deli, bakery,
espresso),
1815 Highway 61 (north of
Ogallala on the lake),
726–2626

MCCOOK
Bieroc Cafe (gourmet
sandwiches, espresso,
cappuccino, and latte;
Italian sodas),
312 Norris Avenue,
345–6500

PAXTON
Ole's Big Game Steakhouse
and Lounge,
downtown,
239–4500

HELPFUL SOUTHWEST NEBRASKA WEB SITES

BIG SPRINGS
www.ci.big-springs.ne.us

CAMBRIDGE
www.cambridgene.org

CHASE COUNTY
www.chasecounty.com

EUSTIS
www.ci.eustis.ne.us

MCCOOK
www.aboutmccook.com

NORTH PLATTE
www.northplatte-
tourism.com

OGALLALA
www.visitogallala.com

PAXTON
www.olesbiggame.com

Land of Cather and Cranes

South-central Nebraska is the land that inspired Pulitzer Prize winner Willa Cather to write: "There was nothing but land: not a country at all, but the material out of which countries are made." This is the land that draws the world's largest concentration of sandhill cranes; up to a half million birds come to the Platte River area in the late winter months. This is the land that saw the passing of immigrants on the Oregon Trail and the Mormon Trail, who watched as Pony Express riders raced across the lands. This is where Kool-Aid was created and liars with tall tales compete for honors. One-of-a-kind museums, historic forts, water recreation, a round barn, and memorabilia from Hollywood stars such as Henry Fonda and David Janssen await your visit to these prairie lands.

Sherman and Howard Counties

Sherman Reservoir, in northeast Sherman County, is popular with boaters, anglers, and campers. There are 65 miles of shoreline, and there is a surface area of nearly 3,000 acres. Drainage areas off the main reservoir provide bays and coves with outstanding fishing opportunities. Walleye fishing is good in the spring, largemouth bass and crappie are good from mid-spring to early summer, and summer brings bites from white bass and catfish. Recreation sites scattered around the reservoir have primitive camping, day-use facilities, drinking water, vault toilets, and shelters. Sherman Reservoir is a good place to get away from it all. It is 4 miles east and 1 mile north of Loup City from Highway 92. A park permit is required. A permit costs $14.00 annually or $2.50 daily. The telephone number is (308) 745–0230.

Here's an interesting historical fact: *Loup City,* near the Sherman Reservoir at the junction of Highways 58, 92, and 10 in Sherman County, was the site of a Depression-era farm strike led by the famous Communist organizer *Ella Reeve "Mother" Bloor.* On June 14, 1934, violence erupted when rumors spread that female poultry workers at

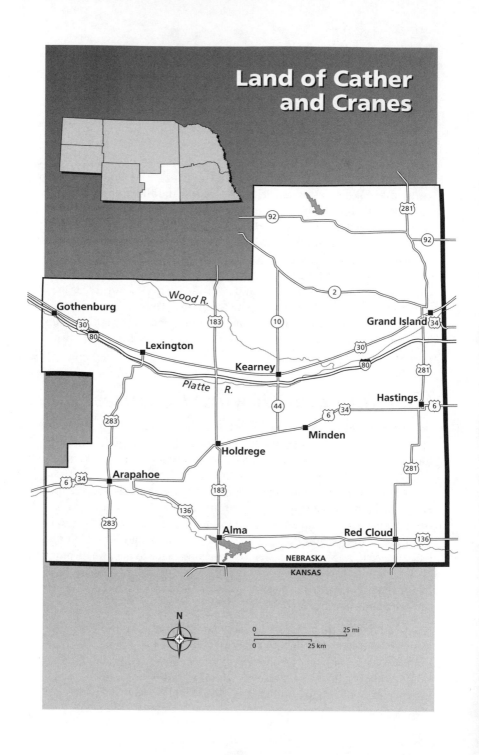

Land of Cather
and Cranes

92
281
92
Wood R.
2
Gothenburg
183
10
Grand Island 34
30
80
Lexington
30
Kearney
80
281
Platte R.
Hastings
283
44
6
6
34
Minden
Holdrege
6
34
Arapahoe
281
183
283
136
Alma
Red Cloud
136
NEBRASKA
KANSAS

N

0   25 mi
0   25 km

AUTHOR'S FAVORITE ATTRACTIONS IN SOUTH-CENTRAL NEBRASKA

Coney Island Cafe,
104 East Third Street,
Grand Island,
(308) 382–7155

Fort Kearney Museum,
131 South Central Avenue,
Kearney, (308) 234–5200

Harold Warp Pioneer
Village, junction of High-
ways 6, 34, and 10, Minden,
(308) 832–1181 or
(800) 445–4447

Hastings Museum and Lied
Superscreen Theater,
1330 North Burlington
Avenue, Hastings,
(402) 461–2399 or
(800) 508–4629

Stuhr Museum of the
Prairie Pioneer,
junction of Highways 34
and 281, Grand Island,
(308) 385–5316

Willa Cather's Home,
tours start from 326 North
Webster, Red Cloud,
(402) 746–2653

the Fairmont Creamery Plant might strike for higher wages. The Communist group and local supporters clashed with its local non-supporters. The resulting fines and jail sentences levied upon "Mother" Bloor and her group marked the end of this attempt to organize farmers and workers in Nebraska.

From Loup City take Highway 58 south 12 miles to *Rockville.* Stop in for a cold one and a meal at *Gin's Tavern.* They've been serving catfish for many years and lobster for fewer years. It's the lobsters that have transformed Rockville into the Lobster Capital of Nebraska. In the mid-1990s the Rasmussen brothers decided to order up a great big batch of lobsters for a special celebration. That event has become "Rockstock," and it draws nearly 3,500 people to feast on Maine lobster on the first Saturday in August. Not bad for a town of 122 people. Then everyone dances the night away at a lively street dance. The phone number at Gin's Tavern is (308) 372–7275.

In neighboring *Howard County* you'll find an attraction as old as the Altamira cave paintings in Spain, as ornate as an East Indian temple, as big as the Pentagon, and as mystifying as the giant Nazco designs in the Peruvian desert that are attributed to alien visitation. No wait, that's a lie, but you *will* find the self-proclaimed *National Liars Hall of Fame* at the *"Lille" Mermaid, Inc.* in *Dannebrog.* Dannebrog is at the junction of Highways 58 and 11. There is, among other things, a tribute to George Washington, who couldn't tell a lie, to Richard Nixon, who couldn't tell the truth, and to Lyndon Johnson, who couldn't tell the difference. The store also has Danish gifts, artwork, and hand-crafted items. The address is 106 South Mill Street, and the phone number is (308) 226–2222.

Northeast of Dannebrog, on Highways 92 and 281, is *St. Paul* and the best homemade pies this side of the Mississippi. Stop in at a little cafe called the *Sweet Shoppe* and sink your teeth into a slice of heaven. The fruit pies are quite delicious, but the very best are the sour-cream raisin and the coconut cream. And they only cost $1.00 per slice. Be sure to thank baker Alice for her magic ways with pies. By all means have a hearty meal, but leave room for pie! The hours are Monday through Friday from 6:00 A.M. to 4:00 P.M. and Saturday and Sunday from 6:30 A.M. to 4:00 P.M. The telephone number is (308) 754–4900.

For a grand slam, check out the *Museum of Nebraska Baseball Greats,* at 619 Howard Avenue, which has displays on Nebraska's five inductees to the Baseball Hall of Fame. These include "Wahoo" Sam Crawford, Bob "Hoot" Gibson, Grover Cleveland Alexander, Arthur "Dazzy" Vance, and Don Richie Ashurn. Open all year Monday through Saturday 10:00 A.M. to 2:00 P.M. On summer weekends open Saturday 10:00 A.M. to 4:00 P.M. and Sunday 1:00 to 4:00 P.M. Admission is $3.00; children ages ten and under are free. The museum is across from the *Howard County Historical Village.* The village itself is pretty cool; there's even an outhouse built by the WPA. For more information call (308) 754–5558.

As you drive south of St. Paul on Highway 281, you'll be nearing *St. Libory* and another gift from heaven—the St. Libory melon. On both approaches to town, you'll see roadside fruit and vegetable stands: Helgoth's Roadside Market, the St. Libory Melon Market, and Kosmicki's Market. Stop and buy

Wing It with Lonnie

*Y*ou know how some people get so excited about something that you just can't help getting excited yourself? Lonnie Logan of Grand Island is like that. A cofounder of a group called Stewards of the Platte, Lonnie gets so excited about sandhill cranes and migrating waterfowl along the Platte River that you find yourself inching closer to him to soak up his enthusiasm and encyclopedic knowledge of these winged creatures. Each spring Lonnie takes groups (children, birdwatchers, retired people, church groups) on tours to teach them about the ecosystem of the Platte region and nearby wetlands. He can tell you why the portions of the Platte suitable for crane habitat have shrunk, and he can tell you what cranes eat, how long they live, how far they can fly, how avian cholera is a serious threat, why little shells are necessary for their diet, and a whole lot more. He will tell you about the many kinds of geese and ducks on the wetlands/lagoons. He can point at an almost invisible speck in the sky and tell you what kind of bird it is. He'll also tell you about competing interests: What's good for the birds might not be good for agriculture, and what's good for agriculture is not necessarily good for birds. Lonnie will have you happily tramping through knee-high grass in boggy marshlands toward a lake covered with ducks and geese and slinking out of a van to see sandhill cranes feeding in cornfields. When he's done with you your shoes will be muddy and your legs will likely be tired, but you'll have a great big smile on your face and a head full of knowledge. To arrange a tour, you can reach Lonnie through Stewards of the Platte at (308) 382–2521.

LAND OF CATHER AND CRANES

some of the legendary melons during the summer and fall. People come from miles away to make these melons their own. You should, too.

Hall County

🖐️**rand Island,** with a population of just under 40,000, is Nebraska's third-largest community, unless you consider the 76,000 fans who attend home football games at the University of Nebraska-Lincoln a community. Located on Interstate 80, at exits 318 and 312 in Hall County, Grand Island offers a grand time to travelers.

First of all, please do not miss the opportunity to eat at the **Coney Island Cafe.** This downtown diner, at 104 East Third Street, is a step across time, with old-fashioned hot dogs topped with mustard, onions, and chili sauce. The cafe has been tempting taste buds since George Katrouzos bought the place in 1933, and his son and grandchildren continue the tradition of great food at great prices. They sell up to 350 dogs on an average Saturday and many more when people are home during the holidays. They also make mouthwatering chili. On a poignant note, former resident Charlie Hunt's daughter fulfilled his dying wish when she arranged for Coney Island to ship some much-loved chili to her dad in California. Other favorites at the cafe are the creamy malts and shakes. Coney Island is cheerfully decorated in red, pink, and white, and it seats about fifty people in the original wooden booths or at the counter. The cafe also serves breakfast, sandwiches, soups, and salads, but if this is your first or only chance to be here, order the dog ($1.40), the chili ($1.85), or both. Take-out is available, too. If you have a cooler in your vehicle, consider buying a pint or quart of the chili and the Coney sauce to go. Coney Island is open Monday through Friday from 8:30 A.M. to 5:30 P.M. and Saturday from 8:30 A.M. to 3:30 P.M. The telephone number is (308) 382–7155.

AUTHOR'S FAVORITE ANNUAL EVENTS IN SOUTH-CENTRAL NEBRASKA
(Call ahead to verify dates)

Crane Watch, March 1–April 15, Kearney, (800) 967–2189

Wings Over the Platte, Sandhill crane festival/ seminars, Grand Island, mid-March, (308) 385–5316

Willa Cather Spring Festival, Red Cloud, early May, (402) 746–2653

Cottonwood Prairie Festival, outdoor celebration with sculpture, art, and entertainment, Hastings, June, (402) 461–2368

Hope Blues Festival, St. Libory, late June, (308) 382–8250

Swedish Midsommarfest, Holdrege, mid-June, (308) 995–4444

Republican River Canoe Race, Franklin, early July, (308) 425–6295

Grover Cleveland Alexander Days, St. Paul, mid-July, (308) 754–5558

Central Nebraska Ethnic Festival, Grand Island, late July, (308) 381–7127

Kool-Aid Days, Hastings, early August, (402) 462–4877

Rockstock (lobster feed), Rockville, first Saturday in August, (308) 372–7275

161

If you plan on being in Grand Island overnight, you'd be well advised to stay at the **Kirschke House B&B,** at 1124 West Third Street. This vine-covered, turreted, and cupolaed Victorian home, which at one time was divided into three apartments, has been restored to its original gracious elegance. Guests can choose from four rooms (two with a private bath) at prices ranging from $55 to $75. The Roses Roses Room, with a canopy bed and lots of windows, is the most popular. A delicious gourmet breakfast is served in one of several places: at the dining room table, which always has fresh flowers and is under a crystal chandelier; on the front porch; on the patio; or in your room. In the backyard the lantern-lit old washhouse no longer has bubbling water where clothes are washed, but it does have bubbling water in an inviting hot tub. The yard is also full of beautiful plants and herbs. The carriage house has a two-level suite that rents for $145. Credit cards are accepted. For reservations call (308) 381–6851 or (800) 381–6851.

The 200-acre **Stuhr Museum of the Prairie Pioneer,** located at the junction of Highways 281 and 34, has been ranked as one of the top ten places to relive America's past by *Good Housekeeping* magazine. The main building, designed by world-famous architect Edward Durrell Stone, is a beautiful white structure on a moat-surrounded island. The Fonner Memorial Rotunda has an excellent collection of Native American and Old West memorabilia. One of the very best things about the museum is the forty-acre Railroad Town; stepping into town makes you feel as though you've walked into one of those wonderfully wistful episodes of *The Twilight Zone.* Suddenly you're one hundred years back in time, and you're in a small western town with wooden sidewalks and posts for tying horses. Among the sixty original buildings are a general store, a depot, a doctor's office, a livery, a railroad hotel, a church, a school, Victorian homes, and the small bungalow where Henry Fonda was born. Many living-history demonstrations are held throughout summer and into fall. Railroad Town is so authentic that it's been the location of three made-for-TV movies, *Sarah Plain & Tall, Home at Last,* and *My Antonia.* Another nice part of the museum is the wooded arboretum, through which you can stroll, feed the ducks, or have a picnic. You'll like this museum a lot. The museum is open daily except for major holidays. The admission fee is $6.40 for adults, $5.85 for seniors, and $3.75 for children ages seven through sixteen; children age six or younger get in free. Call (308) 385–5316 or visit www.stuhrmuseum.org on the Internet.

There are two things in this world I am sure I do not like: martinis and cigars. (Although I do admit to bending—all right, breaking—the law

LAND OF CATHER AND CRANES

when it comes to cigars. I regularly smuggle back a few Cuban cigars from Mexico and Canada for friends and people I feel I must impress.) Given that I do not like these two things at all I will, ironically, heartily recommend a place in Grand Island that specializes in both. *J. Alfred Prufrocks,* at 308 Pine Street, is just way too pretty and well designed not to like. Little cloth napkins with names of drinks embroidered on them. Beautiful comfy chairs, which I assure you are not standard in Nebraska bars. Astonishing light fixtures. Really cool glasses. The stainless steel counter. Artwork. The women's bathroom is nicer than my house, and they have better hand towels than I do. Oh, yes, those martinis . . . there's a bunch of them, like about thirty. And great wines, bourbon, champagne, double and single malt scotch, vodka, cognac, tequila, gin, rum, and a lot of liqueurs.

> **OTHER ATTRACTIONS WORTH SEEING IN SOUTH-CENTRAL NEBRASKA**
> *(Call ahead to verify dates; all area codes are 308)*
>
> **GIBBON**
>
> *Lillian Annette Rowe Sanctuary* *(visitors centers, sandhill cranes tours),* 44450 Elm Island Road, (308) 468–5282
>
> **GRAND ISLAND**
>
> *Fonner Park (horse racing),* open mid-February to early May, (308) 382–4515
>
> **KEARNEY**
>
> *Children's Museum,* 2013 Avenue A, (308) 236–5437

And there are cordials, something I've always wondered about. What the hell *is* a cordial? Now's your chance to find out even though I chickened out; give me a beer any day. Thank God, yes, they do have beer and a very nice selection. And they'll bring you a nice cheese-and-cracker tray if you give them money for it. Now the cigars. There are a lot, and none of them meant anything to me, but you can buy one called Lars Tetens Asadach. I am given to understand that this is a very good thing. This truly wonderful place is open Wednesday through Saturday from 5:00 P.M. to 1:00 A.M. The telephone number is (308) 370–8466.

West of Grand Island is the *Crane Meadows Nature Center,* which is on the south side of Interstate 80 exit 305. There are 7¹/₂ miles of hiking trails on 250 acres that encompass wetlands, woodlands, and prairie. This is a great way to see several landscapes in a relatively small space. On your hike you might see coyotes, deer, turkeys, turtles, ducks, and many other native creatures. The visitors center is full of interesting displays on endangered local species, a model of the Platte River, hands-on activities, and a few live animals. During the late-winter sandhill crane migration you can arrange for tours to blinds along the river. The hours are Monday through Saturday from 9:00 A.M. to 5:00 P.M. and Sunday from 1:00 to 5:00 P.M. The admission fee is $3.00. For additional information call (308) 382–1820.

Do you gotta have art? Then a stop at the *Art Farm* near *Marquette* is in order. This artists-in-residence program in rural Hall County has offered residencies to artists from around the world since 1993. Studio space, workshops, and a gallery have been reconstructed from old farm buildings. Artists live in a century-old farmhouse. Owners and artists Ed Dadey and Janet Williams live in a structure put together from several old barns moved onto the property and joined together. They call it the Mutant Little House on the Prairie. Artists are required to leave one art-work on-site, so the place is sprinkled with pieces, some permanent, some that will devolve back into the prairie. Ed and Janet have turned some of the former cropland back into prairie grasses. It's very fun to wander through the prairie looking at art. The Louvre? MONA? The Tate or the Prado? Not quite yet, but it's still wonderful. In the fall visitors are invited to the annual "Art Harvest" to see the latest crop. Admission is free, and there are no regular hours; folks just drop by. To get there go 8 miles north of Interstate 80 at Aurora on Highway 14 and then 2½ miles west on West 21 Road. The phone number is (402) 854–3120.

Buffalo County

ort Kearny, which was built in 1848 to protect Oregon Trail travel-ers, was also on the Pony Express route. It is located 4 miles south of Kearney on Highway 44 and 4 miles east on L50A. Before it was abandoned in 1871, it played an important role in the expansion of the Amer-ican West. It was the base of operation for Maj. Frank North and his brother, Luther, who organized the famous Pawnee Indian Scouts. At present the fort is a state historical park, and it makes an interesting stop. The visitors center has exhibits about the military on the Plains and on the fort itself. The most poignant displays feature ordinary items like uni-form buttons and pieces of china that were unearthed during the re-creation of the fort. It makes you wonder what sort of items that belong to you might be unearthed in a century or so. A blacksmith shop, a stockade, and an ammunition storage building are on the site, too. The visitors cen-ter is open from Memorial Day weekend through Labor Day weekend from 8:00 A.M. to 8:00 P.M. During the rest of the year, it's open 9:00 A.M. to sunset. The center is also open mid-March to mid-April for sandhill crane tours. The grounds are open daily year-round. A park permit is required. The telephone number is (308) 865–5305; the Internet address is www.ngpc.state.ne.us/parks.

Drive into *Kearney* to see the *Fort Kearney Museum,* at 131 South Central Avenue. The museum is one of those delightful places that are crowded with the most amazingly curious stuff from all around the world. You'll see a full Samurai warrior costume, a shrunken head, an axe that disconnected people from their heads in the Middle Ages, Zulu spears, an original Ghost Dance shirt, cuneiform tablets, a fragment of a dinosaur eggshell, the first American-made coin-operated music box, Palestinian wedding shoes (they look exceedingly uncomfortable), mummified bread from Egyptian tombs, a Sharp's fifty-caliber carbine buffalo gun, seashells, mastodon teeth—but wait, there's more! After you see the collection, you should ride on the glass-bottom boat (in reality, a boat with a glass panel on the bottom). Underneath it, with the inducement of some fish-food pellets, giant catfish, Japanese koi, and scary-looking gar will gather for your enjoyment. It's pretty cool. Take exit 272 off the interstate, turn north at the first place you can, go 1 block, and then turn 1 block east. The museum is open from Memorial Day through Labor Day, Thursday through Saturday, 10:30 A.M. to 5:00 P.M.; and Sunday, 1:00 to 5:00 P.M. The telephone number is (308) 234–5200. Admission is $2.00 for adults; children age eleven or younger visit free when accompanied by an adult.

At 2401 Central Avenue there's a museum that is the polar opposite of the Fort Kearney Museum but equally as wonderful. The collection at the **Museum of Nebraska Art (MONA)** is not from around the world; it all has a Nebraska connection of some sort. Don't even think about smirking when you hear the words *Nebraska* and *art* in the same sentence. MONA

A River Runs through It

*T*he **Platte River** *has been called many things. It's said to be like a politician: shallow, yet wide at the mouth. It's said to be too thick to drink and too thin to plow. It's also said to be a mile wide and an inch deep. Okay, it's true—it's not your ragin' river, except maybe during the spring thaw, when it can create some highly unpleasant floods. Washington Irving said the Platte was "the most magnificent and most useless of rivers." Well! It does have its good points, though. It was fairly easy to cross in a covered wagon, and it is the major reason why sand-*

hill cranes annually flock here in numbers up to a half million during their northward migration. The shallow river gives them a place to roost overnight on sandbars, where predators can't reach them. They spend their days foraging in the fields, and the young, unmated birds spend time "dancing" to attract lifelong mates. Much has been written about the migration; Forbes FYI *magazine says it's the number-one place in the world for bird-watchers, and one travel writer called it the Serengeti of the Plains. The Platte River useless? I don't think so.*

is an excellent museum, with twelve exhibition galleries. The permanent collection is admirable, and there is always at least one fascinating temporary exhibit. The museum is housed in a large, elegant old post office, with a beautiful newer addition and a peaceful sculpture garden out back. The gift shop is sure to tempt even those with the most discriminating of tastes. Hours are Tuesday through Saturday from 11:00 A.M. to 5:00 P.M. and Sunday from 1:00 to 5:00 P.M. Call (308) 865–8559 for additional information. The Web site is www.monet.unk.edu/mona/.

Just east of Kearney on Insterstate 80 you'll see something you don't see very often, that being a great big huge thing over the interstate. This is called the *Great Platte River Road Archway Monument.* It most decidedly is not off the beaten path, but it is worth a stop. Right about where the Archway is located marks the spot of many important westward expansion factors. Near here is where these things traversed: Native American paths, fur trader routes, the Oregon Trail, the Mormon Trail, the Pony Express, the Lincoln Highway, and the first transcontinental railroad. The museum inside explains all these old things in a very whiz-bang, modern way. It's a nice way to learn about history; you'll like it. There's a restaurant and gift shop on-site. The Archway is open Wednesday through Sunday from 10:00 A.M. to 4:00 P.M. Closed Monday and Tuesdays. Admission is $8.50 for adults, $7.50 for AAA members and those over fifty-five years of age, $5.00 for children six through twelve, and free for children under six. To get there, take exit 272 north at Kearney, continue north to Talmadge Street, turn right (east) at Talmadge to Central Avenue, turn right again, go to Archway Parkway (or East First Street), turn left (east), and drive for a bit until you see the parking lot. The telephone number is (877) 511–2724. The Web site is www.archway.org.

West of Kearney, on Interstate 80 at Highway 183, you'll come to *Elm Creek* and two unique attractions. The first is the *Chevyland U.S.A. Antique Car and Cycle Museum.* Owner Monte Hollertz has one of the largest and most complete collections of Chevrolets in the country. There are more than 115 cars. The oldest, a Royal Mail Roadster, dates from 1914. There's a rare 1947 Fleet Line Country Custom Club Sedan, with the original wood paneling that came in a kit for do-it-yourselfers. The museum also has a car that was used as the getaway vehicle in a 1965 robbery. No matter if running boards on cars from the 1920s or fins from the 1950s put you in mind of your glory days, this is the place to relive old memories. Be sure to check out the fuzzy dice in several of the vehicles. The collection also has about fifty motorcycles and has expanded to include Volkswagens, Toyotas, Audis, Cadillacs, and Fords. The hours are Memorial Day through Labor Day, Thursday through Tuesday, from 8:00 A.M. to 5:00 P.M. Admission is $4.00 for adults, $2.00 for children age ten through fifteen; kids nine and under get in free. The telephone number is (308) 856–4208. To get there, take exit 257 north on Highway 10 and turn east on the gravel road across the highway from Bosselman Travel Center.

Another worthwhile attraction is the **Nebraska Wild Horse and Burro Facility.** This forty-acre facility houses up to 500 wild horses and burros that have been removed from Bureau of Land Management areas in the West and Southwest. The animals rest here before they are adopted by someone who will love and care for them. The facility is open Monday through Friday, 7:45 A.M. to 4:30 P.M. There's no admission fee. The telephone number is (308) 856–4498. To get there, travel 3 miles north of Elm Creek on Highway 183.

Dawson County

exington, at Interstate 80 and Highway 21, was at one time known as Plum Creek. At present it has a plum of an attraction in the ***Dawson County Historical Museum.*** For a town with a population of just 8,544, this is one great museum. One of the most popular exhibits is the McCabe Aeroplane, or Baby Biplane, which has unusual elliptical wings and was built here in 1915. Another exceptional exhibit features the preparation and preservation of a Big Al (they thought at first it was Big Alice, but something about the configuration of the hip bones made them change their minds), a 15,000-year-old mammoth that was unearthed in the county in 1993. The main gallery has period rooms, and the military hall contains artifacts from Civil War swords to medals awarded during Desert Storm. There's an 1888 schoolhouse, an 1880 railroad depot, and a 1903 locomotive. A clever photography display shows shots of the same locations in the city, taken every ten years, to demonstrate how the city has changed. There's also a display about the Olive family, who were cattle ranchers, and the trouble they got into with settlers, who wanted to fence the land and farm it. Two settlers ended up hanged in 1878, without benefit of trial, as cattle rustlers. The ensuing legal battle received national attention and is well documented in the museum, located at 805 North Taft Street. There's also a nice gift shop and a section of great books. To find it, go north from Interstate 80 over the viaduct and turn east on Seventh Street; then go 5 blocks to Taft Street. The hours are Monday through Saturday, 9:00 A.M. to 5:00 P.M.; and Sunday by appointment. Closed major holidays. Admission is free, but donations are welcome. Call (308) 324–5340 for more information.

The *Heartland Museum of Military Vehicles,* just north of Interstate 80 at exit 237, opened in June 1994 with an exceptional collection of about one hundred vehicles that were used by the military during the last fifty years. The meticulously restored vehicles are still operational. You'll find ambulances, helicopters, one of the first jeeps, tanks, half-tracks, a rare snow tractor, one of the world's few remaining Downed Airman Retrievers, and the only Bradley Fighting Vehicle in private ownership. There's a wrenching display of a Huey UH-1 helicopter perched on a roof with the silhouetted figure of a crew chief reaching a hand to assist desperate refugees aboard the last flight to freedom. The museum is open Monday through Saturday from 10:00 A.M. to 5:00 P.M. and Sunday from 1:00 to 5:00 P.M. There's no admission fee, but do leave a donation so that they can acquire more vehicles and continue construction. The phone number is (308) 324–6329; the Web site is www.capc.com/heartland/.

You would expect a good B&B to be charming, but there's something indefinably welcoming about *Memories B&B,* at 900 North Washington. Maybe the builders had good karma back in 1903, maybe the families that lived and loved there imbued the walls with laughter, maybe it's the good-for-settin'-a-spell porch, maybe it's the gazebo and the soothing waters of the fish pond, or maybe the house is situated on a very small spiritual-power vortex. In any case, this five-bedroom house is big and wonderful—and it has a pretty-dang-cool cookie-jar collection in the kitchen. There's even an antiques shop attached to the house (or you can stop at the eleven antiques stores in town). A large country breakfast is served. Rooms range from $50 to $60. To get there, take exit 237 north to Ninth Street, turn left, and go 2 blocks. For reservations call (308) 324–3290.

If you like art, the 13-mile drive from Lexington to *Cozad* will be lucky for you. The *Robert Henri Museum,* at 213 East Eighth Street, is a restored hotel and the boyhood home of an internationally famous painter. The young Robert Henry left Cozad as a boy, and at present we know him as Robert Henri. His work hangs here, in New York City's Museum of Modern Art, and in forty-three other museums around the world. Henri was one of the founders of a group of influential artists who called themselves the Eight, or the Ashcan School. The adjacent walkway takes you through the Avenue of Flags to a Pony Express station, a pioneer church, and a school. The museum is open daily from Memorial Day through Labor Day. The hours are Monday through Saturday, 10:00 A.M. to 5:00 P.M., and Sunday by appointment. If you go there in the off-season, there's a list of names and numbers on the door of people who will give you a tour. The admission is $2.00 for adults and 50 cents for children age fifteen and younger. The telephone number is (308) 784–3930.

If you feel as though you're right on the verge of some change, it's because you are: Cozad is located on the 100th meridian, or the geographical line of demarcation between what is considered East and West—you are now right at the spot where the West begins. The *100th Meridian Museum,* at 206 East Eighth Street near downtown Cozad, features pioneer artifacts. The prize of the collection is the antique touring coach used in 1907 by President William Taft and his family on a trip to Yellowstone Park. The museum is open Memorial Day through Labor Day, Monday through Friday, 10:00 A.M. to 5:00 P.M.; and Saturday, 1:00 to 5:00 P.M. Admission is $2.00. Call (308) 784–1100 for more information.

Continuing west on Interstate 80, you'll come to *Gothenburg,* home to the legendary Swedish strongman Febold Feboldson, a mythical character akin to Paul Bunyan and Pecos Pete. Feboldson was said to have accidentally carved the Platte River with a plow and to have named the "mugwump" bird as such because, when perched on a fence, its "mug" was on one side of the fence and its "wump" was on the other. Here's

Here's a Line for Ya

*T*he **100th meridian,** *which runs smack dab through* **Cozad,** *is not a line you'll see on a state map, but it's a significant line nonetheless. This is the line of demarcation where the East officially becomes the West, and what some say is the line where the humid East becomes the arid West. You won't notice the difference in the landscape immediately, especially if you're speeding across Nebraska on the interstate. But you can bet this line is as serious as a heart attack to people who make their living from the land; the East gets in excess of 20 inches of rain per year while the West can expect less than half of that. You won't notice the decided change in attitudes if you don't get out of your car and talk to people, and there's a real difference in how people on either side of the 100th meridian view themselves. People west of the 100th meridian are honest-to-god westerners, and they'll tell you so. Check out the newspaper racks as you head west across the state; you'll see the* Denver Post *with increasing frequency but not the Lincoln and Omaha papers. The first time someone in the western part of the state called me an Easterner, I couldn't figure out what he meant, because he knew I lived in Lincoln, and I'm hardly an Easterner. New Yorkers are Easterners. But, duh, there you go, that darn 100th meridian.*

some trivia for football fans: Another strongman, Jay Novacek, a former tight end for the Dallas Cowboys, is from Gothenburg.

There are two attractions well worth a stop in Gothenburg. The first is the *Sod House Museum,* just north of the interstate on Highway 47 at exit 211. Owners Merle and Linda Block, descendants of pioneers, built an authentic sod house in 1990 with one-hundred-pound sod rectangles in a labor of love. The sod is knitted together with the roots of bluestem and buffalo grasses. Grass and cacti grow on the roof, and the 3-foot-thick interior walls are whitewashed with lime and water. There's a bed inside with ropes serving as bedsprings under a lumpy, grass-stuffed mattress. This is significant because we've all heard the phrase "sleep tight," and just where do you think that came from? It came from pulling bed ropes tighter for a more comfortable night. Also on the site are two wooden windmills, a life-size buffalo fashioned by Merle from 4½ miles of barbed wire, and a second barbed-wire sculpture of a Native American can seated on a horse. Another building at the site contains historical artifacts that pertain to the era of the sod house. The gift shop has cool stuff, including the only Mexican jumping beans I'd seen in about twenty years. The museum is open daily from May through September, 9:00 A.M. to 6:00 P.M.; in June, July, and August, daily hours are 8:00 A.M. to 8:00 P.M. There's no admission fee. The telephone number is (308) 537–2680. In the off-season, call the Gothenburg Chamber of Commerce at (308) 537–2607 for information.

The second attraction is the *Pony Express Station,* which was moved to Ehmen Park from its original location, 15 miles southwest of Gothenburg. The Pony Express operated for only eighteen months, beginning in April 1860, and at that time was called the Greatest Enterprise of Modern Times. The 2,000-mile express route from St. Joseph, Missouri, to Sacramento, California, took ten days to traverse. See if the letters or postcards you mail from here bearing a Pony Express seal get home before you do. Hours at this free museum are the same as those at the Sod House Museum. The telephone number is (308) 537–2143. Horse-drawn carriage rides around the park are available from Memorial Day through Labor Day weekend.

Geology buffs will be interested to know that the steep canyon lands southwest of Gothenburg are the *Dissected Loess Plains National Natural Landmark.* It is made up of 200 feet of loess soil, and that's *really* deep for loess soils, which have been carried in by the wind and have eroded over time into canyons and valleys.

Adams County

The largest community in Adams County is *Hastings,* with a population of just under 23,000. This is an energetic college town, with a great downtown area and plenty of activities for everyone in the family. Hastings is south of Grand Island, at the junction of Highways 281 and 6.

Champions Sports and Recreation is just off Highway 281 at the end of the viaduct if you're coming from the north. You can't miss it; there's a big sign. And you shouldn't miss it because there's a world of things to do. There are three indoor water slides, swimming, basketball, handball, racquetball, volleyball, indoor tennis, a game room, space ball, a weight room, video archery, go-carts, and miniature golf. Costs depend on which activity you select. Hours are Monday through Friday from 5:30 A.M. to 10:00 P.M., Saturday from 8:00 A.M. to 10:00 P.M., and Sunday from noon to 10:00 P.M. The telephone number is (402) 462–6220.

The *Hastings Museum* is not only the premier attraction in Adams County, but it is among the finest attractions in the state. The fully accredited museum features the Lied Superscreen Theater, with a screen that's five stories tall and 70 feet wide. Also featured is the J. M. McDonald Planetarium. The museum has three floors, with well-designed exhibitions that include natural history, wildlife, Native American culture, a Discovery Center, pioneer history and Americana, local history, and a new fantastic wing about Kool-Aid, which was created in Hastings by Edwin Perkins. (In 1998 Kool-Aid became the Official Soft Drink of

A Little Flight Music

*I*f you have ever questioned your belief in a higher power, or call it what you will, those thoughts will be forever banished as you crouch in a freezing riverbank blind to see up to 10,000 sandhill cranes swirl up in a dark cloud to greet the day in an unduplicatable, deafening cacophony. (Check with the Grand Island, Kearney, or Hastings chambers of commerce for information about local events where you can see and learn more about these special birds.)

One more reason why I love Nebraska is that it is the only state on the migratory route where hunting sandhill cranes is prohibited. This meant much more to me after a park ranger in New Mexico told me a story about the mate of a freshly killed sandhill crane. She attacked the hunters when they tried to retrieve her mate's body, and she then held a silent vigil by the carcass for several days until hunger and the undeniable pull of instinct called her north.

Nebraska, whereupon the milk producers of Nebraska had milk designated as the Official Drink of Nebraska.) On the first floor is a very old wooden case with realistic-looking stuffed rattlesnakes. Go stand over there, express loud amazement to your traveling companions, and, when they come over to see what you've discovered, press the secret button and make the rattles buzz. It never fails to elicit a scream. If you're traveling with children, be prepared to press that button again and again and again. Kids love it. This is a must-see museum; there's even someone *buried* in there. The address is 1330 North Burlington (just a couple blocks from Champions). The museum is open Monday from 9:00 A.M. to 5:00 P.M., Tuesday through Saturday from 9:00 A.M. to 8:00 P.M., and Sunday from 10:00 A.M. to 6:00 P.M. Admission prices with museum and/or Superscreen admission. Be sure to take a short walk to the adjacent cemetery, with Oregon Trail–era graves. Call (800) 508–4629 or (402) 461–2399, or visit the Web site at www. hastingsmuseum.org.

Murphy's Wagon Wheel, at 107 North Lincoln in downtown Hastings, is a popular watering hole for locals and sports enthusiasts. You'll know you're there when you see the shamrock on the sign and the statue of St. Patrick in the window. Owner Bob Murphy is proud of his Irish heritage. Murphy's serves prodigious amounts of good bar food. In particular, you should try the Macho Nachos ($6.48); the Murphy Burger with bacon, mushrooms, and Swiss cheese ($5.89); and the Hot Wings ($4.99). It's a fun place, and you'll likely make a few new friends from Hastings. Hours are Monday through Saturday, 11:00 A.M. to 1:00 A.M. The telephone number is (402) 463–3011.

Kearney County

In *Minden* you'll see what is best described as a small version of the Smithsonian Institution's National Museum of American History. The Smithsonian calls itself America's Attic, whereas the *Harold Warp Pioneer Village* invites you to "See the Story of America and How It Grew." Minden is 12 miles south of the interstate at exit 279. You'll be well aware of its approach; you'll likely have seen dozens of signs for it no matter what direction you're coming from. There really is no way to begin to describe the sheer magnitude and volume of the exhibits. Twenty-six buildings occupy more than twenty acres, whereas the twelve historic buildings circle a shady commons area that features a steam-powered carousel, built in 1879, with rides that cost only a nickel. More than 50,000 historic items from "every field of human endeavor" are on display. Some buildings are so full of items dating back to the 1830s that you might approach sensory overload. The most famous collections are the 350 antique cars, including one built by Henry Ford in 1906, one hundred vintage tractors, and a huge display of antique farm machinery. In addition, you'll see a Pony Express station, a sod house, a pioneer church, a one-room school, an oceangoing vessel, a steam engine, and lots more. The Home Appliance Building alone has a zillion gadgets and machines designed to "make mother's workday easier." If you take your time and see everything you should see, you'll never make it through Pioneer Village in a single day. Take time to read the remarks in the guest book; one couple from Minnesota described it as "historical overload" while one gearhead wrote, "very good—cars!" One admission fee gets you in for more than one day. Plan on staying at the adjacent motel or campground. The museum is open daily year-round from 8:00 A.M. to sundown. Admission is $8.00 for adults, $3.50 for children age five and younger. Call (800) 445–4447 or (308) 832–1181, or visit them on the Internet at www.pioneer-village.org.

Phelps and Gosper Counties

The **Nebraska Prairie Museum** in **Holdrege** is housed in a new, two-story building, with well-designed exhibits that cover every facet of the county's development. You can't turn around without seeing something interesting. The Native American collection alone is very impressive. You'll see dolls, bikes, cars, a collection of radios and early televisions, furniture, dishes, clothes, hats, sewing machines, weapons, and all sorts of neat stuff. There's a nice exhibit on the Orphan Trains. One of the more popular exhibits is about Camp Atlanta, a World War II German prisoner-of-war camp, which was located south of town at Highways 6 and 34. All the artifacts in the Prisoner of War Room were donated by former POWs and the military or civilian workers at the camp. There's a scale model of the camp, too. A short video tells the Camp Atlanta story with moving personal stories of German prisoners who became friends with the locals and the farmers for whom they worked. The prisoners were highly important to the area because they worked in many of the businesses and on farms while a lot of American men were off to war. The National Sod House Society is based in the museum, as is a fine genealogical library. You'll find the museum on the north edge of town on Highway 183. Hours are Monday through Saturday, 10:00 A.M. to 5:00 P.M.; and Sunday, 1:00 to 5:00 P.M. Admission is free.

The telephone number is (308) 995–5015 or (308) 995–4944. The Web site is www.nebraskaprairie.org.

In **Gosper County, Johnson Lake** has long been a favorite with boaters, anglers, campers, and picnickers. The lake has 2,060 water acres and most everything you'd need for your outdoor adventure. On or near the lake, abundant services are available: boat rentals, boat ramps, camping, cabins, a grocery store, a golf course, gas, bait and tackle, fish-cleaning stations, boat-repair facilities, refreshments, restaurants, lounges, a go-cart track, and even a car wash. Johnson Lake is 7 miles south of Lexington on Highway 283. A park permit is required and costs $14.00 for a year and $2.50 for a day. It is open year-round. The telephone number is (308) 785–2685. The Web site is www.johnsonlake.org.

If you're in the area during the cold winter months, you might consider viewing the **bald eagle** population at the **J-2 Hydro Plant.** Peak viewing times, when you might see as many as two dozen bald eagles, are mid-December through mid-January. The colder it is, the more eagles you'll see. They come to feed on the open water at J-2 when streams and lakes freeze over. It's really quite a wonderful sight. You can observe the eagles from a warm indoor viewing area. Spotting scopes are provided, and attendants can answer your questions. The hydro plant is south of the interstate, at the Lexington exit. Watch for signs that will lead you to the plant. The viewing areas are open from mid-December until the eagles leave in early spring. Call (308) 995–8601 to find out about free Saturday or Sunday viewing on winter weekends.

Webster County

Nebraska's most famous author and Pulitzer Prize winner is **Willa Cather.** She came to **Red Cloud,** at Highways 281 and 136, in Webster County, as a small girl and lived here until she left for college in Lincoln. Cather's experiences, and those of the settlers whose lives were shaped by the land, led her to write extraordinary books about ordinary people. She was awarded the Pulitzer for *One of Ours* in 1922. Six of her twelve novels are set in the Red Cloud of her youth. Her childhood home, now a State Historic Site, is open to the public. Her upstairs bedroom still has the wallpaper she chose and put up herself as a teenager. If you're a Cather fan, this stop is a must. For a tour of the house, go to 326 North Webster in downtown Red Cloud. For only $5.00 you can see the house and other buildings associated with Cather, such as the Burlington Depot, St. Juliana Falconieri Catholic Church, and Grace Episcopal Church.

More than 9,000 people visit these sites yearly. The old Opera House has been restored; check out the backstage, where teenage Cather's signature is scrawled on the wall. Hours for daily scheduled tours are 9:30 and 11:00 A.M., and 1:30 and 3:00 P.M. Call (402) 746–2653 or visit the Web site at www.willacather.org.

The **Willa Cather Memorial Prairie,** 5½ miles south of Red Cloud on the west side of Highway 28, is a 609-acre stretch of mixed-grass prairie, the sort of land that inspired Cather to write so movingly about the Plains. See if you have the same reaction to the land as Cather, who wrote this: "that shaggy grass country had gripped me with a passion that I never have been able to shake." Much of the land has never been plowed due to its proximity to the Republican River and concomitant susceptibility to erosion. The tract is owned and maintained by the Nature Conservancy and is open to the public free of charge. Some of the land is rented out for grazing, so you may see an occasional cow.

Boning up on History

*H*istorian Will Durant once said that history is lies agreed upon. That may be so, but sometimes once-reasonable, undisputed historical facts are viewed differently with the passing of time. Take the situation of David McCleery, whose great-grandfather, Asa T. Hill, was a Nebraska State Museum and Field Archaeology director who unearthed many a Pawnee burial ground. McCleery's short essay, called "A Brief History of Sacred Places, Archaeology, and Grave Robbing in the Hill Family" (Nebraska Voices, Nebraska Humanities Council), is one of the most sensible, succinct, and poignant things I've ever read about historical perceptions, the quest for scientific knowledge, and indigenous peoples. McCleery wrote: "My great-grandfather, Asa T. Hill, was a grave robber. He wasn't known as a grave robber until about ten years ago. Up until that point he

was known as an archaeologist. He dug up a lot of dead Pawnee.... If A. T. Hill thought folks would be calling him a grave robber forty years after his death, he probably wouldn't have dug so many holes on his farm near Red Cloud, Nebraska. I bet he's rolling over in his grave, but I'm not going to look. As it is, he's safe in a cemetery in Hastings, and as far as I know no one has any plans of digging him up." He concludes with an apology to the Pawnee tribe, saying he regrets his great-grandfather "was such a bonehead and fouled so much sacred ground. From the stories I've heard he seemed like a decent enough guy—he just couldn't stay out of your graveyards." If you'd like to see a historical marker about the Pawnee villages and burial grounds, go east of **Red Cloud** on Highway 136 and turn south to **Guide Rock** on Highway 78.

Willa Cather childhood home

And on occasion the Conservancy has a controlled "prairie burn," when they deliberately set fire to the dry prairie to mimic the old days, when such fires were natural. It truly helps maintain a healthy prairie. The telephone number is (402) 694–4191.

Five miles east of Red Cloud on Highway 136 is the **Starke Round Barn,** the largest in Nebraska and one of the largest of its kind in the nation. The three-story barn was built in 1902–3 by the four Starke brothers. It's 130 feet in diameter and is built of 12-by-12 lumber, held together by balanced tensions and stress rather than nails and pegs. To find it, turn south just at the railroad tracks. The owners live at the site and don't have a phone, so please don't stop at inappropriate times and do conduct yourself accordingly.

Franklin County

unique eight-sided, or octagonal, *church* was built in *Naponee* more than one hundred years ago. Legend has it that it was built in that configuration to keep the devil out, as there'd be no corner in which to hide. It remains devil-free and now houses the **Naponee Museum,** which contains, in addition to the usual historical artifacts, the memorabilia of native son David Janssen, famous for his role as the innocent but hunted man in the original television series *The Fugitive.* It also has memorabilia from Pierce Lyden, another native son who made it in Hollywood. Lyden played the bad guy in his nearly seventy movies with such conviction that he was voted the Villain of the Year in 1944. He played a despicable scout in the movie *Red River,* with stars John Wayne and Montgomery Clift. His scenes, according to a book he wrote, are often cut from television versions of the movie in order to leave time for commercials. The museum has more than 200 articles, such as Lyden's saddle, spurs, and gunbelt, that were used in his long movie and television career, which spanned thirty years. The museum is generally open only on holiday weekends in summer, but if you call (308) 269–2791 during the workday or on Saturday morning, someone will likely let you in. Naponee is south of Highway 136 on S31C.

Harlan County

f it's true that all the world's a stage, then the ***Theater of the American West,*** in ***Republican City,*** on Highway 136 in eastern Harlan County, offers you a world of entertainment. Each summer this fine repertory theater features dramas, musicals, and comedies directed by nationally known figures and performed by a combination of rep, local, and regional actors. An old, large school has been transformed into the production facility, and plays are staged in the 234-capacity former gymnasium. Weekend plays are preceded by a buffet dinner (barbequed ribs, chicken, and catfish), and the bar offers a full selection of drinks unless, as one of the bartenders said, you order "some weird, off-the-wall concoction." Both dinner and the performance are yours for a mere $18.95. You don't have to have dinner, though; prices for performances are up to $10 depending on your age. The recent productions have included comedies, musicals, a ragtime review, and *Dr. Wizard's Sagwa Medicine Show.* The play's the thing on Friday and Saturday nights or on Sunday afternoons in the summer (dinner follows the matinee). Call (308) 799–2113 or (888) 443–8696 for reservations.

Republican City and ***Alma*** are two communities that are very close to ***Harlan County Reservoir,*** Nebraska's second-largest lake, at 13,250 acres, and surrounded by nearly 20,000 acres of federal land. The lake is popular for boating, fishing, swimming, and camping. There is no entry fee. Campgrounds range from primitive for no fee to Class A, with electricity and showers, for $10.00. The Army Corps of Engineers operates three boat ramps you can use for $2.00 daily or $25.00 annually. Tubing on the nearby Republican River is also popular; you can put in on either side of the reservoir's spillway areas. A 600-acre area is reserved for motorcycle and ATV use. Hunting is allowed in season provided you have a Nebraska hunting license. In the spring months the lake is home to up to 5,000 pelicans who are on their northward migration. Other migratory waterfowl in evidence are a multitude of geese and ducks. A three-day women's wilderness weekend offered every summer teaches everything from archery to canoeing, Dutch oven cooking, and scuba diving. The lake can be reached by several exits off Highway 136. Golden Age Passports are honored here. For more information call (308) 799–2105 or visit the Web site at www.nwk.usace.army.mil/haco/harlan-home.htm.

There's a nice little museum with a gift and thrift shop on the reservoir called the *Lighthouse Antique Museum and Flea Market Gift & Thrift.* Displays include kitchens, living rooms, and bedrooms of the early 1900s through the 1950s. There's even vintage clothing on mannequins to complete the setting. It's not hard to imagine June asking Ward how his day was and telling him of Beaver's latest shenanigans. More than 5,000 pieces of Depression glass grace the tables and china cabinets. There's an extensive toy collection of cap guns and dolls from TV westerns and more than 500 McCoy pieces. The museum is open from May 1 through November 1 on Saturday and Sunday from 11:00 A.M. to 5:00 P.M. There's a small admission fee of $2.50 for all ages. Call (308) 779–2033 or (888) 243–0333 for more information.

Furnas County

Every little town has at least one big showcase of a house that makes you slow down to admire it as you wonder, "Who lives there?" In *Cambridge* the answer is Gloria and Gerald Hilton. The *Cambridge B&B,* on Highways 34 and 6, is heart-stoppingly beautiful inside and out. Outside, the big front porch of the 1910 home invites a good sit. And inside, stained and leaded glass, original hardwoods, and more than thirty-five Greek columns are among just a few of the artistic features. There are five rooms; three have private baths. The large, sunny rooms with old-fashioned furnishings all have the most modern conveniences, such as modem access, cable television, and desktop work areas. The inn is open daily. Room rates are $55 to $75; credit cards are accepted. For reservations call (308) 697–3220.

While you're in town, stop at the county museum to get a feel for the area. And, thanks to a state-sponsored project, you can have free, unlimited access to the Internet at the public library while you're in town. Be sure to look up the Nebraska Tourism home page at www.visitnebraska.org. If you're a golfer, the Cambridge Golf Course is said to be one fine course.

Fifteen miles to the east of Cambridge on Highway 34 is **Arapahoe** and the result of a promise made in Dachau, in southern Germany. Father Henry Denis, a Polish priest and prisoner of war, made a promise to the Blessed Virgin Mary that he would erect a shrine in her honor if he lived through the horrors of the Nazi prison camp. He did, and he ultimately made his way to the United States, where he became a pastor at Arapahoe's St. Germanus Catholic Church. Stop and see the **Our Lady of Fatima Shrine** on the grounds of the church. It's right on the highway through town.

PLACES TO STAY IN SOUTH-CENTRAL NEBRASKA

AURORA
Miss Lizzie's
Boardin' House,
1505 Ninth Street,
(402) 694–4200

CAMBRIDGE
Cambridge B&B,
606 Parker Street,
(308) 697–3169

DANNEBROG
The Heart of Dannebrog
B&B,
121 East Elm Street,
(308) 226–2303

Nestle Inn B&B,
209 East Roger
Welsch Avenue,
(308) 226–8252,
www.innsite.com/inns/
A002592

GRAND ISLAND
Kirschke House B&B,
1124 West Third Street,
(309) 381–6851,
www.kirschkehouse.com

HASTINGS
Grandma's Victorian Inn
B&B,
1826 West Third Street,
(402) 462–2013,
www.virtualcities.com/
ons/he/h/neh9501.htm

HOLDREGE
Crow's Nest B&B,
503 Grant Street,
(308) 995–5440

LEXINGTON
Memories B&B,
900 North Washington,
(308) 324–3290

RAVENNA
Aunt Betty's B&B,
804 Grand Avenue,
(308) 452–3739 or
(800) 632–9114,
www.auntbettysbb.com

PLACES TO EAT IN SOUTH-CENTRAL NEBRASKA

CAMPBELL
Farmer's Lounge & News
Room (American,
Mexican, Italian),
Main Street,
(402) 756–8888

DONIPHAN
Doniphan Steak House,
113 West Plum,
(402) 845–2932

GRAND ISLAND
Bonzai Beach Club & The
Wave Pizza Company,
107 North Walnut,
(308) 398–9283

Coney Island Lunch Room
(chili dogs, malts),
104 East Third Street,
(308) 382–7155

El Tapatio (Mexican),
2610 South Locust,
(308) 381–4511

Nonna's Palazzo (Italian),
820 West Second Street,
(308) 384–3029

HASTINGS
Murphy's Wagon Wheel
(pub fare),
107 North Lincoln,
(402) 463–3011

OK Cafe (diner),
806 West Sixteenth,
(402) 461–4663

KEARNEY
Alley Rose (continental
and American),
2013 Central Avenue,
(308) 234–1261

The French Cafe,
2202 Central Avenue,
(308) 234–6808

Oriental Express,
1304 West Twenty-
fourth Street,
(308) 236–6767

Sydney's (fresh pasta, great
wine, crepes and
omelettes for breakfast),
1010 Third Avenue,
(308) 236–6550

Thai American Buffet
Restaurant,
2302 Thirteenth Avenue,
(308) 234–9393

**HELPFUL SOUTH-CENTRAL
NEBRASKA WEB SITES**

ALMA
www.megavision.net/
hctour/

CAMBRIDGE
www.cambridgene.org

CLAY CENTER
www.ci.clay-center.ne.us

GOTHENBURG
www.ci.gothenburg.ne.us

GRAND ISLAND
www.visitgrandisland.com

HASTINGS
www.visithastings
nebraska.com

HOLDREGE
www.ci.holdrege.ne.us/

KEARNEY
www.kearneycoc.org

Index

A

Adams County, 171–72

Agate Fossil Beds National Monument, 118

Ainsworth, 87

Ainsworth Inn, 87, 103

Ak-Sar-Ben Aquarium and Outdoor Education Center, 1

Alley Rose, 180

Alliance, 119

Alma, 177

American G.I. Forum, 47

Andrew Jackson Higgins National Memorial, 71

Angel's Strawbale Saloon, 104

Angela's Eatery, 121

Angus, 38

Angus Automobile Company, 38

Annie's B&B, 73

Anselmo, 100

Antelope County, 65–69

Antioch, 108

Antique Alley, 53

Arapahoe, 179

Arbor Day Farm, 18

Arbor Day Farm Lied Conference Center, 19, 39

Arbor Lodge State Historical Park and Arboretum, 17

Arbor Manor, 21–22

Argo Hotel, The, 74

Arrow Hotel, The, 100, 103

Art Farm, 164

Arthur, 98

Arthur Bowring Sandhills Ranch State Historical Park, 79, 82

Arthur County, 98–99

Arturo's Restaurante, 39

Ashby, 96

Ashfall Fossil Beds State Historical Park, 43, 69

Ash Hollow State Historical Park, 133

Ashland, 6

Atkinson, 90

Atkinson State Recreation Area, 91

Auburn, 21

Aunt Betty's B&B, 179

Aunt Emma's Tea and Gift House, 36

Aurora, 35, 179

B

B&B Bunkhouse, 121

Bald eagles, 174

Bancroft, 62

Bank-Quit Restaurant, 55

Banner County, 130–31

Banner County Historical Museum and Village, 130

Barada, 25

Bar M Corral, 29

Barn Anew B&B, 125, 127, 137

Barrymore's Lounge, 12

Bassett, 92

Battle Creek, 71

Battle of Blue Water, 136

Bayard, 129

Bayside Golf Course, 142

Beatrice, 28

Beatrice Public Library, 28

Beaver Wall, 107

Beemer, 64

Bellevue, 50

INDEX

Belmont, 111
Benkelman, 151
Bennett, 39
Benson B&B, 55, 74
Bergstrom Rock and
    Gem Collection, 135
Bess Streeter Aldrich Home
    and Museum, 5
Best Western Chief Motel, 155
Bieroc Cafe, 154, 155
Big Canyon Inn, 84, 103
Big Springs, 136
Bill's Food Mart, 72
Bistro on the Butte, 121
Blackbird Hill, 56, 57
Black Crow Restaurant, 29
Blacksmith Shop, 128
Blaine County, 97–98
Blair, 52
Bloor, Ella Reeve "Mother", 157
Blue Colonial B&B Inn, 155
Bluebird Nursery, 73
Bluebird Trail, 91
Bluestem Bookstore, 9
Bob's Bar, 59, 75
Bohemian Cafe, 45
Bonzai Beach Club & The Wave Pizza
    Company, 179
Boot Hill, 141
Borsheim's, 49
Box Butte County, 119–20
Boyd County, 87–89
Boys Town, xi, 44
Brewster, 97
Brock, 21
Broken Bow, 100
Brown County, 85–87
Brownville, 22
Brownville Mill, 23

Brownville Village Theater, 23
Brule, 155
Buffalo Bill Scouts Rest Ranch State
    Historical Park and State
    Recreation Area, 144–45
Buffalo County, 164–67
Burchard, 26
Burchard Lake, 26
Burkholder Artists Cooperative, 10
Bush's Gaslight Lounge, 137
Burt County, 55–57
Burton, 84
Burwell, 91
Butler County, 29–30

C

C&E Antique Mall, 53
Cabela's, 131
Cafe Poulet, 5
Calamus Reservoir State
    Recreation Area, 92
Calamus River Lodge, 92
Calamus State Fish Hatchery, 92
Cambridge, 155, 178
Cambridge B&B, 155, 178
Campbell, 179
Camp Duke Alexis Recreation
    Area, 148
Camp Rulo River Club, 25
Captain Bailey House/
    Brownville Museum, 22
Captain Meriwether Lewis Museum
    of River History, 23
Carey's Cottage, 53, 74
Carhenge, 119
Carol's Cafe, 121
Carolyn's Hair Studio and Day Spa, 64
Cass County, 1–6
Cather, Willa, 159, 174–75

Cedar Creek, 93
Centennial Lanes, 75
Central City, 35
Chadron, 109
Chadron State Park, 111
Champion, 148
Champion Mill State
    Historical Park, 148
Champions Sports and
    Recreation, 171
Chances R, 30
Chappell, 135, 136
Chappell Memorial Art Gallery, 135
Chase County, 148
Cheers Smokehouse Grill, 137
Cherry County, 77–83
Chevyland U.S.A. Antique Car and
    Cycle Museum, 166
Cheyenne County, 131–33
Children's Museum, 163
Chimney Rock National
    Historic Site, 125, 129
China House, 121
Clarkson, 73
Clarkson Bakery, 73
Clarkson Historical Museum, 73
Clay Center, 36
Clay County, 36
Clown 'N Country, 155
Colby, Clara, 28
Coldwater Fish Farm, 134
Colfax County, 72–74
Columbus, 71
Comstock, 102
Coney Island Cafe, 159, 161
Coney Island Lunch Room, 179
Conner's Architectural Antiques, 10
Convent House B&B, 27, 39
Cook, 21

Coop, The, 4
Coop de Ville, 4
Corner Cafe, 137
Cornhusker Hotel, 39
Coryell Park, 22
Country Neighbor Restaurant, The, 104
Courthouse Rock, 130
Covered Wagon, The, 163
Cowboy Trail, 70
Cozad, 168, 169
Crane Meadows Nature Center, 163
Crane River Brewpub & Cafe, 39
Crawford, 111, 112
Crete, 39
Crofton, 61
Crofton Lakeview Golf Course, 61–62
Crow's Nest B&B, 179
Crystal Palace Revue, 141
Cuming County, 62–64
Custer County, 100–103
Cuthills Vineyards, 43, 64
Czech Festival, 32
Czech Museum, 32

D

Dakota County, 58–60
Dancing Leaf Earth Lodge and
    Cultural Learning Center, 147
Dannebrog, 159
Dawes County, 109–16
Dawson County, 167–70
Dawson County Historical
    Museum, 167
DeSoto National Wildlife Refuge, 52
Deuel County, 135–36
DeWitty, 81
Dime Store Days, 53
Dissected Loess Plains National
    Natural Landmark, 170

INDEX

Dixon, 59
Dixon County, 58–60
Dobby Lee's Frontier Village, 119–20
Dodge, 54
Dodge County, 53
Doniphan, 179
Douglas County, 41–50
Dowse Sod House, 102
Dream Weavers Cabin, 91
Drifter's Cookshack, 115
Dr. Susan LaFlesche Picotte Center, 57
Dude's Steakhouse, 137
Duffy's, 12
Dundy County, 151–52
Dundy County Museum, 152
Durham Western Heritage Museum, 47
Dusters, 71, 74

E

Eagle Raceways, 5
Edgerton Explorit Center, 3, 35
El Alamo, 47
El Charrito, 137
Elgin, 74
Elkhorn Acres, 63
Elkhorn Valley Museum and
    Research Center, 70
Ell Bee's, 50
Ellsworth, 107
Elm Creek, 166
Elms Ballroom, 20
El Museo Latino, 46
Elmwood, 5
El Tapatio, 179
El Toro, 39
Elyria, 95
Emerald, 39
Endicott, 34
Endicott Clay Products, 34

Ericson, 95
Euni's Place, 59, 74
Eustis, 149
Evelyn Sharp Airfield, 94

F

Fairbury, 33
Farm and Ranch Museum, 125
Farmer Brown's Steak House, 50
Farmer's Lounge and News Room, 179
Filley, 29
Filley Stone Barn, 29
Fillingham & Sons
    Exotic Animal Farm, 132
Fillmore County, 30–32
Flying A Ranch B&B, 155
Flying Bee Beefmaster Ranch, 137
Fonner Park, 163
Fontenelle Forest Nature Center, 43, 51
Fort Atkinson State Park, 51
Fort Calhoun, 51
Fort Cody Trading Post, 141, 145
Fort Hartsuff State Historical
    Park, 95
Fort Kearney, 164
Fort Kearney Museum, 159, 164
Fort McPherson National
    Cemetery, 147
Fort Niobrara National Wildlife
    Refuge, 93
Fort Robinson Museum, 114
Fort Robinson State Park, 112
Fort Sidney Complex, 133
436 Main Steakhouse, 75
Franklin County, 176–77
Fremont, 53
Fremont Dinner Train, 43, 53
French Cafe, The, 180
From Nebraska, 10

Frontier County, 148
Front Street, 141
Frosty Mug, 30
Full-Size Fashion Outlet, 20
Furnas County, 178–79

G

Gage County, 27–29
Gage County Historical Museum, 28
Gandy, 100
Garden County, 133–34
Garfield County, 91–93
Gavins Point Dam, 61
General Crook House, 47
Genoa, 47
Genoa Indian School, 47
Gering, 123
Gibbon, 163
Gin's Tavern, 159
Giovanni's, 121
Girls and Boys Town, xi, 44
Gladys Lux Historical Gallery, 14
Glenn Miller, 147
Glenn Miller Memorial Highway, 147
Glur's Tavern, 71
Golden Hotel, The, 103
Gordon, 121
Gosper County, 173–74
Gothenburg, 169
Gottberg Brew Pub, 71
Gotte Park, 131
Grand Island, 161, 163
Grandma Butch's B&B, 74
Grandma's Victorian Inn B&B, 179
Grant County, 96–97
Grateful Bread Bakery, 39
Great Plains Black History
    Museum, 46

Great Platte River Road
    Archway Monument, 166
Greeley County, 93–95
Green Gables, 75
Gretna, 39
Gross, 88
Guide Rock, 175

H

Half-Breed Tract, 24
Hall County, 161–64
Hallie's, 40
Halsey, 98
Hamilton County, 35
Hansen's Homestead, 121
Happy Jack Chalk Mine and
    Peak, 79, 93
Harlan County, 177–78
Harlan County Reservoir, 178
Harold Warp Pioneer Village, 159, 172
Harrisburg, 130
Harrison, 116, 117
Harr's Family Restaurant, 50
Harry Strunk Lake, 148
Harvard, 36
Harvard Waterfowl Production
    Area, 36
Hastings, 171
Hastings Museum and Lied
    Superscreen Theater, 159, 171
Hayes Center, 148
Hayes County, 148
Haymarket District, 10
Hay Springs, 107
Heartland Elk Guest Ranch, 79, 80, 103
Heartland Museum of
    Military Vehicles, 168
Heart of Dannebrog B&B, The, 179
Hebron, 34

INDEX

Hemingford, 121
Henry Doorly Zoo, 43
Heritage Hills Golf Course, 154
Hidden Paradise, 104
High Plains Homestead
    Bunkhouse, 115
Historic Argo Hotel, 62, 74
Hitchcock County, 151–52
Holdrege, 173
Holt County, 90–91
Homer, 58
Homestead National Monument
    of America, 3, 27
Hooker County, 96–97
Hooper, 74
Horse Thief Cave Ranch, 121
Hotel Wilber, 32, 39
House of Plants and Gifts, 87
Howard County, 157, 61
Howard County Historical Village, 160
Howells, 72
Hudson-Meng Bison Bone
    Bed Enclosure, 114
Hungry Horse Saloon, 95, 105
Hyannis, 96

I

Imperial Palace, 39
Indian Cave State Park, 3, 24
Indian Trails Country Club
    golf course, 64
International Quilt Study Center, 15
Ionia Volcano, 58
Italian Inn, 121

J

J. Alfred Prufrocks, 163
James Arthur Vineyard, 3, 17

Jail Rock, 130
Jan's Strang Tavern, 31
J. C. Robinson House B&B, 49, 74
Jefferson County, 33–34
J-2 Hydro Plant, 174
Joe Tess Place, 46
John G. Neihardt Center and State
    Historic Site, 43, 62
Johnson County, 21
Johnson Lake, 174
Johnstown, 87
Jordan's, 104
Joslyn Art Museum, 43
Junie Mae's Roadhouse
    Barbeque, 141, 155
JX Cattle Ranch and Guest Ranch, 116

K

Kearney, 163, 164
Kearney County, 172–73
Keith County, 139–44
Keller State Park Recreation Area, 86–87
Kenfield Petrified Wood Gallery, 141
Keya Paha County, 83–85
Keystone, 150, 155
Kimball, 131
Kimball County, 130–31
King of Hearts Antiques and
    Things, 81
Kirschke House B&B, 162, 179
Klown Kapital, Band, and Museum, 65
Knoll's Country Inn, 155
Knox County, 60–62
Kreycik Riverview Elk Farm, 60

L

La Casita, 146
Lady Vestey Victorian Festival, 38

Lake Babcock, 72
Lake McConaughy, 143
Lake Minitare State
  Recreation Area, 128
Lake North, 71
Lancaster County, 8–17
La Pazadita, 137
Larrington's Guest Cottage, 84, 103
Lauritzen's B&B, 39
Lewellen, 133, 136
Lewis and Clark Lake, 61
Lexington, 167
Lighthouse Antique Museum and
  Flea Market Gift & Thrift, 178
"Lille" Mermaid, Inc., 159
Lillian Annette Rowe
  Sanctuary, 163
Lincoln, 8
Lincoln County, 144–47
Lincoln Highway, 135
Linoma Beach, 39
Lisco, 134
Little Red Hen Theatre, 58
Lobby Restaurant, The, 104
Lofte Community Theater, 3
Logan County, 99–100
Loma, 29
Long Pine, 85
Long Pine State Recreation
  Area, 93
Louisville, 4
Louisville Lakes State Recreation
  Area, 1
Loup City, 157
Loup County, 91–93
Lovejoy Ranch B&B, 79, 82, 104
Lovers Leap Vineyards, 112
Lynch, 88
Lynn Theater, 88

M

Mac's Trailside Inn, 155
Macy, 56
Madison, 71
Madison County, 70–71
Madison County Historical
  Society Museum, 71
Madrid, 155
Maggie's, 39
Maggie's Main Street Grill & Bar, 137
Malcolm X Birthsite, 48
Mamasita's, 39
Mari Sandoz High Plains
  Heritage Center, 111
Mari Sandoz Room, 107
Marquette, 164
Martinsburg, 59
Martin's Family Restaurant, 121
Maskethine Recreation Area, 63
Massey Waterfowl Production Area, 36
Mayhew Cabin and Historical
  Village Foundation, 19
May's Place, 99
McCawley House B&B, 103
McCook, 152
McPherson County, 99–100
Meadville, 84
Medicine Creek, 148
Melbeta, 137
Memories B&B, 168, 179
Merle's Food and Drink, 39
Merrick County, 35–36
Merriman, 83
Mill, The, 10, 39
Milligan, 30
Minden, 172
Miss Lizzie's Boardin' House, 179
Mitchell, 123
Mom's Cafe, 3, 40

Monowi, 87
Monowi Tavern, 87
Montrose, 119
Morgan's, 107
Mormon Pioneer Winter Quarters,
   Cemetery, and Visitors Center, 48
Morrill, 137
Morrill County, 129–30
Mullen, 96
Murphy's Wagon Wheel, 172, 180
Museum of Nebraska Art, 165
Museum of Nebraska
   Baseball Greats, 160
Museum of the Fur Trade, 109
Museum of the Odd, 8
My Backporch Friends, 81
My Blue Heaven B&B, 39

N

Naper, 89
Naponee, 176
Naponee Museum, 176
National Liars Hall of Fame, 159
National Museum of
   Rollerskating, 12–13
Neale Woods Nature Center, 49
Nebraska City, 17
Nebraska Inn, 88, 104
Nebraska Motorplex, 54
Nebraska National Forest, 79, 98
Nebraska Prairie Museum, 173
Nebraska's Big Rodeo, 91
Nebraska State Capitol, 10
Nebraska Wild Horse and
   Burro Facility, 167
Neligh, 66
Neligh Mills State Historical Site, 66
Nemaha County, 21–24

Nestle Inn B&B, 179
Newcastle, 58
Nine-Mile Prairie, 15
Niobrara, 47, 60
Nonna's Palazzo, 179
Norden, 84
Norfolk Arts Center, 70
North Loup River Trails, 94
North Platte, 144, 150
North Platte Valley Museum, 126, 132
Northern Plains Art Gallery, 61
Nuckolls County, 37

O

Oak, 38
Oak Ballroom, 74
Oakland, 55
O'Conner House Museum Complex, 58
Odell, 34
Odell diamonds, 34
Office Bar and Grill, The, 74
Ogallala, 139, 150
Oglala National Grasslands, 117
OK Cafe, 180
OK Market, 7
Old Baldy, 88
Old Market, 41
Olde Main Street Inn, 109, 110, 121
Ole's Big Game Steakhouse
   and Lounge, 141, 143, 155
Omaha, 41, 47
Omaha Community Playhouse, 45
Omaha Indian Reservation, 56
100th Meridian Museum, 169
O'Neill, 90
Ord, 94
Oregon Trail, Thayer County, 34
Oregon Trail Wagon Train, 125, 129

Oriental Express, 180
O'Rourke's, 12
Otoe County, 17–21
Our Lady of Fatima Shrine, 179
Outlet shopping, 20
Oven, The, 10
Ox-Bow Trail, 6

P

Panorama Point, 131
Park Avenue Antiques, 53
Parson's House B&B, The, 39
Pawnee City, 26
Pawnee City Historical
    Society Museum, 26
Pawnee County, 26–27
Paxton, 143
Peppermill, 79, 104
Pendleton Outlet Store, 20
Phelps County, 173–74
Phelps Hotel B&B, 137
Pierce, 64
Pierce County, 64–65
Pierson Wildlife Museum
    Learning Center, 68
Pine Valley Resort, 85
Pines, The, 85
Pioneer Grave Sites, 128
Pioneers Park, 13
Pioneers Park Nature Center, 14
Plainsman Museum, 35
Plains Trading Company
    Booksellers, 79, 81
Plainview, 65
Plantation House B&B, 65, 74
Platte County, 71
Platte River, 165
Platte River State Park, 1

Plattsmouth, 3
Pleasant Dale, 40
P. O. Pears, 39
Polk County, 29–30
Ponca, 59
Ponca State Park, 59
Ponca Trail of Tears, 68
Ponca Tribe Museum, 61
Pony Express Station, 170
Pool Hall, 141, 149, 155
Porky's, 40
Prairie Garden B&B, 72, 74
Prairie Peace Park, 15
President Gerald Ford's Birthsite, 48
Princeton Tavern, 16

Q

Quarry Oaks Golf Course, 4, 21

R

Ravenna, 179
Rebecca Winters' Grave, 127
Red Cloud, 174, 175
Red Willow County, 152–54
Red Willow Reservoirs, 148
Republican City, 177
R. F. Goeke, 90
R. F. Goeke Variety, 92
Richardson County, 24–26
Ricketts Folsom House B&B, 8, 39
Riverside Zoo, 126
Robber's Cave, 56
Robert Henri Museum, 168
Robidoux Pass, 128
Robidoux Trading Post, 128
Rock County, 91–93
Rock Creek Station
    State Historical Park, 3, 33

Rock 'N Roll Runza, 39
Rockville, 159
Rogers House B&B, 8, 39
Roman L. Hruska Meat Animal
    Research Center, 36–37
Rose Garden Inn B&B, 65, 74
Rosita's, 137
Round the Bend Bar, 4
Royal, 75
Rulo, 25

S

Saint Benedict Center, 73
Saints and Shillelaghs, 90
Saline County, 32
Sallows Arboretum and
    Conservatory, 120
Sandhills Golf Club, 96
Sandhills Guest Ranch B&B, 98
Santee Sioux Indian Reservation, 61
Sarpy County, 50–51
Saunders County, 6–8
Saunders County Courthouse, 8
Saunders County
    Historical Complex, 6
Schilling Wildlife Management Area, 4
Scotia, 93
Schuyler, 74
Scottsbluff, 123
Scotts Bluff County, 123–28
Scotts Bluff National
    Monument, 123, 125
Scribner, 54, 75
2nd Wind Ranch, 103
Senator George Norris State
    Historic Site, 154
Seven Springs Water, 85
Seward, 30
Seward County, 29–30

Sheldon Memorial Art Gallery and
    Sculpture Garden, 13
Shepherd's Dairy, 100
Sheridan County, 105–9
Sherman County, 157–61
Sherman Reservoir, 157
Shubert, 25
Sidney, 132
Sioux County, 116–19
Sioux Lookout, 146
Sioux Sundries, 116–17, 121
Sisters' House B&B, The, 104
Smith Falls State Park, 82
Sod House Museum, 170
Soldier Creek Wilderness
    Area, 112
South Bend, 4
Sowbelly Canyon, 117
Sowbelly Canyon B&B Hideaway, 121
Spalding, 93
Sparks, 80
Special Occasions Outlet, 20
Spencer, 104
Spring Creek Prairie, 16
Spring Ranche, 37
Springview, 84
St. Anthony's Catholic Church, 27
St. Libory, 160
St. Michael's Church, 93
St. Paul, 159
Stanton, 63
Stanton County, 62–64
Stapleton, 100
Starke Round Barn, 176
Starlite Drive-In, 67
Steamboat Trace Trail, 3, 23
Steele City, 34
Steinauer, 27
Strang, 31

Strategic Air and Space Museum, 15, 21
Stratton, 152
Stromsburg, 30
Stuhr Museum of the Prairie Pioneer, 159, 162
Sunrise Cafe, 40
Super 8, 143
Superior, 38
Sutton, 36
Swedish Heritage Center, 56
Sweet Shoppe, 159
Sydney's, 180
Syracuse, 20

T

T&T Canoe Service, 93
Taco Town, 137
TaHaZouka Park, 70
Tarnov, 72
Taylor, 93
Tecumseh, 21
Ted & Wally's, 39
Thai American Buffet, 180
Thai House, 39
Thayer County, 34
Theater of the American West, 177
Thomas County, 97–98
Thurston County, 55–57
Toadstool Geologic Park, 115
Toman's Meat Market, 74
Tower of the Four Winds, 52
Trenton, 152
Tri-State Oldtime Cowboy Museum, 105
Troll Stroll, 56
Tryon, 100, 147
Twisted Pine Ranch B&B, 121

U

Unadilla, 18
Uncle Buck's Lodge, 97, 104
Union Pacific Bailey Yard, 146
University of Nebraska State Museum at Trailside, 113
Upper Room B&B, The, 87, 103
Uptown Brewery, 63, 75

V

Valentine, 81
Valentine National Wildlife Refuge, 93
Valley County, 93–95
Valley View Guest Ranch, 147
VF Factory Outlet, 20
Vic's Steakhouse and Lounge, 137
Victoria Springs State Recreation Area, 103
Virginia's Travelers Cafe, 40
Vogie's Quilts and Treasures, 54

W

Wahoo, 6
Wahoo Bakery, 7
Walgren Lake Monster, 108
Walgren Lake State Recreation Area, 108
Walthill, 57
Warbonnet Battlefield, 118
Wasabi, 40
Washington County, 51–52
Waterloo, 49
Way Home Music and Books, 10
Wayne, 74
Webster County, 174–76
Weeping Water, 3

Wellfleet, 147
Wheeler County, 95–96
Whiskey Run Creek Vineyards &
    Winery, 22–23
Whispering Pines B&B, 20, 39
White Horse Ranch, 89
Whitman, 96
Whitman General Store, 96
Wigwam Cafe, 7
Wilber, 32
Wildcat Hills State Recreation
    Area and Nature Center, 125–26
Wildlife World at the
    Wyo-Braska Museum, 126
Willa Cather Memorial Prairie, 175
Willa Cather's Home, 159
Willetta Lueshen Bird Library, 70
Willow Point Gallery and Museum, 6
Willow Rose B&B, 65, 74
Wind turbines, 84

Winnebago, 57
Winnebago Indian Reservation, 56
Winnetoon, 60
Winnetoon Mini-Mall, 60
Winslow, George, marked grave, 33
Woodland Hills Golf Course, 5
World's largest porch swing, 34
Wyuka Cemetery, 14

Y

Yankee Peddlers West, 53
Yia Yia's Pizza, 40
York, 30
York County, 30–32

Z

Zoo Bar, 11–12
Zoo Nebraska, 68–69

About the Author

Hannah McNally is a native Nebraskan. She considers herself lucky to live in the state and hopes to live there forever.